OCR
LATIN
ANTHOLOGY
for GCSE

Peter McDonald
Margaret Widdess

OCR
RECOGNISING ACHIEVEMENT

OXFORD
UNIVERSITY PRESS

Official Publisher Partnership

OXFORD
UNIVERSITY PRESS

Great Clarendon Street, Oxford OX2 6DP

Oxford University Press is a department of the
University of Oxford. It furthers the University's
objective of excellence in research, scholarship,
and education by publishing worldwide in

Oxford   New York

Auckland   Cape Town   Dar es Salaam
Hong Kong   Karachi   Kuala Lumpur   Madrid
Melbourne   Mexico City   Nairobi   New Delhi
Shanghai   Taipei   Toronto

With offices in

Argentina   Austria   Brazil   Chile
Czech Republic   France   Greece   Guatemala
Hungary   Italy   Japan   South Korea   Poland
Portugal   Singapore   Switzerland   Thailand
Turkey   Ukraine   Vietnam

Oxford is a registered trade mark of Oxford
University Press in the UK and in certain
other countries

British Library Cataloguing in Publication Data

Data available

ISBN 978 019 832932 9

10 9 8 7 6 5 4 3 2 1

Printed in Spain by Cayfosa-Impresia Ibérica

Paper used in the production of this book is a
natural, recyclable product made from wood
grown in sustainable forests. The manufacturing
process conforms to the environmental regulations
of the country of origin.

Acknowledgements

The authors are very grateful to a number
of people for their generous assistance and
encouragement: Liz Lucas (OUP), our copy-editor
Sarah Newton, Anna Davey (OCR) James Morwood
for kind permission to use his biographies of
Latin authors; Richard Widdess; all who read the
material and made suggestions, especially Stephen
Spowart, Tim Hands, and Steffan Griffiths. We are
also indebted to our colleagues and pupils over the
years and to our own teachers who introduced us
to Latin literature.

The Publisher wishes to thank Stephen Anderson
(Winchester College), Chris Burnand (Abingdon
School), Jeff Shaw (Wilson's School), Polly Caffrey
(Cheney School) and Tony Bartlett for reviewing
the manuscript. Also James Morwood, Ian
McAuslan, David Langslow and Philomen Probert
for the verse recordings, which were produced by
Daniel Calvert.

Cover image: Oxford University Press; p7; Musée
des Beaux-Arts, Orléans, France/Giraudon/The
Bridgeman Art Library, p11: Bridgeman Art Library/
Louvre, Paris, France/Peter Willi; p17: Roger
Dalladay; p21: Araldo de Luca/Corbis; p27: Roger
Dalladay; p29: Wallace Collection, London, UK/The
Bridgeman Art Library; p31: Roger Dalladay;
p35: Roger Dalladay; p41: Roger Dalladay;
p47: Araldo de Luca/Corbis; p53 Birmingham
Museums and Art Gallery/The Bridgeman Art
Library; p57: French School/Private Collection/The
Stapleton Collection/The Bridgeman Art Library;
p65: Gian Berto Vanni/Corbis; p69: Mimmo Jodice/
Corbis; p77: Araldo de Luca/Corbis; p79: Bettmann/
Corbis; p83: Roger Dalladay; p85: Bettmann/Corbis;
p89: Roger Dalladay; p91: Francesco Venturi/Corbis;
p103: Roger Dalladay; p105: Vittoriano Rastelli/
Corbis; p115: Roger Dalladay; p119 Roger Dalladay;
p125: Pujol, Abel de (1787-1861)/Musée des Beaux-
Arts, Valenciennes, France/Lauros/Giraudon/
The Bridgeman Art Library; p126: Bibliothèque
Nationale, Paris, France/The Bridgeman Art Library,
p139: Araldo de Luca/Corbis; p148: Leefdael,
J. v. & Strecken, G. v. der (fl.1647-77) (studio)/
Musée de la Révolution Française, Vizille, France/
The Bridgeman Art Library; p150: Werner Forman/
Corbis.

Contents

INTRODUCTION

This *OCR Latin Anthology* provides a basis for studying literature options to be examined in the new Latin GCSE. The purpose of the *Anthology* is to make Latin literature enjoyable to read and accessible to students. We have selected passages that we consider to be representative of fine Latin writing, some of which also reflect the great themes of Roman culture.

We have endeavoured to provide passages from a range of authors, balanced equally between prose and verse, which will appeal both to students and to their teachers. Some familiar pieces are included, but we have taken the opportunity to include authors such as Sulpicia and Persius who are less well known, so that the range of literature is a broad and fresh selection. The texts themselves are genuine Latin, with only some abridgement to ensure accessibility or satisfying narrative. Above all, we hope that these selections will develop knowledge of the language and inspire an understanding and a love of Latin literature.

Facing the text there is thorough glossing of words that are unlikely to be familiar. Familiar words are also glossed if they have any specialised or unusual meaning. The form of the word in which it appears in the text is given first, followed by the nominative singular for nouns and the 1st person singular present for verbs. Several meanings are sometimes given, indicating the range of meanings of a word, and inviting students to choose a suitable translation using these or other appropriate meanings.

There are also some questions designed to encourage the students both to read the text closely and also to consider the themes raised in a wider or modern-day context.

Every word in the texts is included in the General Vocabulary at the back of the book, and further help and guidance on features of language, content and background are provided in the Teacher's Handbook.

Finally, Latin poetry was intended to be read out loud. We very much hope that students will listen to the verse recordings on the audio CD whilst reading the passages, and be inspired to read Latin aloud themselves.

SECTION

ONE

VICE AND VIRTUE

In this section we find a mixture of saints and sinners. Pride comes before a fall, and in Niobe's case, others suffer as a result. Virgil reminds his readers of the good things in store for those who are virtuous—and who set an example by their hard work or memorable deeds. Plautus, however, tells us that men and women are not judged by the same standards. In the prose selections, Cloelia provides a suitable antidote to the pride of Niobe, and Mucius Scaevola is exceptionally brave on behalf of his country. The motivation of the latter is sharply in contrast with that of Verres and Cleomenes as presented by Cicero.

Children of Niobe

1. Niobe's pride brings about her downfall

When Arachne is turned into a spider by Minerva, after not recognising Minerva as the best weaver, Niobe does not learn from her fate, and refuses to honour the gods. She has boasted of her husband (Amphion), their family, their kingdom, and most particularly of her children. The prophetess, Manto, has ordered the women of Thebes to worship Latona, mother of Phoebus (Apollo) and Phoebe (Diana). Whilst the other women worship, Niobe's pride gets the better of her.

> ecce venit comitum Niobe celeberrima turba
> vestibus intexto Phrygiis spectabilis auro
> et, quantum ira sinit, formosa; movensque decoro
> cum capite immissos umerum per utrumque capillos
> 5 constitit, utque oculos circumtulit alta superbos,
> 'quis furor auditos' inquit 'praeponere visis
> caelestes? aut cur colitur Latona per aras,
> numen adhuc sine ture meum est? mihi Tantalus auctor,
> cui licuit soli superorum tangere mensas;
> 10 Pleiadum soror est genetrix mea; maximus Atlas
> est avus, aetherium qui fert cervicibus axem;
> Iuppiter alter avus; socero quoque glorior illo.
> me gentes metuunt Phrygiae, me regia Cadmi
> sub domina est, fidibusque mei commissa mariti
> 15 moenia cum populis a meque viroque reguntur.
> in quamcumque domus adverti lumina partem,
> inmensae spectantur opes; accedit eodem
> digna dea facies; huc natas adice septem
> et totidem iuvenes et mox generosque nurusque.
> ...

1. In the first five lines, what do we learn of Niobe's physical appearance, and what does this tell us about her character?
2. What features of Niobe's speech make it forceful?
3. Sketch Niobe's family tree.
4. List those things of which Niobe is proud.

Niobe sees her children as a way to increase her own power and thinks everyone else must too. Latona was cast out by earth, sea and heavens until she found a home on Delos.

> 20   illa duorum
> facta parens; uteri pars haec est septima nostri.
> sum felix; quis enim neget hoc? felixque manebo;

comitum: comes, -itis, _m.f._ companion

celeberrima: celeber thronged by

turba: turba, _f._ crowd

vestibus: vestis, -is, _f._ clothing

intexto: intexo weave into

Phrygiis: Phrygius Phrygian

spectabilis well worth looking at

auro: aurum, _n._ gold

quantum in as much as

sinit: sino allow

formosa: formosus beautiful

decoro: decorus graceful, noble

immissos umerum per utrumque capillos '[shaking] her hair flowing down over both shoulders'

5 **constitit: consisto** halt, stop

ut as

oculos: oculus, _m._ eye, _here_ 'gaze'

superbos: superbus proud

quis what

furor, -oris, _m._ madness

auditos ... caelestes 'gods that have only been heard about'

praeponere: praepono prefer

visis: video see

colitur: colo worship

per aras 'at the altars'

numen, -inis, _n._ deity

adhuc still

sine ture 'without incense', 'unworshipped'

auctor, -oris, _m._ father

cui licuit soli ... 'who alone was allowed ...'

avus, _m._ grandfather

superorum: superi, _m._ the gods

tangere: tango touch

10 **Pleiadum: Pleiades, _f. pl._** the daughters of Atlas, i.e. 'one of the daughters'

soror, -oris, _f._ sister

genetrix, _f._ mother

aetherium: aetherius heavenly

cervicibus: cervix, -icis, _f._ neck

axem: axis, -is, _m._ vault of heaven, sky

socero: socer, _m._ father-in-law

glorior boast in

metuunt: metuo fear

Phrygiae: Phrygia Phrygia in Anatolia, from where Niobe originates

regia, _f._ palace

Cadmi: Cadmus _here_ 'of Cadmus' (in Thebes)

fidibus: fides, _f._ trust

commissa: committo entrust

mariti: maritus, _m._ husband

15 **moenia, _n. pl._** town walls

in quamcumque ... partem 'in whichever direction'

adverti: adverto turn

lumina: lumen, -inis, _n._ light, _here_ eye

opes, _f. pl._ wealth

accedit: accedo there is added

digna: dignus worthy

natas: nata, _f._ daughter

adice: adicio add

totidem the same number

generos: gener, _m._ son-in-law

nurus: nurus, -us, _f._ daughter-in-law

20 **parens, -tis, _m.f._** parent

uteri: uterus, _m._ womb, _here_ 'offspring'

septima: septimus seventh

pars septima 'one seventh'

felix lucky

neget: nego deny

hoc quoque quis dubitet?: tutam me copia fecit.
maior sum quam cui possit Fortuna nocere,
25   multaque ut eripiat, multo mihi plura relinquet.
excessere metum mea iam bona. fingite demi
huic aliquid populo natorum posse meorum:
non tamen ad numerum redigar spoliata duorum,
Latonae turbam, qua quantum distat ab orba?
30   infectis propere ite sacris laurumque capillis
ponite.' deponunt et sacra infecta relinquunt,
quodque licet, tacito venerantur murmure numen.
indignata dea est summoque in vertice Cynthi
talibus est dictis gemina cum prole locuta:
35   'en ego vestra parens, vobis animosa creatis,
et nisi Iunoni nulli cessura dearum,
an dea sim, dubitor perque omnia saecula cultis
arceor, o nati, nisi vos succurritis, aris.
nec dolor hic solus; diro convicia facto
40   Tantalis adiecit vosque est postponere natis
ausa suis et me, quod in ipsam reccidat, orbam
dixit et exhibuit linguam scelerata paternam.'
        ...

5. **What do Niobe's questions and her use of language tell us about her
   confidence in lines 20–25?**
6. **Why is the women's worship of Niobe done with 'tacito murmure'?**
7. **How does Ovid make Latona's speech to her children forceful?**

Latona pleads to her children for vengeance, and they descend to Thebes where they
proceed to shoot Niobe's seven sons with arrows. Niobe does not realise what has
happened, so great is her pride, until her husband Amphion commits suicide.

corporibus gelidis incumbit et ordine nullo
oscula dispensat natos suprema per omnes;
45   a quibus ad caelum liventia bracchia tollens
'pascere, crudelis, nostro, Latona, dolore,
pascere' ait 'satiaque meo tua pectora luctu!
corque ferum satia!' dixit. 'per funera septem
efferor; exsulta victrixque inimica triumpha!
50   cur autem victrix? miserae mihi plura supersunt
quam tibi felici; post tot quoque funera vinco.'
dixerat, et sonuit contento nervus ab arcu;

dubitet: dubito doubt
tutam: tutus safe
copia, _f._ abundance
nocere: noceo + _dat._ harm
25 **eripiat: eripio** snatch
excessere = excesserunt: excedo exceed
metum: metus, -us, _m._ fear
bona, _n. pl._ advantages
fingite: fingo imagine
demi: demo take away from
huic ... populo
natorum: nati _m. pl._ children
redigar: redigo reduce
spoliata: spolio plunder, rob
quantum how much
distat: disto be distant
orba: orbus bereft, deprived
30 **infectis: infectus** unfinished
propere: properus speedy
laurum: laurus, _m._ laurel
capillis: capilli, _m. pl._ hair
ponite: pono remove
licet it is allowed, it is possible
tacito: tacitus silent, quiet
venerantur: veneror worship
indignata est: indignor be
indignant
summoque in vertice Cynthi
'on the highest peak of Mount
Cynthus'
gemina cum prole 'with her
twin offspring'
35 **en** behold
animosa: animosus strong,
proud
creatis: creo create, produce
Iunoni: Iuno, -onis, _f._ Juno
cessura: cedo yield
an whether
saecula: saeculum, _n._ age,
century
cultis: colo worship, honour
arceor: arceo prevent, keep
from
succurritis: succurro help
diro: dirus dreadful
convicia: convicium, _n._ insult
40 **Tantalis** the daughter of
Tantalus, i.e. Niobe
postponere: postpono esteem
less than
natis ... suis
ausa: audeo dare
reccidat: recido rebound
exhibuit: exhibeo display
linguam: lingua, _f._ tongue
scelerata: sceleratus wicked
paternam: paternus of one's
father

gelidis: gelidus cold
incumbit: incumbo bend over
ordine nullo
ordine: ordo, -inis, _m._ order
oscula: osculum, _n._ kiss
dispensat: dispenso dispense,
add
suprema: supremus final
45 **liventia: liveo** be discoloured
bracchia: bracchium, _n._ arm
tollens: tollo raise
pascere, pasco _here, imperative_
'feed on'
ait: aio say
satia: satio sate, satisfy
luctu: luctus, -us, _m._ grief
cor, cordis, _n._ heart
ferum: ferus cruel
funera: funus, -eris, _n._ death
exsulta: exsulto rejoice, exult
50 **victrix, -icis, _f._** female victor
inimica: inimicus hostile
supersunt: supersum + _dat._
survive
sonuit: sono sound, make a
noise
contento: contentus tense,
tight
nervus, _m._ bowstring
arcu: arcus, -us, _m._ bow

Death of the Niobids

qui praeter Nioben unam conterruit omnes;
illa malo est audax. stabant cum vestibus atris
55 ante toros fratrum demisso crine sorores.
e quibus una trahens haerentia viscere tela
imposito fratri moribunda relanguit ore.

...

8. **What does Niobe's body language tell us about her state of mind in the first three lines of this extract?**
9. **What is the tone of Niobe's speech here?**
10. **What effect do the words 'et sonuit contento nervus ab arcu' have?**

The slaughter of Niobe's daughters continues.

haec frustra fugiens conlabitur, illa sorori
immoritur; latet haec, illam trepidare videres.
60 sexque datis leto diversaque vulnera passis
ultima restabat; quam toto corpore mater,
tota veste tegens 'unam minimamque relinque;
de multis minimam posco' clamavit 'et unam.'
dumque rogat, pro qua rogat, occidit. orba resedit
65 exanimes inter natos natasque virumque
deriguitque malis; nullos movet aura capillos,
in vultu color est sine sanguine, lumina maestis
stant immota genis; nihil est in imagine vivum.
ipsa quoque interius cum duro lingua palato
70 congelat, et venae desistunt posse moveri;
nec flecti cervix nec bracchia reddere motus
nec pes ire potest; intra quoque viscera saxum est.
flet tamen et validi circumdata turbine venti
in patriam rapta est; ibi fixa cacumine montis
75 liquitur, et lacrimas etiamnum marmora manant.

Ovid *Metamorphoses* 6.165–183, 191–213, 277–291, 295–312

11. **How does the Latin convey the effect that Niobe's daughters are picked off one by one?**
12. **In what ways is Niobe's final speech made moving?**
13. **Describe the various stages of the metamorphosis of Niobe.**
14. **Niobe's story could be said to be one of divine retribution. What is divine retribution? Explain how applicable it is in this case, and whether or not, in your opinion, Niobe gets what she deserves.**

praeter + *acc.* except
conterruit: conterreo terrify
illa malo est audax 'is
  emboldened in misfortune'
atris: ater black
55 **toros: torus, *m.*** funeral bier
demisso crine 'with hair
  dishevelled'
trahens: traho pull, drag
haerentia: haereo cling, stick
viscere: viscus, -eris, *n.* heart
tela: telum, *n.* shaft, arrow
imposito: impono place upon
moribunda: moribundus
  dying
relanguit: relanguesco fall
ore: os, oris, *n.* face

conlabitur: conlabor fall, slip
immoritur: immorior die
latet: lateo hide
trepidare: trepido tremble in
  alarm
60 **leto: letum, *n.*** death
diversa: diversus different
passis: patior suffer
ultima: ultimus last
restabat: resto remain
tegens: tego cover
de multis 'from many'
posco demand
resedit: resido sit back down
65 **exanimes: exanimis** lifeless
deriguit: derigesco become
  stiff, motionless
aura, *f.* breeze
vultu: vultus, -us, *m.* face
maestis: maestus sad,
  sorrowful
genis: gena, *f.* cheek
interius inside
duro: durus hard
palato: palatum, *n.* palate
70 **congelat: congelo** harden,
  congeal
venae: vena, *f.* vein
desistunt: desisto stop, cease
flecti: flecto turn, bend
motus: motus, -us, *m.* motion,
  movement
pes, pedis, *m.* foot
intra within, inside
viscera, *n. pl.* internal organs
saxum, *n.* rock
flet: fleo weep
validi: validus strong
circumdata: circumdo
  surround

turbine: turbo, -inis, *m.*
  whirlwind, tornado
venti: ventus, *m.* wind
cacumine: cacumen, -inis, *n.*
  peak
75 **liquitur: liquor** waste away,
  dissolve
etiamnum even now
marmora: marmor, -oris, *n.*
  marble, stone
manant: mano drip

2. The Elysian Fields, resting place of the virtuous

On his visit to the Underworld with the prophetess, the Sibyl, Aeneas has just seen the area of Tartarus which is devoted to the punishment of those who have done wrong during their lives. He has made the due offering of the Golden Bough (his Underworld entry ticket) to Proserpina, queen of the Underworld.

> his demum exactis, perfecto munere divae,
> devenere locos laetos et amoena virecta
> fortunatorum nemorum sedesque beatas.
> largior hic campos aether et lumine vestit
> 5   purpureo, solemque suum, sua sidera norunt.
> pars in gramineis exercent membra palaestris,
> contendunt ludo et fulva luctantur harena;
> pars pedibus plaudunt choreas et carmina dicunt.
> nec non Threicius longa cum veste sacerdos
> 10   obloquitur numeris septem discrimina vocum,
> iamque eadem digitis, iam pectine pulsat eburno.
> hic genus antiquum Teucri, pulcherrima proles,
> magnanimi heroes nati melioribus annis,
> Ilusque Assaracusque et Troiae Dardanus auctor.
> 15   arma procul currusque virum miratur inanes;
> stant terra defixae hastae passimque soluti
> per campum pascuntur equi. quae gratia currum
> armorumque fuit vivis, quae cura nitentes
> pascere equos, eadem sequitur tellure repostos.
> 20   conspicit, ecce, alios dextra laevaque per herbam
> vescentes laetumque choro paeana canentes
> inter odoratum lauris nemus, unde superne
> plurimus Eridani per silvam volvitur amnis.
> hic manus ob patriam pugnando vulnera passi,
> 25   quique sacerdotes casti, dum vita manebat,
> quique pii vates et Phoebo digna locuti,
> inventas aut qui vitam excoluere per artes
> quique sui memores aliquos fecere merendo:
> omnibus his nivea cinguntur tempora vitta.
>
> Virgil *Aeneid* 6.637–665

One of the spirits of the blessed, Musaeus, points out where Aeneas can find his father Anchises.

his ... exactis 'these tasks finished'
demum at last
perfecto: perficio complete, fulfil, accomplish
munere: munus, -eris, n. gift, dutiful offering
divae: diva, f. goddess
devenere = devenerunt: devenio arrive at
amoena: amoenus pleasant
virecta: virectum, n. area of greenery, glade
nemorum: nemus, -oris, n. grove, wood
sedes: sedes, -is, f. seat, home, residence
beatas: beatus blessed, fortunate
largior: largus ample, bountiful
aether, -eris, m. sky
vestit: vestio clothe, cover, bathe (of light)
5 **purpureo: purpureus** bright, radiant
solem: sol, solis, m. sun
sidera: sidus, -eris, n. star
norunt = noverunt: novi know
pars, partis, f. some
gramineis: gramineus grassy
exercent: exerceo exercise
membra: membrum, n. limb
palaestris: palaestra, f. wrestling-ground, exercise area
contendunt: contendo compete
fulva: fulvus tawny
luctantur: luctor wrestle
harena: harena, f. sand
plaudunt: plaudo beat out
choreas: chorea, f. dance
carmina dicunt 'sing songs'
nec non 'and'
Threicius Thracian
veste: vestis, -is, f. clothing, robe
sacerdos, -otis, m. priest (Orpheus)
10 **obloquitur numeris septem discrimina vocum** 'sings a seven-noted tune' (lit. accompanies to rhythms seven distinct levels of voice)
digitis: digitus, m. finger
pectine: pecten, -inis, m. the quill with which a lyre is struck, plectrum

eburno: eburnus of ivory
genus, -eris, n. race
antiquum: antiquus ancient, of old
Teucri: Teucer Teucer, an ancient king of Troy
proles, -is, f. offspring
magnanimi: magnanimus brave, heroic
nati: natus born
Ilus Trojan hero, a son of Dardanus, or son of Tros
Assaracus Trojan hero, son of Tros
Dardanus son of Zeus and Electra
auctor, -oris, m. founder
15 **procul** at a distance
currus: currus, -us, m. chariot
virum = virorum
miratur: miror wonder at
inanes: inanis empty
defixae: defixus fixed
hastae: hasta, f. spear
passim everywhere
soluti: solvo untie
pascuntur: pasco feed, pasture
quae gratia ..., quae cura ..., eadem ... 'those whose interest whilst they were alive was ..., those whose care was ..., the same care ...'
vivis: vivus alive, living
nitentes: niteo shine, gleam
tellure: tellus, -uris, n. ground, earth
repostos 'those laid to rest'
20 **dextra laevaque** 'on the right and on the left'
herbam: herba, f. grass
vescentes: vescor take food, eat
choro: chorus, m. choir, chorus, dance,
paeana: paean, paeanis, m. here Greek acc., hymn
canentes: cano sing
odoratum: odoratus sweet-smelling, fragrant
lauris: laurus, f. laurel tree, bay tree
superne above, at a higher level
plurimus mighty
Eridani: Eridanus the river Eridanus
volvitur 'flows'
amnis, -is, m. river
ob + acc. on account of
patriam: patria, f. homeland

passi: patior suffer
25 **casti: castus** pure, chaste
pii: pius dutiful, devout
vates: vates, -is, m. seer, soothsayer, diviner
Phoebo digna locuti 'who spoke (or sang) utterances worthy of (Phoebus) Apollo
inventas ... per artes 'through new skills' (lit. through discovered arts)
excoluere = excoluerunt: excolo improve
quique sui memores ... merendo 'and those who made some remember them by their service'
sui 'of them'
memores: memor mindful, remembering
aliquos: aliquis someone, so here, some
fecere = fecerunt
merendo 'by their service'
nivea: niveus snow-white
cinguntur: cingo surround
tempora, n. pl. temples (of the head), forehead
vitta: vitta, f. linen or woollen head-band

1. How in the first five lines of this extract does Virgil make the Elysian Fields sound pleasant?
2. In what activities are the spirits of the blessed engaged?
3. What categories of spirits are listed here?
4. How is Virgil's portrayal of the Elysian Fields similar to other representations of the after life for those who are considered good?

3. A hard-working wife

Virgil uses a simile to compare Vulcan (husband of Venus and stepfather of Aeneas) getting up early to make armour for Aeneas, to a virtuous and hard-working wife and mother.

> inde ubi prima quies medio iam noctis abactae
> curriculo expulerat somnum, cum femina primum,
> cui tolerare colo vitam tenuique Minerva
> impositum, cinerem et sopitos suscitat ignes
> 5   noctem addens operi, famulasque ad lumina longo
> exercet penso, castum ut servare cubile
> coniugis et possit parvos educere natos:
> haud secus ignipotens nec tempore segnior illo
> mollibus e stratis opera ad fabrilia surgit.
>
> Virgil Aeneid 8.407–415

1. In what ways is this simile appropriate? Vulcan has just been seduced by Venus, as she seeks to persuade him to make this armour.
2. In what ways is this woman 'virtuous'?

4. Different standards for men and women

Plautus depicts an old female slave complaining about the different rules by which men and women must live.

> ecastor lege dura vivont mulieres
> multoque iniquiore miserae quam viri.
> nam si vir scortum duxit clam uxorem suam,
> id si rescivit uxor, impunest viro;
> 5   uxor virum si clam domo egressa est foras,
> viro fit causa, exigitur matrumonio.
> utinam lex esset eadem quae uxori est viro;
> nam uxor contenta est quae bona est uno viro:
> qui minu' vir una uxore contentus siet?

quies, quietis, *f.* quiet, deep sleep

medio ... curriculo 'from the mid-course'

iam noctis abactae 'of night now driven away'

expulerat: expello drive out

somnum: somnus, *m.* sleep

cui 'on whom'

tolerare: tolero bear, endure

colo: colus, *f.* distaff (staff on which wool or flax is wound during weaving)

tenuique Minerva 'with simple craft' (Minerva was goddess of weaving)

impositum = impositum est

cinerem: cinis, -eris, *m.* ashes

sopitos: sopio sleep, *so here*, 'smouldering' *or* 'slumbering'

suscitat: suscito rouse to flame, kindle

5 **addens: addo** add

operi: opus, operis, *n.* work

famulas: famula, *f.* female slave, maid-servant

ad lumina 'by the firelight'

exercet: exerceo administer, manage

longo ... penso

penso: pensum, *n.* task

castum: castus chaste

castum ... cubile

servare: servo keep, preserve

cubile: cubile, *n.* bed

coniugis: coniunx, coniugis, *m.f.* husband/wife, *here* husband

educere: educo rear, raise

natos: nati, *m. pl.* children

haud secus not otherwise

ignipotens, ignipotentis, *m.* god of fire

tempore ... illo

segnior: segnis sluggish, inactive, slow

mollibus e stratis 'from his soft bed'

fabrilia: fabrilis of or belonging to a metal worker (**opera ... fabrilia** 'his work at the forge')

ecastor 'by Castor!'

lege dura

lege: lex, legis, *f.* law

dura: durus hard, tough

Virgil writing the *Aeneid* with two of the Muses

vivont = vivunt: vivo live

mulieres: mulier, -eris, *f.* woman

multoque iniquiore 'much more unfair'

scortum: scortum, *n.* prostitute

clam uxorem suam 'without his wife knowing'

rescivit: rescisco find out

impunest 'goes unpunished', 'gets away with it'

5 **virum ... clam = clam virum**

foras out of doors

causa, *f.* cause, grounds for divorce

exigitur matrumonio 'she is driven out of the marriage'

matrumonio = matrimonio

utinam would that

contenta: contentus happy

qui minu' vir ... siet? 'why should a husband be less ...?'

minu' = minus

siet = sit

10   ecastor faxim, si itidem plectantur viri,
       si quis clam uxorem duxerit scortum suam,
       ut illae exiguntur quae in se culpam commerent,
       plures viri sint vidui quam nunc mulieres.

Plautus Mercator 817–829

3. **What differences are listed between the behaviour of men and women? What are the consequences of their behaviour?**
4. **How, according to the slave, should men be treated?**
5. **Looking at both the Plautus and the Virgil extracts, how do you think the expectations of men and women's behaviour have changed since classical times?**

5. The corruption and cruelty of Verres and Cleomenes

Cicero, in his speech to prosecute Verres, the corrupt Roman governor of Sicily, describes how Cleomenes, Verres' corrupt henchman, is in charge of the Sicilian defence fleet against pirates, which is in a very poor state (depleted and ill-fed) through Verres' neglect, whilst Verres enjoys the high life with Cleomenes' wife.

       egreditur in Centuripina quadriremi Cleomenes e portu; sequitur
       Segestana navis, Tyndaritana, Herbitensis, Heracliensis,
       Apolloniensis, Haluntina, praeclara classis in speciem, sed inops et
       infirma propter dimissionem propugnatorum atque remigum. tam
5   diu in imperio suo classem iste praetor diligens vidit quam diu
       convivium eius flagitiosissimum praetervecta est; ipse autem, qui
       visus multis diebus non esset, tum se tamen in conspectum nautis
       paulisper dedit. stetit soleatus praetor populi Romani cum pallio
       purpureo tunicaque talari muliercula nixus in litore. iam hoc istum
10   vestitu Siculi civesque Romani permulti saepe viderant.
       posteaquam paulum provecta classis est et Pachynum quinto die
       denique adpulsa, nautae coacti fame radices palmarum agrestium,
       quarum erat in illis locis, sicuti in magna parte Siciliae, multitudo,
       colligebant et iis miseri perditique alebantur; Cleomenes autem,
15   qui alterum se Verrem cum luxurie ac nequitia tum etiam imperio
       putaret, similiter totos dies in litore tabernaculo posito perpotabat.
       ecce autem repente ebrio Cleomene esurientibus ceteris nuntiatur
       piratarum esse navis in portu Odysseae; nam ita is locus
       nominatur; nostra autem classis erat in portu Pachyni. Cleomenes
20   autem, quod erat terrestre praesidium non re sed nomine, speravit
       iis militibus quos ex eo loco deduxisset explere se numerum

10 **faxim** 'I'd suppose that'
itidem in the same way
plectantur: plecto punish
si quis ... if any man ...
ut illae ... as those women ...
culpam: culpa, _f._ blame
commerent: commereo merit
vidui: viduus single; _here m. pl._
  'single men'

egreditur: egredior go out,
  leave
in Centuripina quadriremi
  'in a Centuripan quadrireme'
  (a quadrireme is a galley with
  four banks of oars)
Segestana: Segestanus 'of
  Segesta'
Tyndaritana: Tyndaritanus
  'of Tyndaris'
Herbitensis 'from Herbita'
Heracliensis 'from Heraclia'
Apolloniensis 'from Apollonia'
Haluntina: Haluntinus 'from
  Haluntium'
praeclara: praeclarus fine,
  noble (_said sarcastically_)
classis, -is, _f._ fleet
in speciem 'in appearance'
inops needy, poor
infirma: infirmus weak
**dimissionem: dimissio, -onis,
  _f._** dismissal, discharge
**propugnatorum:
  propugnator, -oris, _m._**
  fighting man, defender
remigum: remex, -igis, _m._ rower
5 **iste** that
praetor: praetor, -oris, _m._
  praetor, governor
diligens careful, diligent, hard-
  working
quam diu as long as
convivium: convivium, _n._
  banquet, feast
flagitiosissimum: flagitiosus
  disgraceful, infamous
**praetervecta est:
  praetervehor** sail by, pass by
se ... dedit 'he showed himself'
**conspectum: conspectus, -us,
  _m._** sight
paulisper for a short time
soleatus 'wearing sandals _or_
  slippers'
pallio: pallium, _n._ cloak
talari: talaris reaching down to
  the ankles
muliercula: muliercula, _f._
  'prostitute'

nixus: nitor lean on
litore: litus, -oris, _n._ shore
10 **vestitu: vestitus, -us, _m._**
  clothing, garb
Siculi Sicilians
permulti very many
provecta: proveho carry
  forward
Pachynum: Pachynus a town
  in south-eastern Sicily
adpulsa: appello drive towards
coacti: cogo force, compel
fame: fames, -is, _f._ hunger
radices: radix, -icis, _f._ root
palmarum agrestium 'of wild
  palms'
sicuti as
multitudo, -inis, _f._ crowd
colligebant: colligo collect,
  gather
perditi: perditus desperate
alebantur: alo nourish
15 **cum ... tum ...** 'not only ... but
  also...'
luxurie ac nequitia 'excess
  and vice'
putaret: puto think, imagine
similiter in similar fashion
**tabernaculo: tabernaculum,
  _n._** tent
perpotabat: perpoto drink
  heavily
repente suddenly
ebrio: ebrius drunk
esurientibus: esurio be
  hungry
20 **terrestre praesidium** 'land-
  based garrison'
non re sed nomine 'not in
  reality but in name only'
deduxisset: deduco lead out
explere: expleo 'make up the
  numbers'

nautarum et remigum posse. reperta est eadem istius hominis
avarissimi ratio in praesidiis quae in classibus; nam erant perpauci
reliqui, ceteri dimissi.

...

1. **How does Cicero make his description of the fleet striking?**
2. **What picture do we gain of Verres from the first paragraph, and what is the tone of Cicero's language here?**
3. **In what state are the sailors, and how does Cicero emphasise this?**
4. **How does Cicero portray Cleomenes as just as awful a character as Verres?**

Cleomenes flees as the pirates attack. One captain is killed, and another later has to be ransomed, whilst the rest beach their ships following Cleomenes' example. The Roman fleet is then burnt by the pirates, who continue to Syracuse, even entering the harbour. Verres tries to pin the blame on the captains of the Roman fleet, but when that fails, he decides they must be put to death to prevent them telling the truth about the dreadful state of the fleet. At the same time he decides to spare Cleomenes.

25   procedit iste repente e praetorio inflammatus scelere furore
      crudelitate; in forum venit, nauarchos vocari iubet. qui nihil
      metuerent, nihil suspicarentur, statim accurrunt. iste hominibus
      miseris innocentibus inici catenas imperat. implorare illi fidem
      praetoris, et quare id faceret rogare. tum iste hoc causae dicit, quod
30   classem praedonibus prodidissent. fit clamor et admiratio populi
      tantam esse in homine impudentiam atque audaciam ut aut aliis
      causam calamitatis attribueret quae omnis propter avaritiam ipsius
      accidisset, aut, cum ipse praedonum socius arbitraretur, aliis
      proditionis crimen inferret; deinde hoc quinto decimo die crimen
35   esse natum postquam classis esset amissa.

      ...

5. **How do we get the impression that Verres acts quickly?**
6. **How is the innocence of the naval captains emphasised?**
7. **Why are people particularly shocked by Verres' behaviour, and how is this shown?**

Despite the fact that they are innocent, and the pleas of their parents, the naval captains are condemned and put in prison. Cleomenes, meanwhile, gets away with it.

      includuntur in carcerem condemnati; supplicium constituitur in
      illos, sumitur de miseris parentibus nauarchorum; prohibentur adire
      ad filios, prohibentur liberis suis cibum vestitumque ferre. patres hi
      quos videtis iacebant in limine, matresque miserae pernoctabant ad
40   ostium carceris ab extremo conspectu liberum exclusae; quae nihil

reperta est: reperio find
avarissimi: avarus stingy, greedy
ratio, -onis, _f._ reasoning, method
in praesidiis 'with the land-based troops'
perpauci very few
reliqui: reliquus remaining

25 **praetorio: praetorium, _n._** praetor's headquarters
inflammatus: inflammo inflame, excite
scelere: scelus, -eris, _n._ crime, wickedness
furore: furor, -oris, _m._ madness
crudelitate: crudelitas, -atis, _f._ cruelty
nauarchos: nauarchus, _m._ ship's captain
metuerent: metuo fear
suspicarentur: suspicor suspect
accurrunt: accurro run up
inici: inicio throw on, put on
catenas: catena, _f._ chain
implorare: imploro invoke, call upon
quare why
hoc causae dicit 'he says this is the reason'
30 **praedonibus: praedo, -onis, _m._** pirate
prodidissent: prodo betray, hand over
admiratio, -onis, _f._ wonder
impudentiam: impudentia, _f._ shamelessness, nerve
audaciam: audacia, _f._ boldness
ut aliis ... attribueret 'that he should attribute to others ...'
calamitatis: calamitas, -atis, _f._ calamity
avaritiam: avaritia, _f._ greed
socius, _m._ ally
arbitraretur: arbitror think
proditionis: proditio, -onis, _f._ betrayal, treason
crimen: crimen, -inis, _n._ charge
quinto decimo die 'on the fifteenth day'
esse natum 'originated'
35 **esset amissa: amitto** lose

includuntur: includo shut in
carcerem: carcer, -eris, _m._ prison
condemnati: condemno condemn
supplicium, _n._ punishment, penalty
constituitur 'is settled upon'
sumitur 'is exacted from'

limine, limen, -inis, _n._ threshold
pernoctabant: pernocto spend the night
40 **ostium: ostium, _n._** entrance
extremo: extremus final
liberum = liberorum 'of their children'
exclusae: excludo shut out from

Cicero

aliud orabant nisi ut filiorum suorum postremum spiritum ore
excipere liceret. aderat ianitor carceris, carnifex praetoris, mors
terrorque sociorum et civium Romanorum, lictor Sextius, cui ex
omni gemitu doloreque certa merces comparabatur. 'ut adeas,
45   tantum dabis, ut cibum tibi intro ferre liceat, tantum.' nemo
recusabat. 'quid? ut uno ictu securis adferam mortem filio tuo, quid
dabis? ne diu crucietur, ne saepius feriatur, ne cum sensu doloris
aliquo spiritus auferatur?' etiam ob hanc causam pecunia lictori dabatur.

8. **How are the naval captains treated in prison?**
9. **In what crimes does Sextius indulge and how is his wickedness emphasised?**

o magnum atque intolerandum dolorem! o gravem acerbamque
50   fortunam! non vitam liberum, sed mortis celeritatem pretio
redimere cogebantur parentes. atque ipsi etiam adulescentes cum
Sextio suo de plaga et de uno illo ictu loquebantur, idque
postremum parentes suos liberi orabant, ut levandi cruciatus sui
causa lictori pecunia daretur. multi et graves dolores inventi
55   parentibus et propinquis, multi; verum tamen mors sit extremum.
non erit. estne aliquid ultra quo crudelitas progredi possit?
reperietur; nam illorum, cum erunt securi percussi ac necati,
corpora feris obicientur. hoc si luctuosum est parentibus, redimant
pretio sepeliendi potestatem. ... quis tam fuit illo tempore ferreus,
60   quis tam inhumanus praeter unum te, qui non illorum aetate
nobilitate miseria commoveretur? ecquis fuit quin lacrimaret, quin
ita calamitatem illam putaret illorum ut fortunam tamen non
alienam, periculum autem commune arbitraretur? feriuntur securi.
laetaris tu in omnium gemitu et triumphas; testes avaritiae tuae
65   gaudes esse sublatos. errabas, Verres, et vehementer errabas, cum
te maculas furtorum et flagitiorum tuorum sociorum innocentium
sanguine eluere arbitrabare.
Cicero *In Verrem* 2.5.86, 87, 106, 117–119, 121 (abridged)

10. **How does Cicero use emotion to convey how awful the situation is?**
11. **In what three ways does Sextius gain money from the young men and their**
    parents?
12. **How does Cicero convey how extreme this cruelty is?**
13. **What effect does the repetition of 'errabas' have?**
14. **Some people say that 'power corrupts'. What modern examples of corruption**
    can you think of? Is power the cause?

postremum spiritum 'dying breath'
excipere: excipio receive
liceret: licet it is allowed
ianitor, -oris, *m.* doorkeeper
carnifex, -icis, *m.* executioner, butcher, torturer
lictor, -oris, *m.* lictor (Roman magistrate's attendant)
gemitu: gemitus, -us, *m.* groan
merces, -edis, *f.* pay, reward
comparabatur: comparo gain

45 **tantum** 'so much'
intro inside
recusabat: recuso refuse, say no
ictu: ictus, -us, *m.* blow
securis: securis, -is, *f.* axe
crucietur: crucio torture
feriatur: ferio strike, hit
sensu: sensus, -us, *m.* feeling
spiritus, -us, *m.* breath, spirit
auferatur: aufero carry away

intolerandum: intolerandus not to be tolerated
acerbam: acerbus bitter
50 **celeritatem: celeritas, -atis, *f.*** speed
pretio: pretium, *n.* price
redimere: redimo buy
plaga: plaga, *f.* blow, stroke
levandi: levo relieve, lessen
cruciatus: cruciatus, -us, *m.* torture
55 **propinquis: propinqui, *m. pl.*** relatives
ultra beyond
percussi: percutio strike
feris: fera, *f.* wild beast
obicientur: obicio throw
luctuosum: luctuosus grievous
sepeliendi: sepelio bury
potestatem: potestas, -atis, *f.* power, right
ferreus iron-hearted
60 **inhumanus** inhuman
praeter + *acc.* except for
aetate: aetas, -atis, *f.* age, youth
miseria: miseria, *f.* wretchedness
commoveretur: commoveo move
ecquis fuit quin ...? 'Was there any man who did not ...?'
lacrimaret: lacrimo cry

alienam: alienus of another
commune: communis common
laetaris: laetor be happy
gemitu: gemitus, -us, *m.* groan, misery
triumphas: triumpho triumph, rejoice
testes: testis, -is, *m.f.* witness
65 **gaudes: gaudeo** rejoice
esse sublatos: tollo eliminate
errabas: erro make a mistake
vehementer 'to a great extent'
maculas: macula, *f.* stain
furtorum: furtum, *n.* theft
flagitiorum: flagitium, *n.* crime
sociorum: socius, *m.* ally
eluere: eluo wash out

6. The bravery of Mucius Scaevola and Cloelia

King Porsenna and his Etruscan forces have attacked, and are now blockading the city of Rome. Gaius Mucius Scaevola, a young nobleman considers this to be a disgrace, and forms a plan to penetrate the enemy camp. For fear of being caught as a deserter, he asks permission from the Senate first.

senatum adit. 'transire Tiberim,' inquit, 'patres, et intrare, si
possim, castra hostium volo, non praedo nec populationum in
vicem ultor; maius si di iuvant in animo est facinus.' adprobant
patres; abdito intra vestem ferro proficiscitur. ubi eo venit,
5   in confertissima turba prope regium tribunal constitit. ibi cum
stipendium militibus forte daretur et scriba cum rege sedens pari
fere ornatu multa ageret eumque milites volgo adirent, timens
sciscitari uter Porsenna esset, ne ignorando regem semet ipse
aperiret quis esset, quo temere traxit fortuna facinus, scribam pro
10   rege obtruncat. vadentem inde qua per trepidam turbam cruento
mucrone sibi ipse fecerat viam, cum concursu ad clamorem facto
comprehensum regii satellites retraxissent, ante tribunal regis
destitutus, tum quoque inter tantas fortunae minas metuendus
magis quam metuens, 'Romanus sum' inquit, 'civis; Gaium Mucium
15   vocant. hostis hostem occidere volui, nec ad mortem minus animi
est quam fuit ad caedem; et facere et pati fortia Romanum est. nec
unus in te ego hos animos gessi; longus post me ordo est idem
petentium decus. proinde in hoc discrimen, si iuvat, accingere, ut
in singulas horas capite dimices tuo, ferrum hostemque in vestibulo
20   habeas regiae. hoc tibi iuventus Romana indicimus bellum. nullam
aciem, nullum proelium timueris; uni tibi et cum singulis res erit.'

1. **What is Gaius Mucius' plan?**
2. **What does he see upon entering the enemy camp?**
3. **How does Gaius Mucius' speech convey his brave and forceful character?**

cum rex simul ira incensus periculoque conterritus circumdari
ignes minitabundus iuberet ... 'en tibi' inquit, 'ut sentias quam vile
corpus sit iis qui magnam gloriam vident'; dextramque accenso
25   ad sacrificium foculo inicit. quam cum velut alienato ab sensu torreret
animo, prope attonitus miraculo rex cum ab sede sua prosiluisset
amoverique ab altaribus iuvenem iussisset, 'tu vero abi' inquit, 'in
te magis quam in me hostilia ausus. iuberem macte virtute esse, si
pro mea patria ista virtus staret; nunc iure belli liberum te, intactum

praedo, -onis, *m.* brigand, *so here*, 'as a brigand'
populationum: populatio, -onis, *f.* plundering
in vicem 'in return'
ultor, -oris, *m.* avenger
maius ... facinus
di = dei
iuvant: iuvo help
facinus, -oris, *n.* crime, deed
adprobant = approbant: adprobo approve
patres, *m. pl.* senators
abdito: abdo hide, conceal
intra + *acc.* inside
vestem: vestis, -is, *f.* clothing
ferro: ferrum, *n.* sword, weapon
eo there, to that place

5 **in confertissima turba** 'in the densest part of the crowd'
regium: regius royal
tribunal: tribunal, -alis, *n.* platform
constitit: consisto stand, halt
stipendium, *n.* pay
scriba, *m.* secretary
pari: par equal, similar
fere almost
ornatu: ornatus, -us, *m.* dress, costume
volgo = vulgo generally
sciscitari: sciscitor enquire
uter which of the two
ignorando: ignoro not know, fail to recognise
semet himself
aperiret: aperio reveal
quo ... facinus 'as fortune directed the deed'
temere blindly

10 **obtruncat: obtrunco** strike, kill
vadentem: vado go, proceed
trepidam: trepidus alarmed, anxious
cruento: cruentus bloody
mucrone: mucro, -onis, *m.* blade, sharp point
concursu: concursus, -us, *m.* rush
comprehensum: comprehendo seize
satellites: satelles, -itis, *m.* attendant, bodyguard
destitutus 'having been left'
minas: minae, *f. pl.* threats
metuendus 'to be feared'

15 **nec ad mortem minus animi est ...** 'I have no less courage to face death ...'
caedem: caedes, -is, *f.* slaughter, murder
animos: animus, *m.* mind, spirit, resolve
ordo, -inis, *m.* line
petentium: peto seek
decus: decus, -oris, *n.* glory
proinde so then
in hoc discrimen 'for this struggle'
accingere: accingo (*passive imperative*) 'prepare yourself'
in singulas horas 'every hour'
capite ... tuo 'for your life'
dimices: dimico fight
vestibulo: vestibulum, *n.* entrance

20 **regiae: regia, *f.*** palace
indicimus: indico declare
aciem: acies, *f.* battle-line
singulis: singuli individuals

ira incensus 'incensed by anger'
conterritus: conterreo terrify
circumdari: circumdo surround
minitabundus threatening
en look!
sentias: sentio feel
quam how
vile: vilis cheap
dextram: dextra, *f.* right hand
accenso: accendo blaze, set alight

25 **ad sacrificium** for sacrifice
foculo: foculus, *m.* fire, brazier
inicit: inicio throw into
quam 'it' (his hand)
velut as if
alienato ab sensu ... animo 'with his mind devoid of feeling'
torreret: torreo scorch, burn
prope almost
attonitus astonished
sede: sedes, -is, *f.* seat
prosiluisset: prosilio leap forth
amoveri: amoveo remove
hostilia 'hostile actions'
ausus: audeo dare
iuberem ... 'I would tell you ...'
macte virtute esse 'continue to be courageous'
iure: ius, iuris, *n.* law
intactum: intactus untouched

30 inviolatumque hinc dimitto.' tunc Mucius, quasi remunerans
meritum, 'quando quidem' inquit, 'est apud te virtuti honos, ut
beneficio tuleris a me quod minis nequisti, trecenti coniuravimus
principes iuventutis Romanae ut in te hac via grassaremur. mea
prima sors fuit; ceteri ut cuiusque ceciderit primi quoad
35 te opportunum fortuna dederit, suo quisque tempore aderunt.'

4. What do we learn of the character of Porsenna from his actions and speech?
5. How does Gaius Mucius respond?

Gaius Mucius gains the name Scaevola from the loss of his right hand, and is granted
a small piece of land across the Tiber, known as the Mucian Meadows. His bravery
inspires that of Cloelia.

ergo ita honorata virtute, feminae quoque ad publica decora
excitatae, et Cloelia virgo una ex obsidibus, cum castra Etruscorum
forte haud procul ripa Tiberis locata essent, frustrata custodes, dux
agminis virginum inter tela hostium Tiberim tranavit, sospitesque
40 omnes Romam ad propinquos restituit. quod ubi regi nuntiatum
est, primo incensus ira oratores Romam misit ad Cloeliam obsidem
deposcendam: alias haud magni facere. deinde in admirationem
versus, supra Coclites Muciosque dicere id facinus esse, et prae se
ferre quemadmodum si non dedatur obses, pro rupto foedus se
45 habiturum, sic deditam intactam inviolatamque ad suos
remissurum. utrimque constitit fides; et Romani pignus pacis ex
foedere restituerunt, et apud regem Etruscum non tuta solum
sed honorata etiam virtus fuit, laudatamque virginem parte
obsidum se donare dixit; ipsa quos vellet legeret. ... pace redintegrata
50 Romani novam in femina virtutem novo genere honoris, statua
equestri, donavere; in summa Sacra Via fuit posita virgo
insidens equo.

Livy *A History of Rome* 2.12–13 (abridged)

6. How is Cloelia described in line 37?
7. What does she do to escape and how does Porsenna respond at first?
8. How is the situation between the Romans and the Etruscans resolved?

30 **inviolatum: inviolatus** unviolated

dimitto send away

tunc then

quasi as if

remunerans: remunero pay back

meritum: meritum, *n.* kindness

quando quidem since

est apud te virtuti honos 'you hold courage in high regard'

beneficio: beneficium, *n.* kindness

tuleris 'you have obtained'

nequisti: nequeo be unable

trecenti three hundred

coniuravimus: coniuro swear

grassaremur: grassor attack

sors, sortis, *f.* lot

ut cuiusque ceciderit 'as each man's lot will have fallen'

quoad until

35 **te opportunum** 'a favourable chance against you', *lit.* 'you as convenient'

quisque each

ergo therefore

honorata: honoro honour, respect

virtute: virtus, -utis, *f.* bravery, courage

publica: publicus public

decora: decus, -oris, *n.* glory, honour

excitatae = excitatae sunt: excito rouse

obsidibus: obses, -idis, *m.f.* hostage

ripa: ripa, *f.* bank (of a river)

locata: loco place, locate

frustrata: frustror deceive

agminis: agmen, -inis, *n.* column, group

tela: telum, *n.* weapon

tranavit: trano swim across

sospites: sospes, -itis safe

40 **propinquos: propinqui** kinsfolk, family

restituit: restituo restore, give back

deposcendam: deposco require, demand

haud magni facere 'he did not care about'

admirationem: admiratio, -onis, *f.* wonder, admiration

versus 'turning'

supra above

dicere *here*, 'he said'

prae se ferre 'he announced that'

quemadmodum si ... , sic ... 'just as if ... , so ...'

dedatur: dedo surrender

pro rupto foedus se habiturum 'he would consider the treaty broken'

45 **intactam: intactus** untouched, unharmed

inviolatam: inviolatus unviolated

remissurum: remitto send back

utrimque on both sides

constitit: consisto stand, hold

fides, *f.* pledge, treaty, trust

pignus: pignus, -oris, *n.* 'as a pledge'

tuta: tutus safe

donare: dono present with, give

legeret: lego choose

redintegrata: redintegro restore

50 **genere: genus, -eris,** *n.* type, sort

equestri: equester of a horse

insidens: insideo sit on

Tiber Island, Rome

FAMILY LIFE AND RELATIONSHIPS

The Roman idea of family duty and closeness is readily found in Ovid's description in the *Tristia* of his parting from his loved ones before exile, whilst Catullus' use of almost formulaic language in his poem at his brother's grave contains and yet conveys his grief. In relationships outside the family with lovers, bounds are broken for Sulpicia, and Horace can only look on from the sidelines. Pliny recounts the conventions and ideals of family life – a situation reinforced by Tacitus' portrayal of education within the family. Others like Cicero and Catullus write of bitter hatreds and jealousies which can become all too consuming.

The young Cicero reading

1. Grief at parting

Sent into exile by Augustus for 'carmen et error' (thought to be a reference to the *Ars Amatoria*, and some connection with a scandal involving Augustus' granddaughter, Julia), Ovid recalls the night on which he had to leave Rome.

cum subit illius tristissima noctis imago,
  qua mihi supremum tempus in urbe fuit,
cum repeto noctem, qua tot mihi cara reliqui,
  labitur ex oculis nunc quoque gutta meis.
5 iam prope lux aderat, qua me discedere Caesar
  finibus extremae iusserat Ausoniae.
nec spatium nec mens fuerat satis apta parandi:
  torpuerant longa pectora nostra mora.
non mihi servorum, comites non cura legendi,
10 non aptae profugo vestis opisve fuit.
non aliter stupui, quam qui Iovis ignibus ictus
  vivit et est vitae nescius ipse suae.
ut tamen hanc animi nubem dolor ipse removit,
  et tandem sensus convaluere mei,
15 alloquor extremum maestos abiturus amicos,
  qui modo de multis unus et alter erat.
uxor amans flentem flens acrius ipsa tenebat,
  imbre per indignas usque cadente genas.
nata procul Libycis aberat diversa sub oris,
20 nec poterat fati certior esse mei.
quocumque aspiceres, luctus gemitusque sonabant,
  formaque non taciti funeris intus erat.
femina virque meo, pueri quoque funere maerent,
  inque domo lacrimas angulus omnis habet.
25 si licet exemplis in parvis grandibus uti,
  haec facies Troiae, cum caperetur, erat.
iamque quiescebant voces hominumque canumque
  Lunaque nocturnos alta regebat equos.
hanc ego suspiciens et ad hanc Capitolia cernens,
30 quae nostro frustra iuncta fuere Lari,
'numina vicinis habitantia sedibus,' inquam,
  'iamque oculis numquam templa videnda meis,
dique relinquendi, quos urbs habet alta Quirini,
  este salutati tempus in omne mihi.
...

subit: subeo come to mind
supremum: supremus final, last
repeto recall
labitur: labor slip, fall
gutta, f. tear
5 **lux, lucis, f.** light
Caesar the Emperor (Augustus)
finibus: fines, m. pl. borders
extremae: extremus furthest
Ausoniae: Ausonia Ausonia, Italy
spatium, n. time, space
apta: aptus suitable
torpuerant: torpesco grow numb
pectora: pectus, pectoris, n. heart
mora: mora, f. delay
legendi: lego gather
10 **profugo** 'for an exile'
opis: ops, opis, f. help, need
-ve or
aliter otherwise
stupui: stupeo be stunned, be numbed
ictus: ic(i)o strike, hit
nescius unaware
nubem: nubes, -is, f. cloud
sensus: sensus, -us, m. sense, emotion
convaluere = convaluerunt: convalesco grow strong, rally, recover
15 **alloquor** address
extremum 'for the last time'
maestos: maestus sad, sorrowful
modo now
flentem: fleo weep
acrius: acer eager, passionate
imbre: imber, -bris, m. constant flow of tears, downpour
indignas: indignus undeserving
usque continuously
genas: gena, f. cheek
nata, f. daughter
procul far away
Libycis: Libycus Libyan
diversa: diversus separate, apart
oris: ora, f. shore
20 **certior esse** 'be informed'
quocumque wherever
aspiceres: aspicio look
luctus: luctus, -us, m. grief, mourning

gemitus: gemitus, -us, m. groaning
sonabant: sono resound, be heard
taciti: tacitus silent
funeris: funus, -eris, n. death, funeral
intus inside, within
maerent: maereo be sad, lament, bewail
angulus, m. corner
25 **licet** it is allowed, possible
exemplis grandibus
grandibus: grandis big, large
uti: utor + *abl.* use
facies, f. appearance
quiescebant: quiesco be quiet
regebat: rego control, drive
suspiciens: suspicio look up
ad hanc 'by her', (i.e. the moon)
Capitolia: Capitolium the Capitol
cernens: cerno look at, determine, make out
30 **iuncta: iunctus** joined, united
fuere = fuerunt
Lari: lar, laris, m. household god
numina: numen, -inis, n. deity
vicinis: vicinus neighbouring
sedibus: sedes, -is, f. home
Quirini: Quirinus Quirinus (Romulus)
este salutati *lit.* 'be greeted', *so here* 'farewell'

Capitol at night, Rome

1. What does Ovid tell us about his physical and mental state?
2. In lines 9–10, what is the effect of the repetition of 'non'?
3. Pick out and translate two Latin phrases where Ovid's grief is emphasised effectively.
4. Ovid talks of missing Rome and its buildings. To what extent do you think this is possible? Or is it the people whom we associate with places that we miss?

35   hac prece adoravi superos ego : pluribus uxor,
        singultu medios impediente sonos.
    illa etiam ante Lares passis adstrata capillis
        contigit exstinctos ore tremente focos,
    multaque in adversos effudit verba Penates
40   pro deplorato non valitura viro.
    iamque morae spatium nox praecipitata negabat.
    ...
    ter limen tetigi, ter sum revocatus, et ipse
        indulgens animo pes mihi tardus erat.
    saepe 'vale' dicto rursus sum multa locutus,
45   et quasi discedens oscula summa dedi.
    saepe eadem mandata dedi meque ipse fefelli,
        respiciens oculis pignora cara meis.
    ...
    dividor haud aliter, quam si mea membra relinquam,
        et pars abrumpi corpore visa suo est.
50   sic doluit Mettus tunc cum in contraria versos
        ultores habuit proditionis equos.
    tum vero exoritur clamor gemitusque meorum,
        et feriunt maestae pectora nuda manus.
    tum vero coniunx umeris abeuntis inhaerens
55   miscuit haec lacrimis tristia verba meis:
    'non potes avelli. simul hinc, simul ibimus:' inquit,
        'te sequar et coniunx exsulis exsul ero.
    et mihi facta via est, et me capit ultima tellus:
        accedam profugae sarcina parva rati.'
                  Ovid *Tristia* 1.3.1–34, 41–47, 55–60, 73–84

5. How is the distress of Ovid's wife emphasised in lines 35–41?
6. How does Ovid make his farewells particularly vivid?
7. How appropriate do you find the description of Mettus?
8. Pick out three expressions in Latin which emphasise how sad Ovid is and explain each choice.

35 **prece: prex, precis, *f*.** prayer
adoravi: adoro worship
superos: superi, *m. pl*. the
  gods
singultu: singultus, -us, *m*.
  sobbing
impediente: impedio hinder
passis ... capillis 'with hair
  untied'
adstrata: adsterno prostrate
  oneself
contigit: contingo touch
exstinctos: exstinguo
  exstinguish
focos: focus, *m*. hearth, ashes,
  fireplace
adversos: adversus
  unfavourable
effudit: effundo pour out
Penates: Penates, *m. pl*.
  household gods
40 **deplorato: deploro** lament for,
  mourn for
valitura: valeo be strong, be
  powerful
praecipitata 'hurtling'
negabat: nego deny
ter three times
limen: limen, -inis, *n*.
  threshold
tetigi: tango touch
indulgens kind
pes, pedis, *m*. foot
tardus slow
vale farewell
45 **quasi** as if, practically
oscula: osculum, *n*. kiss
summa: summus 'the last'
mandata: mandatum, *n*.
  order, instruction
fefelli: fallo cheat, escape the
  notice of
respiciens: respicio look back
pignora: pignus, pignoris, *n*.
  pledge, *here* children
dividor: divido divide, separate
haud not
aliter otherwise, other
quam than
membra: membrum, *n*. limb
abrumpi: abrumpo tear away
  from
50 **doluit: doleo** suffer
tunc = tum
in contraria 'in opposing
  directions'
versos: verto turn, drive
ultores: ultor, -oris, *m*.
  avenger

proditionis: proditio, -onis, *f*.
  betrayal, treachery
exoritur: exorior arise
feriunt: ferio strike
umeris: umerus, *m*. shoulder
inhaerens: inhaereo cling
55 **miscuit: misceo** mix
avelli: avello tear from, separate
  by force
exsulis: exsul, -is, *m.f*. exile
ultima: ultimus farthest
tellus, -uris, *f*. land, earth
accedam: accedo be added
profugae: profugus refugee
sarcina: sarcina, *f*. burden,
  here, 'as a (small) burden'
rati: ratis, -is, *f*. ship

2. Love and Loss

a. Farewell to a brother

Catullus, after a long journey, visits his brother's grave.

> multas per gentes et multa per aequora vectus
>> advenio has miseras, frater, ad inferias,
> ut te postremo donarem munere mortis
>> et mutam nequiquam alloquerer cinerem.
> 5   quandoquidem fortuna mihi tete abstulit ipsum,
>> heu miser indigne frater adempte mihi,
> nunc tamen interea haec, prisco quae more parentum
>> tradita sunt tristi munere ad inferias,
> accipe fraterno multum manantia fletu,
> 10   atque in perpetuum, frater, ave atque vale.

Catullus 101 ad inferias

1. **How do the sounds of the poem reflect its sad tone?**
2. **What aspects of this poem make it particularly personal?**
3. **What is the effect of the last line?**

b. Rejection in love

Catullus talks to himself and tries to reassure himself.

> miser Catulle, desinas ineptire,
> et quod vides perisse perditum ducas.
> fulsere quondam candidi tibi soles,
> cum ventitabas quo puella ducebat
> 5   amata nobis quantum amabitur nulla.
> ibi illa multa cum iocosa fiebant,
> quae tu volebas nec puella nolebat,
> fulsere vere candidi tibi soles.
> nunc iam illa non vult: tu quoque impotens noli,
> 10   nec quae fugit sectare, nec miser vive,
> sed obstinata mente perfer, obdura.
> vale, puella. iam Catullus obdurat,
> nec te requiret nec rogabit invitam.
> at tu dolebis, cum rogaberis nulla.
> 15   scelesta, vae te, quae tibi manet vita?
> quis nunc te adibit? cui videberis bella?
> quem nunc amabis? cuius esse diceris?

Street of the Tombs, Pompeii

aequora: aequor, aequoris, **_n._** sea
vectus: vehor travel
inferias: inferiae, _f. pl._ funeral rites, sacrifices or offerings in honour of the dead
postremo: postremus final
donarem: dono present with
munere: munus, -eris, _n._ gift
mutam: mutus dumb, silent
nequiquam in vain
alloquerer: alloquor address
cinerem: cinis, -eris, _m._ ashes
5 **quandoquidem** since indeed
tete = te
heu alas
indigne: indignus unworthy
adempte: adimo take away
prisco ... more 'in the ancient custom'
parentum: parentes, _m. pl._ ancestors
fraterno: fraternus brotherly, of a brother
manantia: mano drip
fletu: fletus, -us, _m._ tears, weeping

10 **in perpetuum** forever
ave atque vale 'hail and farewell'

desinas 'cease!'
ineptire: ineptio be silly
perisse: pereo perish
perditum: perdo ruin, destroy
ducas: duco consider, reckon
fulsere = fulserunt: fulgeo shine
quondam once
candidi: candidus bright
soles: sol, solis, _m._ sun
ventitabas: ventito come repeatedly
5 **quantum** 'as much as'
iocosa 'pleasant things'
impotens powerless
10 **sectare: sector** follow, pursue
obstinata: obstinatus determined, steady, stubborn
perfer: perfero endure, see something through
obdura: obduro persist, endure
requiret: requiro seek, look for
invitam: invitus unwilling

dolebis: doleo grieve, suffer
rogaberis nulla '(when) you are not asked for'
15 **scelesta: scelestus** wicked
vae ah! woe! alas!
bella: bellus beautiful, pretty
cuius esse diceris? 'Whose will you be said to be?'

quem basiabis? cui labella mordebis?
at tu, Catulle, destinatus obdura.

Catullus 8 ad se ipsum

1. What image does Catullus use in line 3 and why? Why is the idea repeated?
2. What stage does it seem this relationship is at?
3. What examples of word-play are there in this poem?
4. What is the effect of the questions at the end of the poem? Who is meant to answer these questions?

c. Jealousy takes over

This poem is directed at Lesbia, Catullus' girlfriend, thought to have been the notorious Clodia, and reveals both Catullus' jealousy and depth of emotional attachment.

ille mi par esse deo videtur,
ille, si fas est, superare divos,
qui sedens adversus identidem te
    spectat et audit
5   dulce ridentem, misero quod omnes
eripit sensus mihi: nam simul te,
Lesbia, aspexi, nihil est super mi
    vocis in ore
lingua sed torpet, tenuis sub artus
10 flamma demanat, sonitu suopte
tintinant aures, gemina teguntur
    lumina nocte.
otium, Catulle, tibi molestum est:
otio exsultas nimiumque gestis:
15 otium et reges prius et beatas
    perdidit urbes.

Catullus 51 ad Lesbiam

1. How does Catullus stress love's physical effects in the second and third stanzas?
2. What is the effect of the final stanza?

basiabis: basio kiss
labella: labellum, *n.* lip
mordebis: mordeo bite
destinatus: destino determine

mi = mihi
par equal
fas, *n. indecin.* right
divos = deos
adversus opposite
identidem repeatedly
5 **dulce: dulcis** sweet
ridentem: rideo smile, laugh
misero mihi
aspexi: aspicio look at
nihil est super 'nothing
   remains'
ore: os, oris, *n.* mouth
lingua, *f.* tongue
torpet: torpeo be numb, be
   paralysed
tenuis slender
sub artus 'through my limbs'
10 **demanat: demano** spread
   down, pour down
sonitu: sonitus, -us, *m.* sound
suopte: suus 'their own'
tintinant: tintino make a
   ringing sound
aures: auris, -is, *f.* ear
gemina: geminus double
gemina nocte
teguntur: tego cover
lumina: lumen, -inis, *n.* light,
   eye
otium, *n.* leisure, free time,
   peace
molestum: molestus
   troublesome, tiresome
exsultas: exsulto rejoice, exult
nimium too much
gestis: gesta, *n. pl.* deeds.
   achievements
15 **beatas: beatus** happy,
   fortunate, blessed, wealthy
perdidit: perdo destroy, ruin

d. Ever-changing love

Two short poems which show the ever-changing dynamics of love and relationships.

> nulli se dicit mulier mea nubere malle
> > quam mihi, non si se Iuppiter ipse petat.
> dicit: sed mulier cupido quod dicit amanti,
> > in vento et rapida scribere oportet aqua.

Catullus 70

> odi et amo. quare id faciam, fortasse requiris?
> > nescio, sed fieri sentio et excrucior.

Catullus 85

1. **What does poem 70 tell us about Catullus' attitude to his lover?**
2. **How does the brevity of poem 85 effectively convey Catullus' feelings?**

3. Sulpicia discovers love

Sulpicia is one of the few female poets whose works remain from the ancient world. Here she expresses her feelings now that she has found love.

> tandem venit amor, qualem texisse pudori
> > quam nudasse alicui sit mihi fama magis.
> exorata meis illum Cytherea Camenis
> > adtulit in nostrum deposuitque sinum.
> 5 exsolvit promissa Venus: mea gaudia narret,
> > dicetur siquis non habuisse sua.
> non ego signatis quicquam mandare tabellis,
> > ne legat ut nemo quam meus ante, velim,
> sed peccasse iuvat, vultus conponere famae
> 10 taedet: cum digno digna fuisse ferar.

Sulpicia 1

1. **What imagery does Sulpicia use for how love came to her?**
2. **How does Sulpicia make the reader aware that she wants everyone to know about her love?**
3. **To what extent is Sulpicia behaving as other people expect her to, and to what extent is she breaking with convention?**

mulier, -eris, *f.* woman
nubere: nubo + *dat.* marry
petat: peto seek, fancy
cupido: cupidus eager, desirous
vento: ventus, *m.* wind
rapida: rapidus swirling
oportet one should

odi hate
quare why
fortasse perhaps
requiris: requiro ask
excrucior: excrucio torture,
   torment

qualem 'of a sort, of a kind
   which ...'
texisse: tego hide, cover up
pudori: pudor, -oris, *m.*
   shame, *here* predicative dative,
   'as a source of shame (to me)'
quam than
nudasse = nudavisse: nudo
   reveal
alicui: aliquis someone, so *here*,
   'to someone'
fama, *f.* rumour, report (*followed
   by indirect statement, so,* 'the
   rumour that ...')
magis more
exorata: exoro win over
Cytherea 'the Cytherean one' i.e.
   Venus
meis ... Camenis 'by my Muses'
Camenis: Camena, *f.* Muse
deposuit: depono drop
sinum: sinus, -us, *m.* lap
5 **exsolvit: exsolvo** perform, fulfil
gaudia: gaudium, *n.* joy,
   happiness
siquis 'if anyone', 'anyone who'
sua 'their own' (joyous
   experience of love)
signatis: signo seal
signatis ... tabellis
quicquam: quisquam anyone,
   anything
mandare: mando entrust
tabellis: tabella, *f.* message
   tablet
meus 'my lover', 'my man'
peccasse = peccavisse: pecco
   sin, do wrong
iuvat it pleases
vultus: vultus, -us, *m.* face
conponere = componere:
   compono compose, arrange
famae: fama, *f.* rumour

10 **taedet** it is tiring
digno: dignus worthy,
   deserving
ferar 'let me be said'

4. Love for a young man

Horace complains that Lydia is ruining Sybaris with too much love.

> Lydia, dic, per omnes
> hoc deos vere, Sybarin cur properes amando
> perdere, cur apricum
> oderit Campum, patiens pulveris atque solis,
> 5   cur neque militaris
> inter aequales equitet, Gallica nec lupatis
> temperet ora frenis?
> cur timet flavum Tiberim tangere? cur olivum
> sanguine viperino
> 10   cautius vitat neque iam livida gestat armis
> bracchia, saepe disco,
> saepe trans finem iaculo nobilis expedito?
> quid latet, ut marinae
> filium dicunt Thetidis sub lacrimosa Troia
> 15   funera, ne virilis
> cultus in caedem et Lycias proriperet catervas?

Horace Odes 1.8

1. In what sort of activities should Sybaris be indulging?
2. Who was the son of Thetis? Why do you think Horace uses this reference?
3. Is Horace more interested in Lydia or Sybaris?

5. A close-knit family

Pliny writes of how a mother, Arria, hides her grief at the death of her son so that her husband (Caecina Paetus), who is also in ill health, does not discover the news.

> aegrotabat Caecina Paetus maritus eius, aegrotabat et filius,
> uterque mortifere, ut videbatur. filius decessit eximia pulchritudine
> pari verecundia, et parentibus non minus ob alia carus quam quod
> filius erat. huic illa ita funus paravit, ita duxit exsequias, ut
> 5   ignoraret maritus; quin immo quotiens cubiculum eius intraret,
> vivere filium atque etiam commodiorem esse simulabat, ac
> persaepe interroganti, quid ageret puer, respondebat; 'bene quievit,
> libenter cibum sumpsit.' deinde, cum diu cohibitae lacrimae
> vincerent prorumperentque, egrediebatur; tunc se dolori dabat;
> 10 satiata siccis oculis composito vultu redibat, tamquam orbitatem
> foris reliquisset. praeclarum quidem illud eiusdem, ferrum

Sybarin *acc.* 'Sybaris'
properes: propero hurry, rush, hasten
perdere: perdo ruin, destroy
apricum: apricus sunny
oderit: odi hate
Campum: Campus, *m.* 'the Campus Martius' (an open area, in Rome, used as an exercise and training ground: 'Field of Mars')
patiens: patior endure
pulveris: pulvis, -eris, *m.* dust
solis: sol, solis, *m.* sun
5 **militaris** 'as a soldier'
aequales: aequalis equal, *so here,* 'his contemporaries' or 'his peers'
equitet: equito ride
Gallica: Gallicus Gallic
lupatis: lupatus with jagged teeth
temperet: tempero control
ora: os, oris, *n.* mouth
frenis: frenum, *n.* bridle, bit
flavum: flavus yellowish
tangere: tango touch
olivum: olivum, *n.* olive-oil
viperino: viperinus of a viper
10 **cautius: cautus** cautious
vitat: vito avoid
livida: lividus bruised
gestat: gesto carry, wear, display
bracchia: bracchium, *n.* arm
disco: discus, *m.* discus
finem: finis, -is, *m. & f.* limit, boundary limit, marker
iaculo: iaculum, *n.* javelin
nobilis noble, famous
expedito: expedio hurl, send forth
quid why?
latet: lateo hide, not be seen
marinae: marinus of the sea
Thetidis: Thetis the sea-nymph, Thetis, mother of Achilles
lacrimosa: lacrimosus sorrowful, weeping, grievous
15 **funera: funus, -eris, *n.*** death
virilis manly
cultus, -us, *m.* dress
caedem: caedes, -is, *f.* slaughter
Lycias: Lycius Lycian (the Lycians supported the Trojans)

Lovers kissing

proriperet: proripio snatch away
catervas: caterva, *f.* squadron, troop

aegrotabat: aegroto be ill
maritus, *m.* husband
uterque each of the two
mortifere terminally
decessit: decedo die
eximia: eximius extraordinary
pulchritudine: pulchritudo, -inis, *f.* beauty, handsomeness, attractiveness
pari: par equal
verecundia: verecundia, *f.* modesty, respect
ob alia 'on account of other factors'
carus dear
funus, -eris, *n.* funeral
duxit exsequias: duco exsequias carry out a funeral
5 **ignoraret: ignoro** be unaware
quin immo 'indeed, on the contrary'
quotiens whenever
cubiculum: cubiculum, *n.* bedroom
commodiorem: commodus well, healthy
simulabat: simulo pretend
persaepe very often
interroganti: interrogo ask, question
quievit: quiesco rest

libenter willingly
sumpsit: sumo eat, consume
cohibitae: cohibeo restrain
prorumperent: prorumpo break through
tunc = tum
dolori: dolor, -oris, *m.* grief, anguish
10 **satiata: satio** satisfy
siccis: siccus dry
composito: compono compose, settle
vultu: vultus, -us, *m.* face, expression
tamquam as if
orbitatem: orbitas, -atis, *f.* bereavement
foris outside
praeclarum ... illud eiusdem 'that noble action indeed is told of the same woman, that she ...'
ferrum: ferrum, *n.* sword, dagger

stringere, perfodere pectus, extrahere pugionem, porrigere marito,
addere vocem immortalem ac paene divinam: 'Paete, non dolet.'
sed tamen ista facienti, ista dicenti, gloria et aeternitas ante oculos
15 erant; quo maius est sine praemio aeternitatis, sine praemio
gloriae, abdere lacrimas operire luctum, amissoque filio matrem
adhuc agere.

1. What do we learn of the son and his relationship with his parents?
2. How does the mother hide the truth from her husband? Describe her behaviour in detail.
3. What picture do we gain of this woman from her subsequent actions?

Scribonianus arma in Illyrico contra Claudium moverat; fuerat
Paetus in partibus, et occiso Scriboniano Romam trahebatur. erat
20 ascensurus navem; Arria milites orabat, ut simul imponeretur.
'nempe enim' inquit 'daturi estis consulari viro servolos aliquos,
quorum e manu cibum capiat, a quibus vestiatur, a quibus
calcietur; omnia sola praestabo.' non impetravit: conduxit
piscatoriam nauculam, ingensque navigium minimo secuta est.
25 eadem apud Claudium uxori Scriboniani, cum illa profiteretur
indicium, 'ego' inquit 'te audiam, cuius in gremio Scribonianus
occisus est, et vivis?' ex quo manifestum est ei consilium
pulcherrimae mortis non subitum fuisse. quin etiam, cum Thrasea
gener eius deprecaretur, ne mori pergeret, interque alia dixisset:
30 'vis ergo filiam tuam, si mihi pereundum fuerit, mori mecum?',
respondit: 'si tam diu tantaque concordia vixerit tecum quam ego
cum Paeto, volo.' auxerat hoc responso curam suorum; attentius
custodiebatur; sensit et 'nihil agitis' inquit; 'potestis enim efficere
ut male moriar, ut non moriar non potestis.' dum haec dicit,
35 exsiluit cathedra adversoque parieti caput ingenti impetu impegit et
corruit. focilata 'dixeram' inquit 'vobis inventuram me quamlibet
duram ad mortem viam, si vos facilem negassetis.' videnturne haec
tibi maiora illo 'Paete, non dolet', ad quod per haec perventum est?

Pliny *Letters* 3.16.3–7

4. How consistently does Arria behave? Is she more selfish or selfless in her relationship?
5. Why is this relationship so close and long lasting? What famous examples of close, long-lasting relationships, based on similar values, can you think of?

stringere: stringo draw (a sword)

perfodere: perfodio stab

pectus: pectus, pectoris, n. chest

extrahere: extraho pull out

pugionem: pugio, -onis, m. dagger

porrigere: porrigo stretch out

dolet: doleo hurt

ista facienti, ista dicenti 'to her doing and saying those things'

gloria et aeternitas 'immortal glory'

15 **quo maius est sine praemio** 'all the greater it is, without the reward of ...'

abdere: abdo hide

operire: operio cover up

luctum: luctus, -us, m. grief, mourning

amisso: amitto lose

adhuc still

agere: ago act as

Illyrico: Illyricum (a province on the east coast of the Adriatic)

in partibus 'on his side'

20 **imponeretur: impono** put on board

nempe clearly

daturi estis 'you will be going to give'

consulari: consularis of consular rank

servolos: servolus, m. young slave

vestiatur: vestio clothe

calcietur: calcio put shoes on

praestabo: praesto provide

impetravit: impetro succeed, obtain by request

conduxit: conduco hire

piscatoriam: piscatorius for fishing

nauculam: naucula, f. small boat

navigium: navigium, n. ship

25 **apud Claudium** 'in the presence of Claudius'

profiteretur: profiteor admit voluntarily, confess

indicium: indicium, n. evidence

gremio: gremium, n. lap, bosom

vivis: vivo live

manifestum: manifestus clear, evident

ei to her, *here*, her

subitus sudden

quin etiam even more so

gener, m. son-in-law (Thrasea)

deprecaretur: deprecor beg

30 **pergeret: pergo** press on, go ahead with

concordia: concordia, f. harmony

vixerit: vivo live

auxerat: augeo increase

curam: cura, f. worry

attentius: attentus attentive, careful

custodiebatur: custodio watch, guard

efficere: efficio effect, bring it about that

exsiluit: exsilio leap up

35 **cathedra: cathedra, f.** chair

adverso: adversus opposite

parieti: paries, parietis, m. wall

impetu: impetus, -us, m. charge, vigour

impegit: impingo drive into

corruit: corruo fall to the ground

focilata: focilo revive, resuscitate

inventuram: invenio find

quamlibet however (hard)

duram: durus hard

negassetis = negavissetis: nego deny

ad quod ... perventum est? 'which point was reached through these remarks?'

6. An ideal daughter

Pliny writes about the death of the daughter of a friend.

GAIUS PLINIUS AEFULANO MARCELLINO SUO S.

tristissimus haec tibi scribo, Fundani nostri filia minore defuncta.
qua puella nihil umquam festivius amabilius, nec modo longiore
vita sed prope immortalitate dignius vidi. nondum annos xiv
5   impleverat, et iam illi anilis prudentia, matronalis gravitas erat et
tamen suavitas puellaris cum virginali verecundia. ut illa patris
cervicibus inhaerebat! ut nos amicos paternos et amanter et
modeste complectebatur! ut nutrices, ut paedagogos, ut
praeceptores pro suo quemque officio diligebat! quam studiose,
10 quam intellegenter lectitabat! ut parce custoditeque ludebat! qua
illa temperantia, qua patientia, qua etiam constantia novissimam
valetudinem tulit! medicis obsequebatur, sororem patrem
adhortabatur ipsamque se destitutam corporis viribus vigore animi
sustinebat. duravit hic illi usque ad extremum, nec aut spatio
15 valetudinis aut metu mortis infractus est, quo plures gravioresque
nobis causas relinqueret et desiderii et doloris. o triste plane
acerbumque funus! o morte ipsa mortis tempus indignius! iam
destinata erat egregio iuveni, iam electus nuptiarum dies, iam nos
vocati. quod gaudium quo maerore mutatum est! non possum
20 exprimere verbis quantum animo vulnus acceperim, cum audivi
Fundanum ipsum, ut multa luctuosa dolor invenit, praecipientem,
quod in vestes margarita gemmas fuerat erogaturus, hoc in tus et
unguenta et odores impenderetur. est quidem ille eruditus et
sapiens, ut qui se ab ineunte aetate altioribus studiis artibusque
25 dediderit; sed nunc omnia, quae audiit saepe quae dixit, aspernatur
expulsisque virtutibus aliis pietatis est totus.

Pliny *Letters* 5.16.1–8

1. Pick out and translate the Latin for four of this girl's characteristics.
2. Pliny recalls the girl's actions in life. By what means does he show he approves of such behaviour?
3. What factor makes this girl's death all the more tragic?
4. How does the girl's father react to her death?
5. What do you want people to remember about you?

AEFULANO MARCELLINO
SUO S. '[Pliny] sends his greetings to his [friend] Aefulanus Marcellinus'
S. = salutem (dicit) greets
Fundani: Fundanus (the father of the girl)
defuncta: defungor die
festivius: festivus agreeable, pretty
amabilius: amabilis pleasant
dignius: dignus worthy, deserving
nondum not yet
5 **impleverat: impleo** complete
anilis of an old woman
prudentia, f. prudence, wisdom
matronalis befitting a married woman
gravitas, -atis, f. seriousness, authority
suavitas, -atis, f. sweetness
puellaris girlish
virginali: virginalis maidenly
verecundia: verecundia, f. modesty
ut how
cervicibus: cervix, -icis, f. neck
inhaerebat: inhaereo cling to
complectebatur: complector embrace
nutrices: nutrix, -icis, f. nurse
paedagogos: paedagogus, m. tutor
praeceptores: praeceptor, -oris, m. teacher
pro suo quemque officio 'each according to their duties'
diligebat: diligo love, esteem highly
studiose: studiosus enthusiastic, keen
10 **lectitabat: lectito** be in the habit of reading
parce: parcus sparing, moderate
custodite: custoditus guarded, careful
ludebat: ludo play
temperantia: temperantia, f. restraint, self-control
constantia: constantia, f. constancy, perseverance
novissimam: novissimus last
valetudinem: valetudo, -inis, f. ill health
medicis: medicus, m. doctor
obsequebatur: obsequor + dat. comply with

sororem: soror, -oris, f. sister
adhortabatur: adhortor encourage
destitutam: destitutus deprived of
sustinebat: sustineo support
duravit: duro endure, last
illi 'for her'
usque ad extremum 'all the way up to the end'
spatio: spatium, n. length, duration
15 **metu: metus, -us, m.** fear
infractus est: infringo break
quo 'on account of which'
desiderii: desiderium, n. longing, regret
plane: planus obvious
acerbum: acerbus grievous
funus, -eris, n. death,end
mortis tempus 'the moment of her death'
indignius: indignus undeserved
egregio: egregius excellent, eminent
electus: eligo choose
nuptiarum: nuptiae, f. pl. wedding, marriage
gaudium, n. joy
maerore: maeror, -oris, m. sorrow
mutatum: muto change
20 **exprimere: exprimo** express
ut although
luctuosa: luctuosus mournful, grievous
praecipientem: praecipio instruct
vestes: vestes, f. pl. clothes
margarita: margaritum, n. pearl
gemmas: gemma, f. jewel
fuerat erogaturus 'he had been about to spend'
tus: tus, turis, n. incense
unguenta: unguentum, n. perfume, ointment
odores: odor, -oris, m. scent
impenderetur: impendo spend, devote to
eruditus learned
ut qui ... 'as one who ...'
se ... dediderit: se dedere to devote oneself to
ab ineunte aetate 'from his early years'
25 **aspernatur: aspernor** despise

expulsis: expello drive out, expel
pietatis: pietas, -atis, f. fatherly duty

7. Education within the family

Tacitus writes of how important it is to pay close supervision to the education of children within the family.

quis enim ignorat et eloquentiam et ceteras artes descivisse ab illa
vetere gloria non inopia hominum, sed desidia iuventutis et
neglegentia parentum et inscientia praecipientium et oblivione
moris antiqui? quae mala primum in urbe nata, mox per Italiam
5   fusa, iam in provincias manant. quamquam vestra vobis notiora
sunt: ego de urbe et his propriis ac vernaculis vitiis loquar, quae
natos statim excipiunt et per singulos aetatis gradus cumulantur, si
prius de severitate ac disciplina maiorum circa educandos
formandosque liberos pauca praedixero.
10   nam pridem suus cuique filius, ex casta parente natus, non in cella
emptae nutricis sed gremio ac sinu matris educabatur, cuius
praecipua laus erat tueri domum et inservire liberis. eligebatur
autem maior aliqua natu propinqua, cuius probatis spectatisque
moribus omnis eiusdem familiae suboles committeretur, coram qua
15   neque dicere fas erat quod turpe dictu neque facere quod
inhonestum factu videretur. ac non studia modo curasque sed
remissiones etiam lususque puerorum sanctitate quadam ac
verecundia temperabat. sic Corneliam Gracchorum, sic Aureliam
Caesaris, sic Atiam Augusti matrem praefuisse educationibus ac
20   produxisse principes liberos accepimus. quae disciplina ac
severitas eo pertinebat ut sincera et integra et in nullis pravitatibus
detorta unius cuiusque natura toto statim pectore arriperet artes
honestas et, sive ad rem militarem sive ad iuris scientiam sive ad
eloquentiae studium inclinasset, id solum ageret, id universum
25   hauriret.

Tacitus Dialogus 28.2–6

1. What four reasons does Tacitus give for the decline in eloquence and the other arts?
2. Find a suitable translation for 'severitate ac disciplina maiorum' (line 8).
3. What special distinction does Tacitus draw about who should and who should not bring up children at the beginning of the second paragraph ('non in cella emptae nutricis sed gremio ac sinu matris educabatur': lines 10–11)?
4. In important families, where mothers have taken charge of education, what does 'disciplina ac severitas' (lines 20–21) produce?

ignorat: **ignoro** be unaware

eloquentiam: eloquentia, *f.*
eloquence, the art of public
speaking, rhetoric

descivisse: descisco diminish,
decline

vetere: vetus, -eris old

inopia: inopia, *f.* shortage

desidia: desidia, *f.* laziness

iuventutis: iuventus, -utis, *f.*
youth

inscientia: inscientia, *f.* lack
of knowledge

praecipientium: praecipio
instruct, teach

oblivione: oblivio, -onis, *f.*
forgetfulness

moris: mos, moris, *m.* custom

antiqui: antiquus of old

nata: natus born, originated

5 **fusa: fundo** spread

manant: mano pervade, trickle

notiora: notus well known

propriis: proprius native,
particular

vernaculis: vernaculus home-
grown

vitiis: vitium, *n.* fault, sin, vice

excipiunt: excipio take hold of

singulos: singulus each, every
individual

aetatis: aetas, -atis, *f.* life

gradus: gradus, -us, *m.* stage,
step

cumulantur: cumulo
accumulate

prius: prior first

maiorum: maiores, *m. pl.*
ancestors

circa about

educandos: educo rear,
educate, bring up

formandos: formo shape,
fashion

praedixero: praedico say
before

10 **pridem** in the past

cuique: quisque each

casta: castus chaste, pure

cella: cella, *f.* chamber, room

emptae: emo buy, hire

nutricis: nutrix, -icis, *f.* wet-
nurse

gremio: gremium, *n.* lap,
bosom

sinu: sinus, -us, *m.* lap,
embrace

praecipua: praecipuus
especial

laus, laudis, *f.* renown, glory

tueri: tueor protect, keep watch
over

inservire: inservio + *dat.*
devote oneself to

eligebatur: eligo choose

aliqua: aliquis someone, *so
here*, 'a woman'

natu by birth

maior ... natu quite old, mature

propinqua, *f.* female relative,
kinswoman

probatis: probo approve of
eiusdem familiae

familiae: familia, *f.* household

suboles, subolis, *f.* offspring

committeretur: committo
entrust

coram qua 'in whose presence'

15 **fas** right, proper

turpe: turpis shameful, foul

dictu 'to say'

inhonestum: inhonestus
dishonourable, disgraceful,
shameful

factu 'to do'

curas: cura, *f.* occupation

**remissiones: remissio, -onis,
*f.*** break, recreation

lusus: lusus, -us, *m.* game

A mother breastfeeds her child

sanctitate: sanctitas, -atis, *f.*
sanctity, piety

verecundia: verecundia, *f.*
modesty, respect

temperabat: tempero control,
moderate

Corneliam Gracchorum
'Cornelia, mother of the
Gracchi'

Aureliam: Aurelia (the mother
of Julius Caesar)

Atiam: Atia (the mother of
Augustus)

praefuisse: praesum + *dat.* be
in charge of

**educationibus: educatio,
-onis, *f.*** upbringing

20 **produxisse: produco** produce,
beget

principes: princeps, -ipis, *m.*
leading figure in the state

accepimus 'we have heard'

eo pertinebat ut 'tended to
ensure that'

sincera: sincerus pure

integra: integer untouched,
virtuous

pravitatibus: pravitas, -atis, *f.*
crookedness, vice

detorta: detorqueo twist, turn
aside

unius cuiusque 'of each one'

pectore: pectus, pectoris, *n.*
heart

arriperet: arripio seize, snatch

honestas: honestus noble,
respectable

sive ... sive ... whether ... or ...

iuris: ius, iuris, *n.* law

scientiam: scientia, *f.*
knowledge

**inclinasset = inclinavisset:
inclino** incline, turn towards

universum: universus whole

25 **hauriret: haurio** drink in

8. Bitter hatred

In 52 BC the two political rivals, Milo and Clodius, each with his own respective entourage, have met in a violent incident outside Rome, and Clodius has been killed. Cicero is defending Milo, and explaining the bitter hatred that existed between the two men.

audistis, iudices, quantum Clodi interfuerit occidi Milonem:
convertite animos nunc vicissim ad Milonem. quid Milonis intererat
interfici Clodium? quid erat cur Milo non dicam
admitteret, sed optaret? 'obstabat in spe consulatus Miloni
5   Clodius.' at eo repugnante fiebat, immo vero eo fiebat magis, nec
me suffragatore meliore utebatur quam Clodio. valebat apud vos,
iudices, Milonis erga me remque publicam meritorum memoria,
valebant preces et lacrimae nostrae, quibus ego tum vos mirifice
moveri sentiebam, sed plus multo valebat periculorum
10   impendentium timor. quis enim erat civium qui sibi solutam Publi
Clodi praeturam sine maximo rerum novarum metu proponeret?
solutam autem fore videbatis, nisi esset is consul qui eam auderet
possetque constringere. eum Milonem unum esse cum sentiret
universus populus Romanus, quis dubitaret suffragio suo se metu,
15   periculo rem publicam liberare? at nunc, Clodio remoto, usitatis
iam rebus enitendum est Miloni, ut tueatur dignitatem suam;
singularis illa et huic uni concessa gloria quae cotidie augebatur
frangendis furoribus Clodianis iam Clodi morte cecidit. vos adepti
estis ne quem civem metueretis; hic exercitationem virtutis,
20   suffragationem consulatus, fontem perennem gloriae suae perdidit.
itaque Milonis consulatus qui vivo Clodio labefactari non poterat
mortuo denique temptari coeptus est. non modo igitur nihil prodest
sed obest etiam Clodi mors Miloni.

1. What does Cicero say others might suggest was the reason for Milo killing Clodius?
2. What factors does Cicero say held sway with the 'iudices'?
3. What does Cicero say the praetorship of Clodius would have caused?
4. What have the Roman people gained, and what has Milo lost, as a result of Clodius' death, according to Cicero?

'at valuit odium, fecit iratus, fecit inimicus, fuit ultor iniuriae,
25   punitor doloris sui.' quid? si haec non dico maiora fuerunt in
Clodio quam in Milone, sed in illo maxima, nulla in hoc, quid
voltis amplius? quid enim odisset Clodium Milo, segetem ac
materiam suae gloriae, praeter hoc civile odium quo omnes

audistis = audivistis

interfuerit: interest + *gen.* it is important to, it is to the advantage of

vicissim in turn

admitteret: admitto commit (a crime)

optaret: opto desire, wish for

obstabat: obsto + *dat.* stand in the way of

5 **eo repugnante** 'with him (Clodius) opposing' (i.e. in spite of his opposition)

fiebat: fio

immo rather

vero indeed

me suffragatore

suffragatore: suffragator, -oris, m. election campaign helper, supporter

utebatur: utor + *abl.* use

valebat: valeo be strong, prevail

erga + *acc.* towards

meritorum: meritum, n. service

preces: prex, precis, f. prayer, entreaty

mirifice: mirificus wonderful, admirable

10 **impendentium: impendeo** impend, be imminent

solutam: solutus unrestrained

praeturam: praetura, f. praetorship

sine maximo ... metu

rerum novarum: res novae, f. pl. revolution

proponeret: propono imagine, conceive

constringere: constringo check, restrain

dubitaret: dubito doubt, hesitate

suffragio: suffragium, n. vote

se metu, rem publicam periculo

15 **liberare: libero** free

usitatis: usitor use frequently

usitatis rebus 'with frequently used things' (i.e. relying upon usual methods)

enitendum: enitor strive to

tueatur: tueor protect, watch

dignitatem: dignitas, -atis, f. position, dignity

singularis singular, outstanding

huic uni 'to this man alone'

concessa: concedo grant

augebatur: augeo increase

frangendis furoribus Clodianis

frangendis: frango break, repress

furoribus: furor, -oris, m. madness, outrageous act

Clodianis: Clodianus of Clodius and his supporters

adepti estis: adipiscor achieve, gain

quem civem 'any citizen'

metueretis: metuo fear

exercitationem: exercitatio, -onis, f. practice, opportunity to practise

20 **suffragationem: suffragatio, -onis, f.** electoral support

fontem: fons, fontis, m. fount, spring, fountain, source

perennem: perennis endless, eternal

perdidit: perdo destroy, lose

labefactari: labefacto overthrow

temptari: tempto attack

prodest: prosum + *dat.* be an advantage to

obest: obsum + *dat.* be a disadvantage to

at but

odium, n. hatred

fecit: facio do, act

ultor, -oris, m. avenger

25 **punitor, -oris, m.** punisher, avenger

in illo ... in hoc 'in the former ... in the latter'

voltis = vultis

amplius more

odisset: odi hate

segetem: seges, segetis, f. 'breeding ground' or 'production area', seed-corn

materiam: materia, f. stuff, substance

praeter + *acc.* except, apart from

civile: civilis civil

improbos odimus? illi erat ut odisset primum defensorem salutis
30   meae, deinde vexatorem furoris, domitorem armorum suorum,
postremo etiam accusatorem suum; reus enim Milonis lege Plotia
fuit Clodius quoad vixit. quo tandem animo hoc tyrannum illum
tulisse creditis? quantum odium illius et in homine iniusto quam
etiam iustum fuisse?

Cicero Pro Milone 34–35

5. What does Cicero suggest others are saying about Milo's anger and hatred?
6. What reasons does Cicero propose Clodius had for hating Milo?

improbos: improbus wicked

illi erat ut *lit.* to that man (Clodius) there was the fact that ... (i.e. Clodius had the reason that ...) *primum ... deinde ... postremo*

30 **vexatorem: vexator, -oris, *m.*** harasser, vexer

domitorem: domitor, -oris, *m.* controller, tamer

reus, *m.* accused, defendant

lege Plotia: lex Plotia, *f.* the Plotian Law

quoad whilst

tandem 'I ask you!'

vixit: vivo live

tulisse: fero bear

in homine iniusto 'for an unjust man (to nurse)'

quam ... iustum 'how justified a hatred'

PASSIONS AND POISONS

Cicero's account of the passions of Sassia and the shenanigans of the imperial family presented by Tacitus may be from a bygone age, but the cult and culture of celebrity displayed is not a million miles from that seen in our own reality television and celebrity magazine driven society. Poisoning found favour in the ancient world and has been seen in more recent times amidst the intrigue of the world of espionage. If passion stirs poison in the *Pro Cluentio*, then in Virgil's portrayal of Amata, we see that it is a poison of sorts which causes the vehement feeling. Ovid in the *Heroides* gives us a Medea who combines both passion and poison with a certain celebrity status. The raw heartache of Catullus forms a very personal tale of passion lived and then later not returned, whilst Ovid's *Ibis* tells of those passions going on beyond the grave.

Medea mixes poison

1. The poisoning of Claudius

In AD 54, the last year of Claudius' reign, Agrippina, Claudius' fourth wife, becomes frightened and impatient. Anxious for power for her son, Nero, she begins through various machinations to ensure his rise over that of Britannicus, Claudius' son by Messalina.

> Marco Asinio Manio Acilio consulibus mutationem rerum in deterius
> portendi cognitum est crebris prodigiis. signa ac tentoria militum
> igne caelesti arsere; fastigio Capitolii examen apium insedit;
> biformes hominum partus et suis fetum editum cui accipitrum
> 5 ungues inessent. numerabatur inter ostenta deminutus omnium
> magistratuum numerus, quaestore, aedili, tribuno ac praetore et
> consule paucos intra menses defunctis. sed in praecipuo pavore
> Agrippina, vocem Claudii, quam temulentus iecerat, fatale sibi ut
> coniugum flagitia ferret, dein puniret, metuens, agere et celerare
> 10 statuit, perdita prius Domitia Lepida muliebribus causis
>
> ...

1. **What is the effect of the list of omens?**
2. **What has Claudius said that has made Agrippina afraid?**

Domitia Lepida was the mother of Messalina. She is charged with trying to use magic against Agrippina, and with not controlling her slaves.
Narcissus, Claudius' freedman, is worried but Agrippina presses ahead shamelessly.

> ob haec mors indicta, multum adversante Narcisso, qui
> Agrippinam magis magisque suspectans prompsisse inter proximos
> ferebatur certam sibi perniciem, seu Britannicus rerum seu Nero
> poteretur; verum ita de se meritum Caesarem, ut vitam usui eius
> 15 impenderet. convictam Messalinam et Silium; pares iterum
> accusandi causas esse, si Nero imperitaret; Britannico successore
> nullum principi metum: at novercae insidiis domum omnem
> convelli, maiore flagitio quam si impudicitiam prioris coniugis
> reticuisset. quamquam ne impudicitiam quidem nunc abesse
> 20 Pallante adultero, ne quis ambigat decus pudorem corpus, cuncta
> regno viliora habere. haec atque talia dictitans amplecti
> Britannicum, robur aetatis quam maturrimum precari, modo ad
> deos, modo ad ipsum tendere manus, adolesceret, patris inimicos
> depelleret, matris etiam interfectores ulcisceretur.

consulibus: consul, -is, _m._ consul

mutationem: mutatio, -onis, _f._ change

deterius: deterior worse

portendi: portendo portend

crebris: creber frequent

prodigiis: prodigium, _n._ omen, portent

signa: signum, _n._ military standard

ac and

tentoria: tentorium, _n._ tent

igne: ignis, -is, _m._ fire

caelesti: caelestis heavenly, divine, from the sky

arsere = arserunt: ardeo blaze, burn

fastigio: fastigium, _n._ summit

Capitolii: Capitolium, _n._ the Capitoline hill

examen, -inis, _n._ swarm

apium: apis, -is, _f._ bee

insedit: insideo sit on, settle on

biformes: biformis two-shaped

partus: partus, -us, _m._ birth

suis: sus, suis, _m.f._ pig

fetum: fetus, -us, _m._ offspring, young

editum: edo publish, proclaim

accipitrum: accipiter, -tris, _m._ hawk

5 **ungues: unguis, -is, _m._** talon

numerabatur: numero count

ostenta: ostentum, _n._ prodigy

deminutus: deminuo diminish, reduce

magistratuum: magistratus, -us, _m._ magistracy

quaestore: quaestor, -oris, _m._ quaestor

aedili: aedilis, -is, _m._ aedile

tribuno: tribunus, _m._ tribune

praetore: praetor, -oris, _m._ praetor

menses: mensis, -is, _m._ month

defunctis: defungor have died

praecipuo: praecipuus particular, especial

pavore: pavor, -oris, _m._ fear

vocem: vox, vocis, _f._ voice, utterance

temulentus drunken

iecerat: iacio utter

fatale: fatalis destined, fated

coniugum: coniunx, -iugis, _m.f._ husband/wife, _here gen. pl._ 'of his wives'

flagitia: flagitium, _n._ crime, scandal, disgrace

dein = deinde

puniret: punio punish

metuens: metuo fear

celerare: celero hasten, quicken

10 **statuit: statuo** resolve, determine

perdita: perdo destroy

prius first, before

muliebribus: muliebris womanly

ob + _acc._ because of

indicta: indico declare publicly

adversante: adversor oppose, resist

suspectans: suspecto suspect, distrust

prompsisse: promo make known

proximos: proximus nearest

ferebatur: fero say, _here_ 'was said'

perniciem: pernicies, _f._ destruction, ruin

seu ... seu whether ... or

poteretur: potior + _gen._ take possession of

ita de se meritum Caesarem 'Claudius deserved such duty from him'

usui: usus, -us, _m._ service

15 **impenderet: impendo** devote, expend

convictam: convinco convict

pares: par equal, fair

imperitaret: imperito rule

successore: successor, -oris, _m._ successor

metum: metus, -us, _m._ fear

novercae: noverca, _f._ stepmother

insidiis: insidiae, _f. pl._ ambush, plot

convelli: convello overthrow, upturn

impudicitiam: impudicitia, _f._ shameless behaviour

reticuisset: reticeo keep silent

ne ... quidem not even

20 **Pallante: Pallas, Pallantis, _m._** Pallas

adultero: adulter, _m._ adulterer, lover

ambigat: ambigo doubt

decus: decus, -oris, _n._ glory, reputation

pudorem: pudor, -oris, _m._ decency, modesty

cuncta: cunctus all

viliora: vilis cheap

dictitans: dictito say often

amplecti: amplector embrace

robur, -oris, _n._ strength, maturity

aetatis: aetas, -atis, _f._ age

quam maturrimum 'as quickly as possible'

precari: precor pray

modo ... modo now ... now

tendere: tendo stretch out

adolesceret: adolesco grow up

inimicos: inimicus, _m._ enemy

depelleret: depello drive out

interfectores: interfector, -oris, _m._ killer

ulcisceretur: ulciscor avenge

3. For what reasons does Narcissus think he is doomed?
4. What effect does referring to Agrippina as 'novercae' have?
5. How does Tacitus effectively set the atmosphere for the poisoning to follow?

Narcissus is recovering from illness whilst Agrippina begins detailed planning.

25   in tanta mole curarum valetudine adversa corripitur, refovendisque
viribus mollitia caeli et salubritate aquarum Sinuessam pergit. tum
Agrippina, sceleris olim certa et oblatae occasionis propera nec
ministrorum egens, de genere veneni consultavit, ne repentino et
praecipiti facinus proderetur; si lentum et tabidum delegisset, ne
30   admotus supremis Claudius et dolo intellecto ad amorem filii
rediret. exquisitum aliquid placebat, quod turbaret mentem et
mortem differret. deligitur artifex talium vocabulo Locusta, nuper
veneficii damnata et diu inter instrumenta regni habita. eius
mulieris ingenio paratum virus, cuius minister e spadonibus fuit
35   Halotus, inferre epulas et explorare gustu solitus.

6. Why does Tacitus bother to tell us that Narcissus is not in Rome?
7. With which two words are 'lentum' and 'tabidum' (line 29) contrasted?
8. Why is Locusta a suitable choice for involvement in this crime?

Slowly ... or quickly?

    adeoque cuncta mox pernotuere ut temporum illorum scriptores
prodiderint infusum delectabili boleto venenum, nec vim
medicaminis statim intellectam, socordiane an Claudii vinolentia;
simul soluta alvus subvenisse videbatur. igitur exterrita Agrippina
40   et, quando ultima timebantur, spreta praesentium invidia provisam
iam sibi Xenophontis medici conscientiam adhibet. ille tamquam
nisus evomentis adiuvaret, pinnam rapido veneno inlitam faucibus
eius demisisse creditur, haud ignarus summa scelera incipi cum
periculo, peragi cum praemio.

9. How, by use of detail, does Tacitus bring out the character of Claudius?
10. What is the effect of the last sentence?
11. In what ways does this account have features in common with 'celebrity' magazines or newspaper gossip columns?

Prayers as cover for further plotting

45   vocabatur interim senatus votaque pro incolumitate principis
consules et sacerdotes nuncupabant, cum iam exanimis vestibus et
fomentis obtegeretur, dum quae res forent firmando Neronis

25 mole: moles, -is, *f.* burden
curarum: cura, *f.* care
valetudine: valetudo, -inis, *f.*
   health
adversa: adversus bad
corripitur: corripio seize
refovendis: refoveo revive,
   refresh
mollitia: mollitia, *f. here*
   pleasantness
salubritate: salubritas, -atis,
   f. health-giving properties
pergit: pergo proceed
sceleris: scelus, -eris, *n.* crime,
   wickedness
oblatae: offero offer
occasionis: occasio, -onis, *f.*
   opportunity
propera: properus quick,
   speedy
ministrorum: minister, *m.*
   servant, accomplice, agent
egens: egeo + *gen.* lack
genere: genus, -eris, *n.* type,
   sort
veneni: venenum, *n.* poison
repentino: repentinus sudden
praecipiti: praeceps
   impetuous, hurried
facinus, -oris, *n.* crime
proderetur: prodo betray
lentum: lentus slow
tabidum: tabidus lingering
delegisset: deligo choose
30 supremis 'death' or 'his dying
   hours'
dolo: dolus, *m.* trick, treachery
exquisitum: exquisitus
   carefully sought out
turbaret: turbo confuse,
   disturb
mentem: mens, -tis, *f.* mind
differret; differo delay
artifex skilful
vocabulo: vocabulum, *n.*
   name
nuper recently
veneficii: veneficium, *n.*
   poisoning
damnata: damno condemn
instrumenta: instrumentum,
   n. tool
regni: regnum, *n.* reign, rule
mulieris: mulier, -eris, *f.*
   woman
ingenio: ingenium, *n.* skill,
   talent
virus, *n.* poison
spadonibus: spado, -onis, *m.*
   eunuch

35 epulas: epulae, *f. pl.* banquet,
   dishes
explorare: exploro test
gustu: gustus, -us, *m.* tasting

cuncta: cunctus all
pernotuere = pernotuerunt:
   pernotesco become widely
   known
prodiderint: prodo hand down,
   declare
infusum: infundo mix with
delectabili boleto 'a favourite
   dish of mushrooms'
vim: vis, *f.* force, strength
medicaminis: medicamen,
   -inis, *n.* drug
intellectam: intellego
   understand
socordia: socordia, *f.*
   sluggishness, lethargy
... ne whether
vinolentia: vinolentia, *f.*
   drunkenness, intoxication
soluta: solvo loosen
alvus, *f.* belly, bowels
subvenisse: subvenio help,
   relieve
exterrita: exterreo scare,
   terrify
40 ultima: ultimus the worst
spreta: sperno disdain, scorn
praesentium: praesens
   present
praesentium invidia
invidia: invidia, *f.* ill-will,
   envy, jealousy

provisam: provideo foresee
   here 'foresee the need for'
medici: medicus, *m.* doctor
conscientiam: conscientia, *f.*
   complicity
adhibet: adhibeo use, make
   use of
tamquam as if, like
nisus: nisus, -us, *m.* effort,
   exertion
evomentis: evomo vomit out
pinnam: pinna, *f.* feather
inlitam = illitam: illino smear
   with
faucibus: fauces, *f. pl.* throat
demisisse: demitto lower, send
   down
ignarus unaware
incipi: incipio begin
peragi: perago complete

45 vota: votum, *n.* prayer
incolumitate: incolumitas,
   -atis, *f.* safety
sacerdotes: sacerdos, -otis,
   m. priest
nuncupabant: nuncupo
   express
exanimis lifeless
vestibus: vestis, -is, *f. here*
   'blankets'
fomentis: fomentum, *n.*
   poultice
obtegeretur: obtego cover
firmando: firmo strengthen

Claudius

imperio componuntur. iam primum Agrippina, velut dolore victa et
solacia conquirens, tenere amplexu Britannicum, veram paterni
50   oris effigiem appellare ac variis artibus demorari ne cubiculo
egrederetur. Antoniam quoque et Octaviam sorores eius attinuit, et
cunctos aditus custodiis clauserat, crebroque vulgabat ire in melius
valetudinem principis, quo miles bona in spe ageret tempusque
prosperum ex monitis Chaldaeorum adventaret.

12. **What is happening to Claudius' body?**
13. **What is being done for Nero's position?**
14. **What does the word 'velut' (line 48) tell us about Agrippina?**
15. **What does Agrippina do to Britannicus, Antonia and Octavia, and why?**

Nero is hailed as emperor

55   tunc medio diei tertium ante Idus Octobres, foribus palatii repente
diductis, comitante Burro Nero egreditur ad cohortem, quae more
militiae excubiis adest. ibi monente praefecto faustis vocibus
exceptus inditur lecticae. dubitavisse quosdam ferunt, respectantes
rogitantesque ubi Britannicus esset: mox nullo in diversum auctore
60   quae offerebantur secuti sunt. inlatusque castris Nero et
congruentia tempori praefatus, promisso donativo ad exemplum
paternae largitionis, imperator consalutatur. sententiam militum
secuta patrum consulta, nec dubitatum est apud provincias.
caelestesque honores Claudio decernuntur et funeris sollemne
65   perinde ac divo Augusto celebratur, aemulante Agrippina proaviae
Liviae magnificentiam. testamentum tamen haud recitatum, ne
antepositus filio privignus iniuria et invidia animos vulgi turbaret.

Tacitus *Annals* 12.64–69 (abridged)

16. **Why do you think that Nero goes before the soldiers?**
17. **Why is it important for the new regime that there are 'caelestes honores' for Claudius?**
18. **What measures do celebrities take in modern times to ensure their own good name and position?**

componuntur: compono arrange

velut as if

dolore: dolor, -oris, _m._ grief, pain

solacia: solacium, _n._ consolation

conquirens: conquiro seek

tenere: teneo hold

amplexu: amplexus, -us, _m._ embrace

veram: verus true

paterni: paternus of a father

50 **oris: os, oris, _n._** face

effigiem: effigies, _f._ image, likeness

appellare: appello call

variis: varius different, various

demorari: demoror delay

sorores: soror, -oris, _f._ sister

attinuit: attineo detain

cunctos: cunctus every

aditus: aditus, -us, _m._ entrance, point of access

custodiis: custodia, _f._ guard

clauserat: claudo close

crebro 'frequently'

vulgabat: vulgo publish, announce

quo 'so that'

ageret: ago act

prosperum: prosperus favourable

ex monitis Chaldaeorum 'from the prophecies of astrologers'

adventaret: advento arrive

55 **tunc** then

tertium ante Idus Octobres '13 October'

foribus: fores, _f. pl._ doors

palatii: palatium, _n._ palace

repente suddenly

diductis: diduco throw open

comitante Burro 'accompanied by Burrus'

militiae: militia, _f._ military service

excubiis: excubiae, _f. pl._ guard duty

praefecto: praefectus, _m._ commanding officer

faustis: faustus favourable, joyful

exceptus: excipio receive

inditur: indo put on

lecticae: lectica, _f._ litter (carriage carried by attendants)

dubitavisse: dubito hesitate

ferunt 'it is said'

respectantes: respecto look around

rogitantes: rogito ask repeatedly

nullo in diversum auctore 'when no one produced an alternative'

60 **congruentia tempori praefatus** 'having spoken as the occasion required'

donativo: donativum, _n._ a gift

largitionis: largitio, largitionis, _f._ generosity, bribery

consalutatur: consaluto hail

sententiam: sententia, _f._ opinion

patrum consulta 'decrees of the Senate'

provincias: provincia, _f._ province

decernuntur: decerno decree

funeris sollemne 'funeral rites'

65 **perinde** just as

celebratur: celebro celebrate

aemulante: aemulor rival, emulate

proaviae Liviae 'of her great-grandmother, Livia' (wife of Augustus)

testamentum, _n._ will

recitatum: recito recite publicly

antepositus: antepono prefer

privignus, _m._ stepson

iniuria et invidia 'with a sense of injustice and dislike'

animos: animus, _m._ mind

vulgi: vulgus, _n._ crowd, people

turbaret: turbo trouble, disturb

2. The passion behind a trumped-up charge of poison

Aulus Cluentius has been accused of poisoning Oppianicus, his mother Sassia's third husband. Oppianicus had previously tried to do the same to Cluentius and had been banished. His mother had attempted a similar prosecution to this one three years earlier, and Cluentius had been acquitted. Cicero succeeds in having Cluentius acquitted once more. Sassia's first husband dies, and she develops a lust for her own son-in-law.

> Aulus Cluentius Habitus fuit, pater huiusce, iudices, homo non solum
> municipi Larinatis ex quo erat sed etiam regionis illius et vicinitatis
> virtute, existimatione, nobilitate princeps. is cum esset mortuus
> Sulla et Pompeio consulibus, reliquit hunc annos XV natum,
> 5   grandem autem et nubilem filiam quae brevi tempore post patris
> mortem nupsit Aulo Aurio Melino, consobrino suo, adulescenti in
> primis, ut tum habebatur, inter suos et honesto et nobili. cum essent
> eae nuptiae plenae dignitatis, plenae concordiae, repente est exorta
> mulieris importunae nefaria libido, non solum dedecore, verum
> 10 etiam scelere coniuncta. nam Sassia, mater huius Habiti – mater
> enim a me in omni causa, tametsi in hunc hostili odio et crudelitate
> est, mater, inquam, appellabitur, neque umquam illa ita de suo
> scelere et immanitate audiet ut naturae nomen amittat; quo enim
> est ipsum nomen amantius indulgentiusque maternum, hoc illius
> 15 matris, quae multos iam annos et nunc cum maxime filium
> interfectum cupit singulare scelus maiore odio dignum esse
> ducetis. ea igitur mater Habiti, Melini illius adulescentis, generi
> sui, contra quam fas erat amore capta primo, neque id ipsum diu,
> quoquo modo poterat, in illa cupiditate continebatur: deinde ita
> 20 flagrare coepit amentia, sic inflammata ferri libidine ut eam non
> pudor, non pietas, non macula familiae, non hominum fama, non
> fili dolor, non filiae maeror a cupiditate revocaret.

1. What sort of a man is Aulus Cluentius Habitus senior?
2. When did he die?
3. Which Latin phrase tells us that Sassia wanted her son dead, and which emphasises the enormity of her intended crime?
4. How in the last sentence does Cicero emphasise how strong Sassia's passion was?

The divorce of Melinus and Cluentia (daughter of Sassia, sister of Cluentius) is followed by the marriage of Melinus and Sassia.

huiusce = **huius**

iudices: iudex, -icis, *m.* judge, member of jury

municipi Larinatis 'of the town of Larinum'

regionis: regio, -onis, *f.* region

vicinitatis: vicinitas, -atis, *f.* neighbourhood

existimatione: existimatio, -onis, *f.* reputation

nobilitate: nobilitas, -atis, *f.* high birth

princeps leading

5 **grandem: grandis** grown up

nubilem: nubilis of marriageable age

nupsit: nubo + *dat.* marry

consobrino: consobrinus, *m.* cousin

adulescenti: adulescens, -entis *m.* young man

ut ... habebatur 'as was then thought'

nuptiae, *f. pl.* marriage

plenae: plenus full of

dignitatis: dignitas, -atis, *f.* merit, dignity

concordiae: concordia, *f.* harmony

repente suddenly

est exorta = **exorta est: exorior** arise, spring up

mulieris: mulier, -is, *f.* woman

importunae: importunus troublesome

nefaria: nefarius wicked, unspeakable

libido, *f.* passion, lust, desire

dedecore: dedecus, -oris, *n.* disgrace, infamy

10 **scelere: scelus, -eris, *n.*** crime

coniuncta: coniungo connect, associate

tametsi even though

hostili: hostilis of an enemy, hostile

odio: odium, *n.* hatred

crudelitate: crudelitas, -atis, *f.* cruelty

appellabitur: appello call, name

immanitate: immanitas, -atis, *f.* brutality

amittat: amitto lose

quo ... hoc

indulgentius: indulgens kind

15 **nunc cum maxime** 'now more than ever'

singulare: singularis singular, remarkable

dignum: dignus + *abl.* worthy of

ducetis: duco *here* 'think'

generi: gener, *m.* son-in-law

fas right, proper

quoquo modo 'in whatever way'

cupiditate: cupiditas, -atis, *f.* desire

continebatur: contineo contain

20 **flagrare: flagro** blaze, flame, be excited

amentia: amentia, *f.* madness

inflammata: inflammo inflame

pudor, -oris, *m.* shame, decency, modesty

pietas, -atis, *f.* duty, goodness

macula, *f.* stain, blemish, disgrace

dolor, -oris, *m.* pain, suffering

maeror, -oris, *m.* grief

revocaret: revoco recall, call back

animum adulescentis nondum consilio ac ratione firmatum pellexit
eis omnibus rebus quibus illa aetas capi ac deleniri potest. filia,
25 quae non solum illo communi dolore muliebri in eius modi viri
iniuriis angeretur, sed nefarium matris paelicatum ferre non posset
de quo ne queri quidem se sine scelere posse arbitraretur, ceteros
sui tanti mali ignaros esse cupiebat; in huius amantissimi sui fratris
manibus et gremio maerore et lacrimis consenescebat. ecce autem
30 subitum divortium, quod solacium malorum omnium fore
videbatur! discedit a Melino Cluentia ut in tantis iniuriis non
invita, ut a viro non libenter. tum vero illa egregia ac praeclara
mater palam exsultare laetitia, triumphare gaudio coepit, victrix
filiae non libidinis; diutius suspicionibus obscuris laedi famam
35 suam noluit; lectum illum genialem quem biennio ante filiae suae
nubenti straverat, in eadem domo sibi ornari et sterni expulsa atque
exturbata filia iubet. nubit genero socrus nullis auspicibus, nullis
auctoribus, funestis ominibus omnium.

5. Why was Cluentia's distress so intense?
6. How does Sassia make her 'crime' even worse?
7. Pick out three Latin examples of strong language which make Cicero's
description particularly vivid here.

Sassia's outrageous behaviour

o mulieris scelus incredibile et praeter hanc unam in omni vita
40 inauditum! o libidinem effrenatam et indomitam! o audaciam
singularem! nonne timuisse, si minus vim deorum hominumque
famam, at illam ipsam noctem facesque illas nuptiales, non limen
cubiculi, non cubile filiae, non parietes denique ipsos superiorum
testes nuptiarum! perfregit ac prostravit omnia cupiditate ac furore;
45 vicit pudorem libido, timorem audacia, rationem amentia. tulit hoc
commune dedecus familiae, cognationis, nominis graviter filius;
augebatur autem eius molestia cotidianis querimoniis et adsiduo
fletu sororis; statuit tamen nihil sibi in tantis iniuriis ac tanto
scelere matris gravius esse faciendum quam ut illa ne uteretur, ne
50 quae videre sine summo animi dolore non poterat, ea, si matre
uteretur, non solum videre, verum etiam probare suo iudicio
putaretur.
...
nihil in vita vidit calamitatis Aulus Cluentius, nullum periculum
mortis adiit, nihil mali timuit quod non totum a matre esset

nondum not yet
ratione: ratio, -onis *f.* reason
firmatum: firmo strengthen
pellexit: pellicio seduce
aetas, -atis, *f.* age
deleniri: delenio bewitch
25 **communi: communis** common, shared
muliebri: muliebris womanly
iniuriis: iniuria, *f.* injury, wrongdoing
angeretur: ango vex, trouble
nefarium: nefarius unspeakable
paelicatum: paelicatus, -us, *m.* prostitution
queri: queror complain
arbitraretur: arbitror think
mali: malum, *n.* misfortune
ignaros: ignarus unaware
amantissimi: amans loving
gremio: gremium, *n.* bosom, lap
consenescebat: consenesco grow old
30 **divortium, *n.*** divorce
solacium, *n.* solace, consolation
invita: invitus unwilling
egregia: egregius eminent, illustrious
praeclara: praeclarus brilliant
palam openly
exsultare: exsulto exult, rejoice
laetitia: laetitia, *f.* happiness
triumphare: triumpho triumph
gaudio: gaudium, *n.* joy
victrix, -icis, *f.* victor
suspicionibus: suspicio, -onis, *f.* suspicion
obscuris: obscurus shady, uncertain
laedi: laedo harm
35 **lectum: lectus, *m.*** bed, couch
genialem: genialis marital
biennio: biennium, *n.* period of two years
straverat: sterno bedeck
ornari: orno adorn, decorate
exturbata: exturbo throw out
socrus, -us, *f.* mother-in-law
auspicibus: auspex, -icis, *m.* supporter
auctoribus: auctor, -oris, *m.* promoter, adviser
funestis: funestus fatal, destructive
ominibus: omen, -inis, *n.* omen

praeter except
40 **inauditum: inauditus** unheard of
effrenatam: effreno unbridle, let loose
indomitam: indomitus untamed, unrestrained
audaciam: audacia, *f.* boldness, daring
si minus if not
vim: vis, *f.* force, power
faces: fax, facis, *f.* torch
nuptiales: nuptialis nuptial
limen: limen, -inis, *n.* threshold
cubiculi: cubiculum, *n.* bedroom
cubile: cubile, *n.* bed
parietes: paries, -etis, *m.* wall
denique finally
superiorum: superior previous, former
testes: testis, -is, *m.f.* witness
perfregit: perfringo break, break through
prostravit: prosterno overthrow
furore: furor, -oris, *m.* madness
45 **commune: communis** common, shared
cognationis: cognatio, -onis, *f.* family, relatives
augebatur: augeo increase
molestia, *f.* misery, annoyance
cotidianis: cotidianus daily
querimoniis: querimonia, *f.* complaint
adsiduo: adsiduus constant, incessant
fletu: fletus, -us, *m.* weeping, tears
statuit: statuo resolve, determine
50 **uteretur: utor** + *abl.* use, have dealings with
verum but
probare: probo approve
iudicio: iudicium, *n.* judgement
calamitatis: calamitas, -atis, *f.* calamity

55   conflatum et profectum. quae hoc tempore sileret omnia atque ea,
         si oblivione non posset, tamen taciturnitate sua tecta esse pateretur;
         sed vero sic agitur ut prorsus reticere nullo modo possit.

Cicero Pro Cluentio 5.11–6.18 (abridged)

8. Pick out the Latin exclamation about Sassia which you find most powerful and explain your choice.
9. How is Cluentius' troubled situation made worse?
10. How does Cicero emphasise that Sassia is to blame for all Cluentius' ills?
11. Sassia is behind the prosecution of her son. Cicero therefore tries to blacken her name. How does Cicero effectively portray Sassia's character as driven by excessive passion?

3. A snake's poison stirs passion

Allecto, one of the Furies, causes a snake to enter Queen Amata's robes and spread its venom throughout her body, firing her hatred of the Trojans.

     exim Gorgoneis Allecto infecta venenis
     principio Latium et Laurentis tecta tyranni
     celsa petit, tacitumque obsedit limen Amatae,
     quam super adventu Teucrum Turnique hymenaeis
5   femineae ardentem curaeque iraeque coquebant.
     huic dea caeruleis unum de crinibus anguem
     conicit, inque sinum praecordia ad intima subdit,
     quo furibunda domum monstro permisceat omnem.
     ille inter vestes et levia pectora lapsus
10   volvitur attactu nullo, fallitque furentem
     viperam inspirans animam; fit tortile collo
     aurum ingens coluber, fit longae taenia vittae
     innectitque comas et membris lubricus errat.
     ac dum prima lues udo sublapsa veneno
15   pertemptat sensus atque ossibus implicat ignem
     necdum animus toto percepit pectore flammam,
     mollius et solito matrum de more locuta est,
     multa super natae lacrimans Phrygiisque hymenaeis:

1. Why are Allecto's poisons described as 'Gorgoneis' (line 1)?
2. From line 7 onwards how does the snake make its way into and around Amata? What picture do we gain of its movement?
3. Who is the 'natae' referred to on the last line? What event is this snake making an attempt to stop?

55 **conflatum: conflo** bring about
sileret: sileo be silent, not speak about
oblivione: oblivio, -onis, _f._ oblivion, forgetfulness
taciturnitate: taciturnitas, -atis _f._ maintaining silence
tecta: tego hide conceal
pateretur: patior allow, endure
vero indeed
prorsus absolutely
reticere: reticeo keep silent

exim: exinde then
Gorgoneis: Gorgoneus of the Gorgons
infecta: inficio infect, corrupt
venenis: venenum, _n._ poison
principio: principium, _n._ beginning _here_ 'straightaway'
Latium 'to Latium'
Laurentis ... tyranni 'of the Laurentine ruler' _or_ 'of the ruler of Latium'
tecta: tectum, _n._ roof, house
celsa: celsus high, lofty
tacitum: tacitus silent
obsedit: obsideo occupy, settle upon
limen: limen, liminis, _n._ threshhold
super + _abl._ about
adventu: adventus, -us, _m._ arrival
Teucrum: Teucri, _m. pl. here gen._ 'of the Trojans'
hymenaeis: hymenaeus _here_ 'marriage'
5 **femineae: femineus** womanly
ardentem: ardens, -tis 'in turmoil'
curae: cura, _f._ care, concern
coquebant: coquo stir up

caeruleis: caeruleus dark
crinibus: crinis, _m._ hair
anguem: anguis, _m.f._ snake
conicit: conicio fling, hurl
sinum: sinus, -us, _m._ bosom
praecordia: praecordia, _n. pl._ chest, breast
intima: intimus inmost
subdit: subdo place, insert
quo ... monstro 'on account of which creature'
furibunda: furibundus raging, maddened, furious
permisceat: permisceo _subj._ confound, disturb thoroughly
vestes: vestis, _f. here acc.pl._ garments, clothing, clothes
levia: levis smooth
pectora: pectus, -oris, _n._ heart
lapsus: labor slip, slide, glide down
10 **volvitur: volvo** turn around, wind
attactu: attactus, -us _m._ touch
fallit: fallo deceive, cheat, escape notice
furentem: furo rage
viperam: vipereus of a viper _or_ of vipers
inspirans: inspiro blow into, inspire, instil
animam: anima, _f._ soul, breath
tortile: tortilis twisted, coiled
collo: collum, _n._ neck
coluber: coluber, _m._ snake, serpent
taenia: taenia, _f._ ribbon
vittae: vitta, _f._ headband
innectit: innecto fasten to, weave
comas: coma, _f._ hair
membris: membrum, _n._ limb
lubricus slippery, sinuous

errat: erro wander, stray about
lues, _f._ plague, pestilience, scourge
udo: udus wet
sublapsa: sublabor sink into
15 **pertemptat: pertempto** agitate thoroughly
sensus: sensus, -us, _m._ feeling, emotions, sense
ossibus: os, ossis, _n._ bone
implicat: implico enfold, entangle
necdum and not yet
animus, _m._ mind
percepit: percipio perceive, take possession of
mollius: mollis soft, tender
solito: soleo be accustomed _here_ 'usual'
locuta est: loquor speak
super + _abl._ about
natae: nata, _f._ daughter
lacrimans: lacrimo weep
Phrygiis: Phrygius Phrygian, Trojan

Snake (House of the Vetii, Pompeii)

'exsulibusne datur ducenda Lavinia Teucris,
20   o genitor, nec te miseret nataeque tuique?
        nec matris miseret, quam primo Aquilone relinquet
        perfidus alta petens abducta virgine praedo?
        at non sic Phrygius penetrat Lacedaemona pastor,
        Ledaeamque Helenam Troianas vexit ad urbes?
25   quid tua sancta fides? quid cura antiqua tuorum
        et consanguineo totiens data dextera Turno?
        si gener externa petitur de gente Latinis,
        idque sedet, Faunique premunt te iussa parentis,
        omnem equidem sceptris terram quae libera nostris
30   dissidet externam reor et sic dicere divos.
        et Turno, si prima domus repetatur origo,
        Inachus Acrisiusque patres mediaeque Mycenae.'

Virgil *Aeneid* 7.341–372

4. How does Virgil make Amata's speech powerful and persuasive?
5. Why is the comparison with Helen's situation especially fitting?
6. What does Amata suggest is the origin of Turnus' family? Why is this appropriate?
7. The 'snake' becomes a symbol of evil, causing problems for the Trojans. What examples can you think of in other books you have read where snakes are symbols of evil?

4. Medea's impassioned plea to Jason

Medea's powers have seemingly deserted her, like her husband, Jason.

        laese pater, gaude! Colchi gaudete relicti!
            inferias umbrae fratris habete mei!
        deseror amissis regno patriaque domoque
            coniuge, qui nobis omnia solus erat.
5   serpentes igitur potui taurosque furentes,
            unum non potui perdomuisse virum.
        quaeque feros pepuli doctis medicatibus ignes,
            non valeo flammas effugere ipsa meas.
        ipsi me cantus herbaeque artesque relinquunt
10   nil dea, nil Hecates sacra potentis agunt.
        non mihi grata dies, noctes vigilantur amarae
            et tener a misero pectore somnus abit.
        quae me non possum, potui sopire draconem.
            utilior cuivis quam mihi cura mea est.

exsulibus: exsul, -ulis, *m.f.* exile

20 **genitor: genitor, *m.*** father

nec te miseret ...? 'do you not feel pity for ...?'

tuique *here*, 'and for yourself'

Aquilone: Aquilo, -onis, *m.* North wind

perfidus treacherous, deceitful

alta: altum, *n.* the sea, deep water

praedo, -onis, *m.* brigand, pirate

penetrat: penetro penetrate, gain entrance

Lacedaemona: Lacedaemon, -onis, *f.* *here Gk. acc.* Lacedaemon, Sparta

pastor, *m.* shepherd

Ledaeam: Ledaeus 'of Leda'

vexit: veho carry off

25 **sancta: sanctus** sacred

fides, *f.* pledge, loyalty

antiqua: antiquus old

consanguineo: consanguineus related by blood

totiens so often

dextera, *f.* right hand, pledge

gener, *m.* son-in-law

externa: externus foreign

gente: gens, gentis, *f.* people, race

sedet: sedeo *here* 'is settled'

Fauni ... parentis 'of father Faunus' (grandson of Saturn and father of Latinus)

premunt: premo prevail, overpower

equidem indeed, I for my part

sceptris: sceptrum, *n.* sceptre

libera: liber free

30 **dissidet: dissideo** be separated

reor think

divos: divus, *m.* god

repetatur: repeto recall, retrace

origo, *f.* origin, source

laese: laedo hurt, injure, *here*, 'Injured father, ...'

Colchi relicti

Colchi: Colchus, inhabitant of Colchis

inferias: inferiae, *f. pl.* offerings to the dead, funeral

deseror: desero desert

amissis: amitto lose

regno: regnum, *n.* kingdom

patria: patria, *f.* homeland

coniuge: coniunx, -iugis, *m.f.* husband/wife, *here* husband

5 **serpentes: serpens, -tis,** serpent

tauros: taurus, *m.* bull

furentes: furo rage

perdomuisse: perdomo tame thoroughly

feros: ferus wild, savage

pepuli: pello banish, drive out

doctis: doctus clever, learned

medicatibus: medicatus, -us, *m.* charm, potion

valeo be strong, have the ability

cantus: cantus, -us, *m.* spell, incantation

herbae: herba, *f.* herb

artes: ars, artis, *f.* skill

10 **Hecates: Hecate** *here gen.* 'of Hecate'

sacra 'sacred rites'

potentis: potens powerful

agunt: ago do

grata: gratus pleasing

vigilantur: vigilo spend awake

amarae: amarus bitter

tener tender, soft

sopire: sopio put to sleep

utilior: utilis useful

cuivis: quivis anyone

15   quos ego servavi, paelex amplectitur artus
        et nostri fructus illa laboris habet.
     forsitan et, stultae dum te iactare maritae
        quaeris et iniustis auribus apta loqui,
     in faciem moresque meos nova crimina fingas.
20   rideat et vitiis laeta sit illa meis.
     rideat et Tyrio iaceat sublimis in ostro—
        flebit et ardores vincet adusta meos.
     dum ferrum flammaeque aderunt sucusque veneni,
        hostis Medeae nullus inultus erit.

1. **Why, in the first four lines, does Medea suggest her father and the people of Colchis should rejoice?**
2. **In the second four lines, how does Medea contrast how powerful she was before with how she is now?**
3. **Pick out and translate (or otherwise explain) the Latin words which tell us that Medea cannot rest by day or night.**
4. **What is the effect of the repetition of 'rideat'?**
5. **What three methods of vengeance does Medea promise to any enemy?**

Medea worries for her children, reminds Jason of the help she has given him, and finally makes more threats.

25   quod si forte preces praecordia ferrea tangunt,
        nunc animis audi verba minora meis.
     tam tibi sum supplex, quam tu mihi saepe fuisti,
        nec moror ante tuos procubuisse pedes.
     si tibi sum vilis, communes respice natos:
30   saeviet in partus dira noverca meos.
     et nimium similes tibi sunt, et imagine tangor
        et quotiens video, lumina nostra madent.
     per superos oro, per avitae lumina flammae,
        per meritum et natos, pignora nostra, duos,
35   redde torum, pro quo tot res insana reliqui!
        adde fidem dictis auxiliumque refer!
     non ego te imploro contra taurosque virosque,
        utque tua serpens victa quiescat ope;
     te peto, quem merui, quem nobis ipse dedisti,
40   cum quo sum pariter facta parente parens.
     dos ubi sit, quaeris? campo numeravimus illo,
        qui tibi laturo vellus arandus erat.

15 **paelex, f.** mistress, love-rival
amplectitur: amplector embrace
artus: artus, m. pl. limbs
fructus: fructus, -us, m. profit, fruit
forsitan perhaps
stultae: stultus stupid
te iactare = te iactaris: se iactari boast of oneself
maritae: marita, f. spouse
iniustis: iniustus unfair
auribus: auris, -is, f. ear
apta: aptus suitable
faciem: facies, f. face, appearance
mores: mos, moris, m. habit, custom; (*pl.*) character
crimina: crimen, -inis, n. charge
fingas: fingo fashion, make up
20 **vitiis: vitium n.** fault, shortcoming
Tyrio: Tyrius Tyrian
sublimis high, lofty, exalted
ostro: ostrum, n. purple
flebit: fleo weep
ardores: ardor, -oris, m. flame of passion
vincet: vinco outdo
adusta: aduro burn
sucus, m. juice, sap
inultus unavenged, unpunished

25 **quod si** 'but if'
preces: prex, precis, f. prayer
praecordia: praecordia, n. pl. breast, vitals, heart
ferrea: ferreus of iron
tangunt: tango touch
supplex suppliant
moror delay, wait
procubuisse: procumbo prostrate oneself
pedes: pes, pedis, m. foot
vilis worthless, contemptible
communes: communis shared, common
respice: respicio consider
natos: nati, m. pl. children
30 **saeviet: saevio** rage
partus: partus, -us m. offspring
dira: dirus horrible
noverca, f. stepmother
nimium too much
imagine: imago, -inis, f. image, likeness
lumina: lumen, -inis, n. light, eye

madent: madeo be wet
superos: superi, m. pl. the gods
avitae: avitus ancestral, of a grandfather
lumina NB *here a different meaning to the previous line*
meritum: meritum, n. service, kindness
pignora: pignus, -oris, n. pledge, bond
35 **torum: torus, m.** marriage, marriage bed
insana: insanus mad, insane
adde: addo add
fidem: fides, f. faith, trust
refer: refero bring
imploro beg, beseech, beg for help
serpens victa

quiescat: quiesco rest, become quiet
tua ope
ope: ops, opis, f. help
merui: mereo deserve, earn
40 **pariter** equally, together
parente: parens, -tis, m.f. parent
dos, dotis f. dowry
quaeris ubi sit dos
numeravimus: numero recall, remember, *lit.* count out
tibi laturo *lit.* 'by you about to carry off'
vellus: vellus, -eris n. fleece
arandus erat: aro plough

Medea and Jason with their children

aureus ille aries villo spectabilis alto,

    dos mea: 'quam' dicam si tibi 'redde,' neges.

45   dos mea tu sospes, dos est mea Graia iuventus.

    i nunc, Sisyphias, inprobe, confer opes.

quod vivis, quod habes nuptam socerumque potentes,

    hoc ipsum, ingratus quod potes esse, meum est.

quos equidem actutum—sed quid praedicere poenam

50   attinet? ingentes parturit ira minas.

quo feret ira sequar. facti fortasse pigebit;

    et piget infido consuluisse viro.

viderit ista deus, qui nunc mea pectora versat.

    nescio quid certe mens mea maius agit.

Ovid Heroides 12.160–213

6. What particular worry does Medea have for her children?
7. Pick out and translate the Latin phrase from Medea's pleas about her children which you find most persuasive.
8. To what two things does Medea equate her dowry, the Golden Fleece?
9. What does Medea say Jason has, thanks to her?
10. What does Medea say she regrets?
11. What, according to myth, will she do to Jason and his new bride?
12. Do you think Medea is justified in feeling the way she does? How much sympathy do you have for her after reading this passage?

5. Catullus struggles with love

Catullus feels he is owed a better deal in love by the gods for his previous good service. He has been a faithful lover to Lesbia, but now he must get over his affair.

siqua recordanti benefacta priora voluptas

    est homini, cum se cogitat esse pium,

nec sanctam violasse fidem, nec foedere nullo

    divum ad fallendos numine abusum homines,

5   multa parata manent in longa aetate, Catulle,

    ex hoc ingrato gaudia amore tibi.

nam quaecumque homines bene cuiquam aut dicere possunt

    aut facere, haec a te dictaque factaque sunt.

omnia quae ingratae perierunt credita menti.

10   quare iam te cur amplius excrucies?

quin tu animo offirmas atque istinc teque reducis,

    et dis invitis desinis esse miser?

aureus golden, of gold
aries, arietis, *m.* ram
villo: villus, *m.* shaggy hair
spectabilis spectacular, worth
   looking at
neges: nego deny, say no
45 **sospes** safe
Graia: Graius Greek
iuventus, *f.* youth, young men
Sisyphias: Sisyphius of
   Sisyphus (former king of
   Corinth) *so* 'Corinthian'
inprobe: inprobus wicked,
   shameful
confer: confero collect
opes: ops, opis, *f.* wealth
nuptam: nupta, *f.* bride
socerum: socer, *m.* father-in-
   law
potentes: potens powerful
hoc ipsum ... meum est ' it's
   down to me that ...'
ingratus ungrateful
quid ... attinet 'how does it
   help ...?'
actutum quickly, instantly
praedicere: praedico declare,
   proclaim
poenam: poena, *f.* punishment,
   penalty
50 **parturit: parturio** bring forth
minas: minae *f. pl.* threats
fortasse perhaps
pigebit: piget regret
infido: infidus treacherous,
   faithless
consuluisse: consulo + *dat.*
   consult the interest of, show
   concern for
ista 'these things'
pectora: pectus, -oris, *n.*
   chest, heart
versat: verso drive, stir
nescio quid 'something'
mens, -tis, *f.* mind

siqua 'if any'
recordanti: recordor call to
   mind, remember
benefacta *acc. pl.* 'good deeds'
priora: prior former
voluptas, -atis *f.* pleasure
cogitat: cogito think *(indirect
   statement)*
pium: pius dutiful
sanctam: sanctus sacred
violasse = violavisse: violo
   violate
fidem: fides, *f.* pledge, trust,
   loyalty

foedere: foedus, -eris, *n.*
   treaty, agreement
divum: divus, *m.* *here gen. pl.*
   'of the gods'
ad fallendos ... homines
fallendos: fallo deceive, cheat
numine: numen, -inis, *n.*
   deity, divinity
abusum: abutor + *abl.* abuse,
   make wrong use of
5 **aetate: aetas, -atis, *f.*** life
   ahead
ex hoc ingrato ... amore
ingrato: ingratus ungrateful,
   unthankful
gaudia: gaudium, *n.* joy
quaecumque: quicumque
   whoever, whatever
cuiquam: quisquam anyone
quae credita
credita: credo entrust
ingratae menti
perierunt: pereo perish
10 **quare** why
amplius more
excrucies: excrucio torment,
   torture
quin why ... not...?, but rather
offirmas: offirmo secure,
   strengthen
istinc from here
invitis: invitus unwilling
desinis: desino leave off, cease,
   desist

difficile est longum subito deponere amorem,
    difficile est, verum hoc qua lubet efficias:
15   una salus haec est. hoc est tibi pervincendum,
    hoc facias, sive id non pote sive pote.
o di, si vestrum est misereri, aut si quibus umquam
    extremam iam ipsa in morte tulistis opem,
me miserum aspicite et, si vitam puriter egi,
20   eripite hanc pestem perniciemque mihi,
quae mihi subrepens imos ut torpor in artus
    expulit ex omni pectore laetitias.
non iam illud quaero, contra me ut diligat illa,
    aut, quod non potis est, esse pudica velit:
25   ipse valere opto et taetrum hunc deponere morbum.
    o di, reddite mi hoc pro pietate mea.

Catullus 76 ad deos

1. How does Catullus use religious and financial language in the first nine lines of this poem?
2. How, in lines 10–16, does he stress how difficult it is to get over his affair?
3. How, in lines 17–26, does Catullus suggest that he is in a dreadful state, and that love, in this case, has been strong and passionate?
4. Catullus' words here might be described as 'self-help' or perhaps ancient 'counselling'. In what ways is his own advice useful, and in what ways would it be useful for a modern relationship?

6. Passion fades

dicebas quondam solum te nosse Catullum,
    Lesbia, nec prae me velle tenere Iovem.
dilexi tum te non tantum ut vulgus amicam,
    sed pater ut gnatos diligit et generos.
5   nunc te cognovi: quare etsi impensius uror,
    multo mi tamen es vilior et levior.
qui potis est, inquis? quod amantem iniuria talis
    cogit amare magis, sed bene velle minus.

Catullus 72

1. What contrast does Catullus make in lines 3 and 4?
2. How is Catullus' word order and choice of words particularly effective in the last line? How contradictory is Catullus' statement?

qua 'in whatever way'
lubet = libet it pleases
efficias: efficio effect, accomplish
15 salus, -utis, *f.* safety, hope of safety
pervincendum: pervinco overcome completely
facias: facio do, *so here, subj.,* 'you must'
sive ... sive ... whether ... or...
pote: potis possible
di = dei
vestrum est *lit.* it is of you, 'it is your habit'
misereri: misereor pity
extremam: extremus last, final
opem: ops, opis, *f.* help
aspicite: aspicio look upon
puriter purely
egi: ago *here* 'I have lived'
20 eripite: eripio snatch
pestem: pestis, -is, *f.* plague, death
perniciem: pernicies, *f.* destruction
mihi: ego *(dative of disadvantage)* 'from me'
subrepens: subrepo creep
imos: imus inmost, deepest
ut as, like
torpor, -oris, *m.* paralysis, numbness, torpor
artus: artus, *m. pl.* limbs
pectore: pectus, -oris, *n.* chest, heart
laetitias: laetitia, *f.* happiness, joy
contra in return
diligat: diligo love
pudica: pudicus chaste
25 valere: valeo be strong
opto pray, desire
taetrum: tacter grim, foul, vile
morbum: morbus, *m.* sickness, disease
pro + *abl.* for, in proportion to
pietate: pietas, -atis, *f.* loyalty, good behaviour

quondam once
nosse = novisse: novi know
prae + *abl.* before
dilexi: diligo love
tantum only
ut as
vulgus, *n.* crowd, ordinary people
gnatos = natos

generos: gener, *m.* son-in-law
5 quare for which reason
etsi although, even if
impensius: impensus excessive
uror: uro burn
mi = mihi
vilior: vilis cheap
levior: levis fickle, unimportant
qui potis est? 'how can this be?'
iniuria, *f.* injustice, wrongdoing

7. The passions of a ghostly fury

Ovid describes how he'll return to torment the man he hates bitterly in life.

> pugnabunt arcu dum Thraces, Iazyges hasta,
> > dum tepidus Ganges, frigidus Hister erit,
> robora dum montes, dum mollia pabula campi,
> > dum Tiberis liquidas Tuscus habebit aquas,
> 5   tecum bella geram; nec mors mihi finiet iras,
> > saeva sed in Manes Manibus arma dabit.
> tum quoque, cum fuero vacuas dilapsus in auras,
> > exsanguis mores oderit umbra tuos.
> tum quoque factorum veniam memor umbra tuorum,
> 10   insequar et vultus ossea forma tuos.
>
> ...
>
> quicquid ero, Stygiis erumpere nitar ab oris,
> > et tendam gelidas ultor in ora manus.
> me vigilans cernes, tacitis ego noctis in umbris
> > excutiam somnos visus adesse tuos.
> 15   denique quicquid ages, ante os oculosque volabo
> > et querar, et nulla sede quietus eris.
> verbera saeva dabunt sonitum nexaeque colubrae:
> > conscia fumabunt semper ad ora faces.

Ovid *Ibis* 133–142; 151–158

1. What contrasts does Ovid put forward in the first three lines?
2. How does Ovid emphasise the personal nature of his complaints?
3. How does Ovid make his threats particularly forceful? How genuine do they seem to you?
4. Ovid's strength of feeling might be regarded as excessive. What do people feel passionately about in today's society?

arcu: **arcus, -us, *m.*** bow
Thraces: Thrax, Thracis, *m.*
   Thracian
Iazyges, *m. pl.* the Iazyges, a
   tribe from the Black Sea coast
hasta: hasta, *f.* spear
tepidus warm
frigidus cold
Hister, *m.* the River Danube
robora: robur, -oris, *n.* oak
   tree
mollia: mollis soft
pabula: pabulum, *n.* fodder,
   grass
campi: campus, *m.* plain
Tiberis, *m.* the River Tiber
liquidas: liquidus clear
Tuscus Tuscan, Etruscan
5 **finiet: finio** end, finish
saeva: saevus savage, fierce
Manes: Manes, *m. pl.* shades,
   gods of the Underworld
vacuas: vacuus empty
dilapsus: dilabor disperse,
   decay
auras: aura, *f.* air
exsanguis bloodless
mores: mos, moris, *m.* custom,
   habit; (*pl.*) character
oderit: odi hate
umbra, *f.* ghost, shade
memor + *gen.* remembering
10 **insequar: insequor** pursue
vultus: vultus, -us, *m.* face
ossea: osseus bony
quicquid = quidquid whatever
Stygiis: Stygius Stygian, of the
   River Styx
erumpere: erumpo break out
nitar: nitor strive, endeavour
oris: ora, *f.* shore
tendam: tendo stretch
gelidas: gelidus icy
ora: os, oris, *n.* face
ultor, -oris, *m.* avenger
vigilans: vigilo watch, stay
   awake
cernes: cerno see, perceive
tacitis: tacitus silent
excutiam: excutio shake off,
   drive out, prevent
15 **denique** finally
oculos: oculus, *m.* eye
volabo: volo fly
querar: queror complain
sede: sedes, -is, *f.* home, seat
quietus quiet, at rest
verbera: verber, -eris, *n.* lash,
   stroke

nexae: necto link, intertwine
colubrae: colubra, *f.* serpent,
   snake
conscia: conscius guilty
fumabunt: fumo smoke
faces: fax, facis, *f.* torch

LAND AND SEA

No one can rely on a straightforward journey from one place to another. In the ancient world, travel by land and sea was more difficult and more dangerous than it is now in many parts of the world, but people still made surprisingly long journeys.

Horace and his travelling companions took about two weeks to travel from Rome to Brundisium. They enjoyed each other's company as they put up with mixed weather, illness, and bad accommodation as well as good. Hannibal made an ambitious journey across the Alps with an army that included elephants and was unused to snow. Pliny's letters about the journey to his province show how the government of the Roman Empire depended on a great deal of travel, while the accounts of Tacitus and Julius Caesar explain how troops that were highly skilled on land could be at the mercy of tides and currents in unfamiliar seas. In the part of the *Aeneid* about the journeys of Aeneas from the ruins of Troy to Italy, the poet Virgil describes a dramatic storm at sea that is the work of jealous gods. In an ode, apparently addressed to a ship, Horace sees the state itself as a ship struggling in troubled waters.

Funerary monument of M. Viriatius Zosimus

1. A governor travels to his province

Pliny the Younger (Gaius Plinius Caecilius Secundus) took up his position as governor of the province of Bithynia and Pontus, on the south coast of the Black Sea, in AD 111. These letters, reporting on his journey and arrival, are from the collection of letters that Pliny wrote to the emperor Trajan from his province. The collection also includes Trajan's replies.

> C. PLINIUS TRAIANO IMPERATORI
> quia confido, domine, ad curam tuam pertinere, nuntio tibi me
> Ephesum cum omnibus meis *hyper Malean*
> navigasse quamvis contrariis ventis retentum. nunc destino partim
> 5   orariis navibus, partim vehiculis provinciam petere. nam sicut
> itineri graves aestus, ita continuae navigationi etesiae reluctantur.
>
> Pliny *Letters* 10.15

> TRAIANUS PLINIO
> recte renuntiasti, mi Secunde carissime. pertinet enim ad animum
> meum, quali itinere provinciam pervenias. prudenter autem
> constituis interim navibus, interim vehiculis uti, prout loca
> 5   suaserint.
>
> Pliny *Letters* 10.16

1. **What problems did Pliny face on the journey? How did he solve them?**

> C. PLINIUS TRAIANO IMPERATORI
> sicut saluberrimam navigationem, domine, usque Ephesum
> expertus ita inde, postquam vehiculis iter facere coepi, gravissimis
> aestibus atque etiam febriculis vexatus Pergami substiti. rursus,
> 5   cum transissem in orarias naviculas, contrariis ventis retentus
> aliquanto tardius quam speraveram, id est xv kal. Octobres,
> Bithyniam intravi. non possum tamen de mora queri, cum mihi
> contigerit, quod erat auspicatissimum, natalem tuum in provincia
> celebrare. nunc rei publicae Prusensium impendia, reditus,
> 10   debitores excutio; quod ex ipso tractatu magis ac magis
> necessarium intellego. multae enim pecuniae variis ex causis a
> privatis detinentur; praeterea quaedam minime legitimis sumptibus
> erogantur. haec tibi, domine, in ipso ingressu meo scripsi.
>
> Pliny *Letters* 10.17a

1. **How does Pliny (lines 7–9) assure Trajan that his delay in arriving was not too great?**
2. **How does he make it clear that he is making up for lost time?**

GAIUS PLINIUS TRAIANO IMPERATORI Pliny [sends greetings to] the Emperor Trajan
quia because
confido trust, be confident that
pertinere: pertineo concern, be of interest to
cum omnibus meis with all my staff/entourage
hyper Malean (Greek phrase) round Cape Malea (southern tip of the Peloponnese in Greece)
navigasse = navigavisse
quamvis although
contrariis: contrarius contrary
ventis: ventus, m. wind
retentum: retineo hold back
destino decide, resolve
partim ... partim ... partly ... partly ...
5 **orariis: orarius** of the coast, coastal
vehiculis: vehiculum, n. vehicle, carriage
provinciam: provincia, f. province
sicut ... (ita) ... while
sicut itineri graves aestus (reluctantur)
graves: gravis *here* intense
aestus: aestus, -us, m. heat
continuae: continuus continuous, uninterrupted
navigationi: navigatio, -onis, f. sailing
etesiae, m. pl. northerly Etesian/trade winds, blowing throughout the summer
reluctantur: reluctor + *dat.* obstruct

TRAIANUS PLINIO Trajan [sends greetings to] Pliny
recte rightly
renuntiasti = renuntiavisti: renuntio report
Secunde: Secundus i.e. Pliny
pervenias: pervenio reach, arrive at
prudenter wisely, sensibly
autem however
interim ... interim ... at one time ... at another ...
uti: utor + *abl.* use
prout + *subj.* as
loca, n. pl. connected places, i.e. region
5 **suaserint: suadeo** urge, recommend, *here* dictate

sicut ... (ita) although
saluberrimam: salubris healthy
usque as far as
Ephesum: Ephesus, f. Ephesus (in modern Turkey)
expertus: experior *here* undergo, experience
inde from there
coepi *perf.* began
febriculis: febricula, f. slight fever
vexatus: vexo distress, trouble
Pergami at Pergamum (a city in Mysia)
substiti: subsisto stop, stay for a while
rursus again
5 **transissem = transivissem: transeo** cross over, transfer
naviculas: navicula, f. little ship
aliquanto somewhat, rather
tardius: tardus late
speraveram: spero hope
ante diem xv kal. (=Kalendas) Octobres 15 days before 1 October (Kalends), *i.e.* 17 September
possum can, be able
mora: mora, f. delay
queri: queror complain
contigerit: contingit + *dat. impers.* fall to
auspicatissimum: auspicatus fortunate, auspicious
(diem) natalem: (dies) natalis, m. birthday (18 September)

celebrare: celebro celebrate
rei publicae: res publica, f. state, city
Prusensium: Prusenses, m. pl. people of Prusa (in Bithynia)
impendia: impendium, n. expense
reditus: reditus, -us, m. revenue
10 **debitores: debitor, -oris, m.** debtor
excutio investigate, examine *lit.* shake out
tractatu: tractatus: -us, m. procedure
magis more
necessarium: necessarius necessary
variis: varius different, various
causis: causa, f. reason
privatis: privatus, m. private citizen
detinentur: detineo keep back, retain
praeterea moreover, in addition
quaedam: quidam some, certain
minime not at all, not in the least
legitimis: legitimus lawful, legitimate
sumptibus: sumptus, -us, m. cost, payment
erogantur: erogo pay out
ingressu: ingressus, -us, m. entrance, commencement (*here* of Pliny's governorship)

Antiquarian map of Roman Empire

2. The army on land and sea

a. A difficult landing

Julius Caesar invaded Britain for the first time with two legions in 55 BC. This is an extract from his own account. The Britons on the south coast (near modern Dover) made landing difficult by throwing weapons from the cliffs.

> hunc ad egrediendum nequaquam idoneum locum arbitratus, dum
> reliquae naves eo convenirent ad horam nonam in ancoris
> exspectavit. interim, legatis tribunisque militum convocatis, et
> quae ex Voluseno cognosset et quae fieri vellet ostendit;
> 5   monuitque ad nutum et ad tempus omnes res ab iis administrarentur.
> his dimissis, et ventum et aestum uno tempore nactus secundum,
> dato signo et sublatis ancoris, circiter milia passuum septem ab eo loco
> progressus aperto ac plano litore naves constituit.

1. Why might it be especially important to respond to orders quickly in a sea battle?

> at barbari, consilio Romanorum cognito praemisso equitatu et
> 10   essedariis, quo plerumque genere in proeliis uti consuerunt,
> reliquis copiis subsecuti nostros navibus egredi prohibebant. erat
> ob has causas summa difficultas, quod naves propter
> magnitudinem nisi in alto constitui non poterant, militibus autem,
> ignotis locis, impeditis manibus, magno et gravi onere armorum
> 15   oppressis simul et de navibus desiliendum et in fluctibus
> consistendum et cum hostibus erat pugnandum, cum illi aut ex
> arido aut paulum in aquam progressi, omnibus membris expeditis,
> notissimis locis, audacter tela conicerent et equos insuefactos
> incitarent. quibus rebus nostri perterriti atque huius omnino generis
> 20   pugnae imperiti, non eadem alacritate ac studio quo in pedestribus
> uti proeliis consuerant utebantur.

2. How did the Britons make it difficult for Caesar's men to disembark (lines 9–11)?
3. Match up the phrases that describe the Romans' disadvantages and the enemy's advantages (lines 13–19).

Caesar then describes how he tried to solve this problem. He ordered his warships to station themselves where the enemy were unguarded, and to attack them with slings, arrows and war-machines. These weapons were unfamiliar, so the enemy were disturbed and withdrew a short distance. In spite of this success, the Romans were still reluctant to join battle.

egrediendum: egredior go out, disembark

nequaquam in no way, not at all

idoneum: idoneus suitable

arbitratus: arbitror think, consider

dum + *subj.* until

reliquae: reliquus remaining

eo to that place, there

convenirent: convenio come together, assemble

horam: hora, *f.* hour

ad horam nonam up to the ninth hour

ancoris: ancora, *f.* anchor

exspectavit: exspecto wait *(Caesar) exspectavit*

legatis: legatus, *m.* deputy

tribunis militum: tribunus militum, *m.* military tribune, commander

convocatis: convoco call together

cognosset = cognovisset

Voluseno: Volusenus, *m.* (a military tribune sent out to reconnoitre)

fieri: fio *here* be done/made, happen

5 **nutum: nutus, -us, *m.*** command, order, *lit.* nod

administrarentur: administro perform, do

dimissis: dimitto send away, dismiss

septem milia passuum seven miles

aestus, -us, *m.* tide

nactus: nanciscor obtain

progressus: progredior advance

aperto: apertus open

plano: planus flat, level

litore: litus, -oris, *n.* shore, beach

constituit: constituo position, draw up, moor

at but

barbari: barbarus, *m.* enemy, *lit.* barbarian

praemisso: praemitto send in advance

equitatu: equitatus, -us, *m.* cavalry

10 **essedariis: essedarius, *m.*** fighter in a war-chariot

plerumque mostly, generally

genere: genus, -eris, *n.* kind, sort

quo ... genere ... of the kind that ...

proeliis: proelium, *n.* battle

uti: utor + *abl.* use

consuerunt = consueverunt: consuesco be accustomed, be in the habit of

copiae, *f. pl.* forces, troops

subsecuti: subsequor follow closely

nostros: nostri, *m. pl.* our men

prohibebant: prohibeo prevent

ob + *acc.* on account of, for

causas: causa, *f.* reason

propter + *acc.* because of, owing to

magnitudinem: magnitudo, -inis, *f.* large size

alto: altum, *n.* *here* deep water

ignotis: ignotus unknown

impeditis: impeditus hindered

impeditis manibus *here* with their hands full

onere: onus, -eris, *n.* load

armorum: arma, *n. pl.* weapons, armour, equipment

15 **oppressis: opprimo** press down, weigh down, burden

desiliendo: desilio jump down

fluctibus: fluctus, -us, *m.* wave, current

consistendum: consisto stand, keep one's footing

militibus (Romanis) ... erat desiliendum et ... consistendum et ... pugnandum ... the soldiers had to jump down ... and keep their footing ... and fight ...

cum *here* while, by contrast *illi (barbari)*

aut ... aut ... either ... or ...

arido: aridum, *n.* dry land

paulum a little, only a little

membris: membrum, *n.* limb

expeditis: expeditus unencumbered

notissimis: notus well known, familiar

audacter boldly, confidently

tela: telum, *n.* weapon

conicerent: conicio throw, hurl

insuefactos: insuefactus trained in/ accustomed to (this kind of warfare)

incitarent: incito urge/spur on

perterriti: perterritus terrified

omnino completely

20 **pugnae: pugna, *f.*** fight

imperiti: imperitus + *gen.* inexperienced

alacritate: alacritas, -atis, *f.* eagerness, keenness, spirit

studio: studium, *n.* zeal, application, enthusiasm

pedestribus: pedester on foot, *here* on dry land

proeliis: proelium, *n.* battle

consuerant = consueverant

atque nostris militibus cunctantibus, maxime propter altitudinem
maris, qui decimae legionis aquilam ferebat, contestatus deos, ut ea
res legioni feliciter eveniret, 'desilite,' inquit, 'milites, nisi vultis
25 aquilam hostibus prodere: ego certe meum rei publicae atque
imperatori officium praestitero.' hoc cum voce magna dixisset, se
ex navi proiecit atque in hostes aquilam ferre coepit. tum nostri
cohortati inter se, ne tantum dedecus admitteretur, universi ex navi
desiluerunt. hos item ex proximis navibus cum conspexissent,
30 subsecuti hostibus adpropinquarunt.

4. Why did an appeal by a standard-bearer have particular force?
5. How is the Romans' team spirit demonstrated?

As the Romans jumped down from their ships, they could not line up in their usual
order. The enemy took advantage, blocking their way and attacking them, until
Caesar brought up reinforcements in ships to protect the troops.

nostri, simul in arido constiterunt, suis omnibus consecutis, in
hostes impetum fecerunt atque eos in fugam dederunt; neque
longius prosequi potuerunt, quod equites cursum tenere atque
insulam capere non potuerant. hoc unum ad pristinam fortunam
35 Caesari defuit.

Caesar Gallic War 4.23–26 (abridged)

6. How did the Romans finally get the upper hand?

b. Land and sea confused
This journey took place during Germanicus' campaign in Germany in AD 15. Tacitus
describes how legionaries lose their footing on land that turns into sea.

at Germanicus legionum, quas navibus vexerat, secundam et
quartam decimam itinere terrestri Publio Vitellio ducendas tradit, quo
levior classis vadoso mari innaret vel reciproco sideret. Vitellius
primum iter sicca humo aut modice adlabente aestu quietum
5 habuit: mox inpulsu aquilonis, simul sidere aequinoctii, quo
maxime tumescit Oceanus, rapi agique agmen.

1. Why did putting some of the troops ashore seem to be a good idea?
**2. 'Vitellius primum ... rapi agique agmen' (lines 3–6). Compare the situation of the
troops at the beginning of this sentence with their situation at the end. What has
changed?**

et opplebantur terrae: eadem freto litori campis facies, neque
discerni poterant incerta ab solidis, brevia a profundis. sternuntur

cunctantibus: cunctor delay, hesitate

altitudinem: altitudo, -inis, f. depth, height

decimae: decimus tenth

legionis: legio, -onis, f. legion

aquilam: aquila, f. eagle (standard of Roman legion)

contestatus: contestor call to witness, call on

feliciter favourably

eveniret: evenio happen, turn out

25 **prodere: prodo** *here* betray

certe *here* at least

rei publicae: res publica f. republic, state

imperator: imperator, -oris, m. general, commander

officium: officium, n. duty

praestitero: praesto stand out, *here* fulfil, perform

proiecit: proicio throw down

cohortati: cohortor urge, exhort

inter se one another

dedecus, -oris, n. disgrace

admitteretur: admitto let in, allow

universi: universi, m. pl. the whole body, everyone together

item in the same way

proximis: proximus nearest

conspexissent: conspicio observe, see, notice

30 **adpropinquarunt = appropinquaverunt**

simul *here* as soon as

constiterunt: consisto stand

consecutis: consequor follow, pursue

Impetum: impetus, -us, m. attack

fugam: fuga, f. flight

eos in fugam dederunt (they) put them to flight

longius: longus far

prosequi: prosequor pursue

equites, -um, m. pl. cavalry

cursum: cursus, -us, m. course

capere: capio *here* enter, reach

defuit: desum + *dat.* fail, be lacking

pristinam: pristinus former

hoc unum ... Caesari defuit Caesar lacked this one thing (*lit.* This one thing was lacking to Caesar) compared to his former good fortune,

Standard bearer (centre)

at but

Germanicus, m. Caesar Germanicus (general and nephew of the emperor Tiberius)

legionum: legio, -onis, f. legion

vexerat: veho transport

legionum ... secundam et quartam decimam the second and fourteenth (of the) legions

terrestri: terrestris of/on the land

itinere terrestri ... ducendas to lead by a land route

quo *here* in order that

levior: levis light, *here* lightly

classis, -is, f. fleet

vadoso: vadosus shallow

innaret: inno float/sail upon

vel or

reciproco: reciprocus turning back, tidal, ebbing

sideret: sido *here* stick (in shallows), 'be grounded'

quo classis innaret levior vadoso mari vel sideret (levior) reciproco (mari)

primum at first

sicca: siccus dry

humo: humus, f. ground

modice moderately, slightly

adlabente: adlabor come in, flow in

aestu: aestus, -us, m. *here* tide

quietus quiet, uneventful

iter ... quietum

5 **inpulsu: inpulsus, -us, m.** blow, onset

aquilonis: aquilo, -onis, m. north wind

simul at the same time

sidere: sidus, -eris, n. *here* season

aequinoctii: aequinoctium, m. equinox

quo *here* when

maxime very, exceedingly

tumescit: tumesco swell, (of the sea) be rough

rapi = rapiebatur snatch/carry away, *here* carry off course

agi = agebatur drive, put under pressure

agmen, -inis, n. column (of army)

opplebantur: oppleo fill, *here* cover

eadem: idem the same

freto: fretum, n. strait (of sea)

litori: litus. -oris, n. shore

campis: campus, m. field

facies, f. shape, face, appearance

eadem (erat) ... facies

discerni: discerno distinguish

poterant: possum be able

incerta: incertus uncertain, treacherous (ground)

solidis: solidus firm (ground)

brevia: brevis *here* shallow (water)

profundis: profundus deep (water)

sternuntur: sterno *here* overthrow, knock down

fluctibus, hauriuntur gurgitibus; iumenta, sarcinae, corpora

10   exanima interfluunt, occursant. permiscentur inter se manipuli,
modo pectore, modo ore tenus exstantes, aliquando subtracto solo
disiecti aut obruti. non vox et mutui hortatus iuvabant adversante
unda; nihil strenuus ab ignavo, sapiens ab inprudenti, consilia a
casu differre: cuncta pari violentia involvebantur.

3. 'et opplebantur terrae' (line 7). What details in the rest of the sentence illustrate
this statement?

4. 'sternuntur ... involvebantur' (lines 8–14). What strengths usually shown by the
Roman army are overcome by the disaster?

15   tandem Vitellius in editiora enisus eodem agmen subduxit.
pernoctavere sine utensilibus, sine igni, magna pars nudo aut
mulcato corpore, haud minus miserabiles quam quos hostis
circumsidet: quippe illic etiam honestae mortis usus, his inglorium
exitium. lux reddidit terram, penetratumque ad amnem, quo Caesar

20   classe contenderat. inpositae dein legiones, vagante fama
submersas; nec fides salutis, antequam Caesarem exercitumque
reducem videre.

Tacitus Annals 1.70

5. What made the night shameful and humiliating for the soldiers as well as
uncomfortable?

6. What does Tacitus mean by saying that 'the day gave back the land' (line 19)?

Both passages (2a. and b.)

1. Could the problems of the troops have been avoided, or were they inevitable in an
unfamiliar country?

2. What problems did the sea cause for Vitellius' troops and Julius Caesar's troops? In
what ways were they similar?

hauriuntur: haurio consume, swallow

gurgitibus: gurges, -itis, *m.* whirlpool, current

iumenta: iumentum, *n.* baggage animal

sarcinae: sarcina, *f.* baggage

10 **exanima: exanimus** dead

interfluunt: interfluo flow between, float among (each other)

occursant: occurso come together, collide

permiscentur: permisceo mix up, throw into confusion

manipuli: manipulus, *m.* maniple, company (of soldiers)

modo ... modo ... now ... now ...

pectore: pectus, -oris, *m.* breast, chest

ore: os, oris, *m.* face

tenus + *abl.* as far as

exstantes: exsto stand out, be visible

modo ... exstantes now their chests visible (above the water), now (only) their faces

aliquando sometimes

solo: solum, *n.* ground

subtracto: subtraho take away from under, remove

subtracto solo the ground cut from under their feet

disiecti: disicio scatter

obruti: obruo overwhelm, sink

vox, vocis, *f.* voice, shouting

mutui: mutuus mutual, to each other

hortatus, -us, *m.* encouragement

iuvabant: iuvo help

adversante unda with the flood/tide against them

nihil differre ... ab ... there was no difference between ... and ...

differre = differebant: differo + a/ab + *abl.* be different from

strenuus energetic, active

ignavo: ignavus lazy, cowardly, *here* 'who were normally "cowardly"'

sapiens sensible, shrewd

inprudenti: inprudens ignorant, thoughtless, inexperienced

casu: casus, -us, *m.* chance, leaving to chance

cuncta: cunctus every, all

pari: par equal

violentia, *f.* *here* onslaught

involvebantur: involvo envelop, cover, overwhelm

15 **editiora, *n. pl.*** *here* higher ground

enisus: enitor force one's way up

eodem to the same place

subduxit: subduco withdraw

pernoctavere = pernoctaverunt: pernocto pass the night

utensilibus: utensilia, *n. pl.* equipment

igni: ignis, -is, *m.* fire

mulcato: mulcatus battered, bruised

haud minus ... quam no less ... than

quam (ei) quos

circumsidet: circumsido besiege

quippe ... etiam and indeed, and in fact

illic there, in that situation

honestae: honestus worthy, honourable

usus, -us, *m.* *here* advantage

inglorium: inglorius shameful, inglorious

exitium, *n.* end, death

lux, lucis, *f.* light, daylight

penetratum (est) = penetraverunt: penetro ad reach

amnem: amnis, -is, *m.* river

quo to which, which

20 **contenderat: contendo** hurry, make an effort to reach

inpositae (sunt): inpono put into, put on board, embark

dein = deinde

vagante: vagor wander, *here* spread

fama: fama, *f.* rumour

submersas = submersas esse: submergo sink, drown

fides, *f.* faith, confidence

salutis: salus, -utis, *f.* safety

fides (erat) salutis

antequam before

videre = viderunt

exercitum: exercitus, -us, *m.* army

reducem: redux coming back, being brought back

Soldiers on a boat

3. Hannibal crosses the Alps

In 218 BC, the Carthaginian general Hannibal left New Carthage (founded by the Carthaginians in Spain). With his army, which included elephants, he aimed to march on Rome, and this passage describes his crossing of the Alps into Italy.

Hannibal and his troops reach the summit

> elephanti sicut per artas vias magna mora agebantur, ita tutum ab
> hostibus quacumque incederent, quia insuetis adeundi propius
> metus erat, agmen praebebant. nono die in iugum Alpium
> perventum est ...

1. What difficulties did the troops face?
2. How did the elephants help?

The exhausted troops are held back by snow but encouraged by the view of Italy.

5   biduum in iugo stativa habita fessisque labore ac pugnando quies
       data militibus; iumentaque aliquot, quae prolapsa in rupibus erant,
       sequendo vestigia agminis in castra pervenere. fessis taedio tot
       malorum nivis etiam casus, occidente iam sidere Vergiliarum,
       ingentem terrorem adiecit. per omnia nive oppleta cum signis
10   prima luce motis segniter agmen incederet pigritiaque et desperatio
       in omnium vultu emineret, praegressus signa Hannibal in
       promunturio quodam, unde longe ac late prospectus erat, consistere
       iussis militibus Italiam ostentat subiectosque Alpinis montibus
       Circumpadanos campos, moeniaque eos tum transcendere non
15   Italiae modo sed etiam urbis Romanae; cetera plana, proclivia fore;
       uno aut summum altero proelio arcem et caput Italiae in manu ac
       potestate habituros.

3. Why did the snow frighten the soldiers?
4. Using the information in lines 11–17 ('praegressus signa ... habituros'), write the speech Hannibal might have made to the troops.

The descent begins. A dead end, a detour and more problems with snow.

> procedere inde agmen coepit iam nihil ne hostibus quidem praeter
> parva furta per occasionem temptantibus. ceterum iter multo quam
20   in adscensu fuerat – ut pleraque Alpium ab Italia sicut breviora ita
> arrectiora sunt – difficilius fuit; omnis enim ferme via praeceps,
> angusta, lubrica erat, ut neque sustinere se ab lapsu possent nec qui
> paulum titubassent haerere adflicti vestigio suo, aliique super alios
> et iumenta in homines occiderent.

elephanti: elephantus, *m.* elephant

sicut *here* although, while

artas: artus narrow

mora: mora, *f.* delay

ita *here* even so

tutum: tutus safe

quacumque *here* wherever

incederent: incedo go, advance

quia because

insuetis: insuetus not used to

adeundi: adeo go to, approach

propius *here* too close

metus, -us, *m.* fear

agmen: agmen, -inis, *n.* column, force

praebebant: praebeo *here* make

(elephanti) tutum ab hostibus ... agmen praebebant

quia ... erat because they (the enemy) were not used to (the elephants) and were afraid to get too close

nono: nonus ninth

iugum: iugum, *n.* yoke, *here* ridge, summit

perventum in: pervenio in arrive at, reach

perventum est they arrived

5 **biduum** for two days

stativa habita (sunt) there was a halt, they halted

fessis: fessus tired out, exhausted

labore: labor, -oris *m.* work, effort

quies, -etis, *f.* rest, respite

quies data militibus fessis labore ac pugnando

iumenta: iumentum, *n.* baggage animal

aliquot some

prolapsa erant: prolabor fall

rupibus: rupis, -is, *f.* rock

sequendo: sequor follow

vestigia: vestigium, *n.* track foothold

pervenere = pervenerunt

taedio: taedium, *n.* weariness

malorum: mala, *n. pl.* *here* hardships, calamities

nivis: nix, nivis, *f.* snow

etiam *here* on top of everything else

casus, -us, *m.* fall

occidente: occido *here* set

sidere: sidus, -eris, *n.* star, constellation

Vergiliarum: Vergiliae, *f. pl.* the Pleiades

terrorem: terror, -oris, *m.* terror

adiecit: adicio add to, bring to

casus nivis (militibus) fessis ... ingentem terrorem adiecit

oppleta: oppleo fill, *here* cover

signa: signum, *n.* sign, military standard

10 **prima luce** at dawn

signis ... motis when they had broken up the camp, got under way, *lit.* the standards having been moved

segniter slowly

pigritia, *f.* sluggishness, reluctance

desperatio, -onis, *f.* hopelessness

vultu: vultus, -us, *m.* face

emineret: emineo stand out, be clearly seen

cum ... agmen incederet pigritiaque et desperatio ... emineret

praegressus: praegredior + *acc.* go ahead of

promunturio: promunturium, *n.* viewpoint

longe ac late far and wide

prospectus, -us, *m.* view, sight, prospect

consistere: consisto stop

iussis: iubeo command

ostentat: ostento show, point out

subiectos: subiectus bordering on, *here* at the foot of

Circumpadanos campos: Circumpadani campi, *m. pl.* lands of the Po Valley

moenia: moenia, -ium, *n. pl.* walls, defences

transcendere: transcendo cross, climb over

non ... modo sed etiam not only ... but also

15 **plana: planus** flat, level

proclivia: proclivis downhill

fore *fut. infin.* **esse**

proelio: proelium, *n.* battle

uno aut summum altero proelio in one or at the most two battles

arcem: arx, arcis, *f.* citadel

potestate: potestas, -atis, *f.* power

(dixit) ... eos transcendere ...; cetera ... fore; ... (eos) habituros (esse)

procedere: procedo advance

inde from there

coepit: coepi began

furta: furtum, *n.* raid, robbery

per occasionem when they had the chance

temptantibus: tempto try, attempt

ceterum but, however

20 **adscensu: adscensus, -us, *m.*** ascent

pleraque: plerique many, most

ab Italia on the Italian side

breviora: brevis short

arrectiora: arrectus steep

ut pleraque Alpium ... arrectiora sunt for just as many slopes of the Alps on the Italian side are shorter, so they are (also) steeper

multo ... difficilius much more difficult

iter multo difficilius fuit quam in ascensu fuerat

ferme almost

praeceps steep

angusta: angustus narrow

lubrica: lubricus slippery

se sustinere: sustineo support oneself, keep/prevent oneself

lapsu: lapsus, -us, *m.* fall, falling

paulum a little, even a little

titubassent = titubavissent: titubo stagger, stumble

haerere: haereo stick, *here* get a grip

adflicti: adflictus *here* having lost

... haerere adflicti vestigio suo (possent) ... could get a grip as they lost their footing

alii ... super alios on top of each other

occiderent: occido fall

ut neque ... possent nec ... (possent)...

-que ... occiderent

5. What were the difficulties of this stage of the journey, and what was the only improvement?

25   ventum deinde ad multo angustiorem rupem atque ita rectis saxis
       ut aegre expeditus miles temptabundus manibusque retinens
       virgulta ac stirpes circa eminentes demittere sese posset. natura
       locus iam ante praeceps recenti lapsu terrae in pedum mille
       admodum altitudinem abruptus erat. ibi cum velut ad finem viae
30   equites constitissent, miranti Hannibali quae res moraretur agmen
       nuntiatur rupem inviam esse.

When Hannibal saw the precipice caused by the landslide, he decided they would have to make a detour, however much it took them out of their way. But neither the men nor the baggage animals could get a foothold on the slush and impacted ice on the ground. They had to return to the precipice and pitch camp.

       tandem nequiquam iumentis atque hominibus fatigatis castra in
       iugo posita, aegerrime ad id ipsum loco purgato; tantum nivis
       fodiendum atque egerendum fuit.
35   inde ad rupem muniendam per quam unam via esse poterat milites
       ducti, cum caedendum esset saxum, arboribus circa immanibus
       deiectis detruncatisque struem ingentem lignorum faciunt eamque,
       cum et vis venti apta faciendo igni coorta esset, succendunt
       ardentiaque saxa infuso aceto putrefaciunt. ita torridam incendio
40   rupem ferro pandunt molliuntque anfractibus modicis clivos ut non
       iumenta solum sed elephanti etiam deduci possent.

6. Why did it seem that the troops had got to the end of the road?
7. What were the two stages in making the road down the precipice?

The descent to the lowlands

       quadriduum circa rupem consumptum, iumentis prope fame
       absumptis; nuda enim fere cacumina sunt et, si quid est pabuli,
       obruunt nives. inferiora valles apricos quosdam colles habent
45   rivosque prope silvas et iam humano cultu digniora loca. ibi
       iumenta in pabulum missa et quies muniendo fessis hominibus
       data. triduo inde ad planum descensum et iam locis mollioribus
       et accolarum ingeniis.
       hoc maxime modo in Italiam perventum est quinto mense a
50   Carthagine Nova, ut quidam auctores sunt, quinto decimo die
       Alpibus superatis.

                                        Livy *A History of Rome* 21.35–38 (abridged)

25 **ventum (est)** they came
deinde then, next
ita rectis saxis with such sheer/perpendicular rocks
aegerrime: aegre with difficulty, hardly
expeditus lightly armed, not carrying much equipment
temptabundus (tempto) *here* by testing the ground, by feeling his way
retinens: retineo hang/hold on to
virgulta: virgultum, *n.* bush
stirpes: stirps, -pis, *f.* tree stump, root
circa eminentes sticking out round about
demittere: demitto let down
sese = se
natura *abl.* by nature
iam ante even before, already
recenti: recens recent, fresh
altitudinem: altitudo, -inis, *f.* height, depth
admodum fully, to the full
pedum: pes, pedis, *m.* foot
in pedum mille admodum altitudinem to a depth of a full thousand feet
abruptus broken off, *here* turned into a precipice/drop
velut as if
30 **equites, equitum, *m. pl.*** cavalry
constitissent: consisto stop, stand still
miranti: miror wonder, be surprised
moraretur: moror delay, hold up
inviam: invius impassable

nequiquam in vain,
fatigatis: fatigatus (fatigo) exhausted
posita (sunt)
ad id ipsum for that very purpose
purgatum: purgo cleanse, *here* clear
loco aegerrime purgato ad id ipsum
tantum nivis so great a quantity of snow
fodiendum: fodio dig
egerendum: egero carry away
35 **muniendam: munio** build a wall around, *here* build a road over

ducti (sunt): duco *here* direct
caedendum: caedo cut, split
immanibus: immanis huge
deiectis: deicio throw down, fell
detruncatis: detrunco lop
struem: strues, struis, *f.* pile
lignorum: lignum, *n.* wood, log
vis, *f.* force
venti: ventus, *m.* wind
apta: aptus + *dat.* fit for, good for
igni: ignis, -is, *m.* fire
coorta: coorior rise
succendum: succendo set fire to
ardentia: ardens burning, hot
infuso: infundo pour over
aceto: acetum, *n.* sour wine, vinegar
putrefaciunt: putrefacio *here* make to crumble, break up
torridam: torridus hot, heated
40 **pandunt: pando** open up
molliunt: mollio soften, *here* make less steep
anfractibus: anfractus, -us, *m.* bend, zigzag
modicis: modicus small, manageable
clivos: clivus, *m.* slope, gradient
deduci: deduco lead down

quadriduum four days
consumptum (est): consumo use up

fame: fames, -is, *f.* hunger, starvation
absumptis: absumptus *here* destroyed
cacumina: cacumen, -inis, *n.* peak
pabuli: pabulum, *n.* fodder
obruunt: obruo cover over, bury
inferiora *here* the lands below
valles: vallis, -is, *f.* valley
apricos: apricus sunny
colles: collis, -is, *m.* upland, hill
45 **rivos: rivus, *m.*** stream
cultu: cultus, -us, *m.* *here* way of life
digniora: dignus worthy
quies, -etis, *f.* rest
missa (sunt) ... data (est)
triduo in after three days
descensum (est) = descenderunt descend, go down
ingeniis: ingenium nature, quality
locis mollioribus et accolarum ingeniis both the regions and the nature of the inhabitants being gentler
mense: mensis, -is, *m.* month
50 **ut quidem auctores sunt** according to some writers
quinto decimo die Alpibus superatis the conquest of the Alps having taken fifteen days

Hannibal

8. How does the description of the lowlands contrast with the journey to reach them?

The whole passage
1. Why do you think Livy gives so many details of the difficulties of the journey and the way Hannibal and his troops overcame them?
2. How might Livy's account of this journey have been of interest or use to the Romans?
3. Do you admire Hannibal?

4. A traveller's tale

71 lines

Day 1   The poet leaves Rome on the Appian Way with a companion.

> egressum magna me accepit Aricia Roma
> hospitio modico: rhetor comes Heliodorus,
> Graecorum longe doctissimus; inde Forum Appi,
> differtum nautis, cauponibus atque malignis.
> 5   hoc iter ignavi divisimus, altius ac nos
> praecinctis unum: minus est gravis Appia tardis.
> hic ego propter aquam, quod erat deterrima, ventri
> indico bellum, cenantes haud animo aequo
> exspectans comites.

1. Which two words in lines 5–6 show that Horace and Heliodorus travelled slowly?
2. What made Horace miss his dinner?

Days 2–3   Night trip on a canal

> 10   iam nox inducere terris
> umbras et caelo diffundere signa parabat.
> tum pueri nautis, pueris convicia nautae
> ingerere: 'huc adpelle!'; 'trecentos inseris: ohe
> iam satis est!' dum aes exigitur, dum mula ligatur,
> 15   tota abit hora. mali culices ranaeque palustres
> avertunt somnos, absentem ut cantat amicam
> multa prolutus vappa nauta atque viator
> certatim: tandem fessus dormire viator
> incipit, ac missae pastum retinacula mulae
> 20   nauta piger saxo religat stertitque supinus.
> iamque dies aderat, nil cum procedere lintrem
> sentimus, donec cerebrosus prosilit unus
> ac mulae nautaeque caput lumbosque saligno
> fuste dolat. quarta vix demum exponimur hora.

egressum: egredior leave
accepit: accipio receive, *here* welcome
hospitio: hospitium, *n.* inn, accommodation
modico: modicus simple, basic
Aricia me, egressum magna Roma, accepit hospitio modico
rhetor, -oris, *m.* teacher of rhetoric (the art of making speeches)
comes, -itis, *m.f.* companion, fellow traveller
rhetor Heliodorus (erat) comes
longe far, a long way, *here* by far
doctissimus: doctus learned
inde from there
inde (venimus) Forum Appi
differtum: differtus + *abl.* stuffed with, full of
nautis: nauta, *m.* sailor, boatman
cauponibus: caupo, -onis, *m.* tradesman, inn-keeper
malignis: malignus evil, spiteful *here* stingy, grasping
differtum nautis atque cauponibus malignis
5 **iter: iter, itineris, *n.*** journey, *here* part of the journey, stage
ignavi: ignavus lazy
divisimus: divido divide
ac *here* than
altius ... praecinctis more energetic *lit.* (with clothes) tucked up higher
hoc iter, unum (iter) altius ac nos praecinctis, (nos) ignavi divisimus
minus less
gravis *here* arduous, tiring
(via) Appia, *f.* the Appian Way
tardis: tardus slow
propter + *acc.* because of
deterrima: deterrimus worst, terrible
ventri: venter, -tris, *m.* stomach
indico bellum + *dat.* declare war on
cenantes: ceno dine, have dinner
haud not
animo aequo patiently

10 **inducere: induco** *here* spread over
umbras: umbra, *f.* shadow
diffundere: diffundo pour over, scatter

signa: signum, *n.* sign, *here* star, constellation
convicia: convicium, *n.* abuse, insult
ingerere = ingerebant: ingero throw into/onto, pile onto
appelle: appello bring (a ship) in, put to land
trecentos: trecenti three hundred
inseris: insero put into, cram in
ohe! hey!
aes, aeris, *n.* bronze, *here* money
exigitur: exigo *here* demand, collect
mula, *f.* mule
ligatur: ligo bind, *here* harness
15 **abit: abeo** go away, pass
culices: culex, -icis, *m.* gnat, mosquito
ranae: rana, *f.* frog
palustres: paluster marshy, swampy
avertunt: averto drive away
somnos: somnus, *m.* sleep
absentem: absens absent, not there
ut *here* while
cantat: canto sing
amicam: amica, *f.* girl friend
prolutus *here* soaked, drunk
vappa: vappa, *f.* flat, bad wine
viator, -oris, *m.* passenger
certatim in competition
(cantat) certatim

fessus tired
incipit: incipio begin
pastum 'to graze, feed'
missae ... pastum mulae the mule sent/put out to graze
retinacula: retinacula, *n.* pl. halter, reins
20 **piger** lazy, sluggish
saxo: saxum, *n.* stone
religat: religo tie up
nauta piger religat saxo retinacula mulae missae pastum
stertit: sterto snore
supinus on his back
aderat: adsum be here
procedere: procedo go forwards, make progress
lintrem: linter, -tris, *f.* boat, barge
donec until
cerebrosus hot-headed, hot-tempered
prosilit: prosilio jump up
lumbos: lumbus, *m.* *here* backside
saligno: salignus made of willow
fuste: fustis, -tis, *m.* stick
dolat: dolo *here* beat
quarta ... hora at the fourth hour, 10 am
vix scarcely, only just
demum at last
exponimur: expono put out, *pass. here* land

Three men in a boat

3. What sounds kept the travellers awake at night?
4. Would you describe the 'cerebrosus' in line 22 as bossy, unreasonable, impatient or public-spirited?

Day 3   Arrival at Anxur; more bad health; more friends

25   ora manusque tua lavimus, Feronia, lympha.
      milia tum pransi tria repimus atque subimus
      impositum saxis late candentibus Anxur.
      huc venturus erat Maecenas optimus atque
      Cocceius, missi magnis de rebus uterque
30   legati, aversos soliti componere amicos.
      hic oculis ego nigra meis collyria lippus
      illinere. interea Maecenas advenit atque
      Cocceius Capitoque simul Fonteius, ad unguem
      factus homo, Antoni non ut magis alter amicus.
      ...

5. In lines 25–27, how does Horace combine descriptions of the places with details of the journey?
6. How do lines 31–32 ('hic oculis ... illinere') contrast with what comes before and afterwards?

Days 5–7   Poets meet at Sinuessae; hospitality simple and grand.

35   postera lux oritur multo gratissima; namque
      Plotius et Varius Sinuessae Vergiliusque
      occurrunt ...
      ...
      o qui complexus et gaudia quanta fuerunt!
      nil ego contulerim iucundo sanus amico.
40   proxima Campano ponti quae villula, tectum
      praebuit et parochi quae debent ligna salemque.
      hinc muli Capuae clitellas tempore ponunt.
      lusum it Maecenas, dormitum ego Vergiliusque;
      namque pila lippis inimicum et ludere crudis.
45   hinc nos Coccei recipit plenissima villa,
      quae super est Caudi cauponas ...
      ...

7. Why is this day so special?
8. Why would Horace and Virgil under normal circumstances have accompanied Maecenas?

25 **ora: os, oris, *n.*** face
lavimus: lavo wash
Feronia, *f.* ancient Italian
   goddess
lympha: lympha, *f.* water
tua ... lympha
milia (passuum) ... tria three
   miles
pransi: prandeo have breakfast
repimus: repo creep, crawl
subimus: subeo come up to
impositum: impono place
   upon, *here* build on
late far and wide
candentibus: candens white,
   shining
huc to this place, here
Maecenas, Maecenatis, *m.*
   Gaius Cilnius Maecenas,
   Horace's patron
Cocceius, *m.* Cocceius Nerva
uterque both, each (of two)
30 **legati: legatus, *m.*** ambassador,
   envoy
soliti: soleo be accustomed to
aversi: aversus turned away,
   here fallen out
componere: compono bring
   together, reconcile
collyria: collyrium, *n.*
   ointment
lippus having sore/inflamed
   eyes
illinere = illino smear
simul at the same time
Fonteius Capito
unguem: unguis, -is, *m.* nail
   (of a person)
ad unguem factus the perfect
   man, i.e. with no rough edges
   felt by the nail
Antoni = Antonii: Antonius,
   m. Marcus Antonius
magis more
ut non alter (sit) magis amicus
   Antoni

35 **postera: posterus** next day's
lux, lucis, *f.* light
oritur: orior rise, dawn
multo gratissima by far the
   most joyful
Sinuessae at Sinuessa
Vergilius, *m.* the poet Virgil,
   who wrote the *Aeneid*
(nobis) occurrunt
occurrunt: occurro + *dat.*
   meet
qui ... ! what ... !

complexus: complexus, -us,
   m. embrace
gaudia: gaudium, *n.* joy
contulerim (*perf. subj.*):
   confero compare
iucundo: iucundus agreeable
iucundo ... amico: iucundus
   amicus *here* good company
40 **ponti: pons, -tis, *m.*** bridge
sanus *here* while in my right
   mind
villula, *f.* little house, *here* lodge
   for travellers on public duty
tectum: tectum, *n.* roof
praebuit: praebeo provide
parochi: parochus, *m.* local
   officer
ligna: lignum, *n.* wood, fuel
salem: sal, -is, *m.* salt
villula quae (erat) proxima
   Campano ponti praebuit tectum,
   et parochi (praebuerunt) ligna
   salemque quae debent (praebere)
45 **hinc** from here, next
muli: mulus, *m.* mule
clitellas: clitellae, *f. pl.* saddle-
   bags
tempore *here* in good time
lusum: ludo play (ball)
lusum to play
dormitum to sleep
pila: pila, *f.* ball
inimicum: inimicus hostile, *here*
   bad for
crudis: crudus *here* suffering
   from an upset stomach
namque pila ludere inimicum (est)
   lippis et crudis
plenissima: plenus full, ample
super + *acc.* above
Caudi = Caudii: Caudium, *n.*
   Caudium
cauponas: caupona, *f.* inn

Days 8–9   Dinner is burnt and the poet sees his homeland.

> tendimus hinc recta Beneventum; ubi sedulus hospes
> paene macros arsit dum turdos versat in igni:
> nam vaga per veterem dilapso flamma culinam

50
> Volcano summum properabat lambere tectum.
> convivas avidos cenam servosque timentes
> tum rapere, atque omnes restinguere velle videres.
> incipit ex illo montes Apulia notos
> ostentare mihi, quos torret Atabulus et quos

55
> numquam erepsemus, nisi nos vicina Trivici
> villa recepisset lacrimoso non sine fumo,
> udos cum foliis ramos urente camino.

9. In lines 47–52, how does Horace make the description of the cooking disaster sound both grand and comical?
10. Which word in line 53 shows that Horace is now in a part of the country he knows well?

Days 10–11   Bread and water; a friend leaves

> quattuor hinc rapimur viginti et milia raedis,
> mansuri oppidulo quod versu dicere non est,

60
> signis perfacile est: venit vilissima rerum
> hic aqua; sed panis longe pulcherrimus, ultra
> callidus ut soleat umeris portare viator.
> nam Canusi lapidosus, ...
>
> ...
> flentibus hinc Varius discedit maestus amicis.

11. In lines 59–62, what practical advice is there for the traveller?
12. In line 63, how does Horace draw attention to the sadness of the event he mentions?

Days 12–15   Bad weather and roads; a fishing port; a miracle; the end of the journey

65
> inde Rubos fessi pervenimus, utpote longum
> carpentes iter et factum corruptius imbri.
> postera tempestas melior, via peior ad usque
> Bari moenia piscosi; dein Gnatia Lymphis
> iratis exstructa dedit risusque iocosque,

tendimus: tendo *here* make for
recta straight, by the direct route
sedulus busy, attentive
hospes, -itis, *m.* *here* host
macros: macer lean, skinny
arsit: ardeo catch fire, burn
turdos: turdus, *m.* thrush
versat: verso turn
igni: ignis, -is, *m.* fire
vaga: vagus wandering, roving
veterem: vetus old
dilapso: dilabor fall apart,
  escape
flamma, *f.* flame
50 **Volcano: Volcanus, *m.*** Vulcan,
  god of fire
properabat: propero hurry,
  rush to
lambere: lambo lick
tectum: tectum, *n.* roof, house
dilapso Volcano per veterem
  culinam, vaga flamma properabat
  lambere summum tectum
convivas: conviva, *m.f.* guest,
  diner
avidos: avidus greedy, hungry,
  starving
restinguere: restinguo put out
  (the fire)
tum videres ... convivas ...
  servosque ... cenam ... rapere
  atque omnes velle (ignem)
  restinguere
ex illo *here* from that point
Apulia, *f.* Apulia, where Horace
  was born
notos: notus familiar
ostentare: ostento show
Apulia incipit ostentare mihi ...
torret: torreo dry, scorch
Atabulus, *m.* Atabulus, local
  name for hot dry wind
55 **erepsemus = erepsissemus:**
  erepo crawl out, *here* climb over
vicina: vicinus + *gen.* close to
Trivici = Trivicii: Trivicum
  Trivicum
lacrimoso: lacrimosus full of
  tears
fumo: fumus, *m.* smoke
udos: udus damp
foliis: folium, *n.* leaf
ramos: ramus, *m.* branch
urente: urens burning
camino: caminus, *m.* fire,
  furnace

raedis: raeda, *f.* carriage (with
  four wheels), wagon

oppidulo: oppidulum, *n.* little
  town
versu: versus, -us, *m.* verse
60 **perfacile: perfacilis** very easy
quod versu (perfacile) dicere non est
  sed signis perfacile (dicere) est
venit: veneo be sold
vilissima: vilis cheap
panis, panis, *m.* bread
longe pulcherrimus by far the
  finest
ultra further, on to the next
  stage
callidus experienced, canny
portare: porto carry
umeris: umerus, *m.* upper
  arm, shoulder
Canusi at Canusium
lapidosus stony, gritty *(panis*
  est) lapidosus
aquae non ditior urna
  (a place) no better off by a jug
  of water
flentibus: fleo weep
maestus sad, sorrowful

65 **Rubos: Rubi, *m. pl.* Rubi**
pervenimus: pervenio arrive
  at
utpote because of
carpentes iter: carpo iter
  make a journey, take a route
factum corruptius made worse
imbri: imber, -bris, *m.* rain,
  rain storm
iter longum et factum corruptius ...
tempestas, tempestatis, *f.*
  weather
melior better
peior worse
ad usque + *acc.* all the way to
Bari = Barii: Barium, *n.*
  Barium
piscosi: piscosus fishy, full of
  fish
dein = deinde
Lymphis iratis where the
  water-goddesses were angry,
  where there were no springs
exstructa: exstructus built on
risus: risus, -us, *m.* laughter
iocos: iocus, *m.* joke, fun
sine flamma

70　　dum flamma sine tura liquescere limine sacro
　　　persuadere cupit.

　　　...

　　　Brundisium longae finis chartaeque viaeque est.

　　　　　　Horace *Satires* 1.5.1–33, 39–41, 43–51, 71–81, 86–91, 93–100, 104

The whole passage

1. In the account of the journey, Horace avoids saying 'We left ...', 'Then we arrived at ...', Next we did ...' etc. How does Horace add variety to the way the stages of the journey are described?
2. What part do Horace's travelling companions play in the account of the journey?
3. What parts of the poem describe sight-seeing on the journey?
4. On the whole, do you think Horace enjoyed the journey? Does he enjoy talking about its discomforts?

5. A storm at sea

Juno wants to destroy Aeneas and the Trojans. At her request Aeolus, the god of the winds, stirs up a storm to shipwreck them.

The storm begins.

　　　haec ubi dicta, cavum conversa cuspide montem
　　　impulit in latus; ac venti velut agmine facto,
　　　qua data porta, ruunt et terras turbine perflant.
　　　incubuere mari totumque a sedibus imis
5　　una Eurusque Notusque ruunt creberque procellis
　　　Africus, et vastos volvunt ad litora fluctus.
　　　insequitur clamorque virum stridorque rudentum;
　　　eripiunt subito nubes caelumque diemque
　　　Teucrorum ex oculis; ponto nox incubat atra;
10　　intonuere poli et crebris micat ignibus aether
　　　praesentemque viris intentant omnia mortem.

1. How does Virgil make the winds seem like an enemy?
2. What sounds does the storm cause?

Aeneas would rather have died in battle.

　　　extemplo Aeneae solvuntur frigore membra;
　　　ingemit et duplices tendens ad sidera palmas
　　　talia voce refert: 'o terque quaterque beati,
15　　quis ante ora patrum Troiae sub moenibus altis

70 **tura: tus, turis, *n.*** incense

liquescere: liquesco melt, turn
  to liquid

limine: **limen, -inis, *n.***
  threshold

sacro: sacer sacred, *here* of the
  temple

Brundisium, *n.* port in
  southern Italy

chartae: charta, *f.* leaf, paper,
  here account, poem

ubi haec dicta (sunt)

cavum: cavus hollow

conversa: converto swing
  round

cuspide: cuspis, -idis, *f.* spear

montem: mons, montis, *m.*
  mountain, rock, cliff

impulit: impello strike

latus: latus, -eris, *n.* side

venti: ventus, *m.* wind

agmine: agmen, -inis, *n.* army
  column, troop

velut agmine facto as if in
  army formation, drawn up like
  an army

porta, *f.* *here* passage

qua data (est) porta

ruunt: ruo rush

turbine: turbo, -inis, *f.*
  whirlwind

perflant: perflo blow through,
  blow over

incubuere = incubuerunt:
  incumbo lie on, press upon

totum ... una *here* altogether

sedibus: sedes, -is, *f.* seat,
  dwelling

imis: imus lowest, deepest

5 **Eurus, *m.*** the east wind

Notus, *m.* the south wind

creber frequent, *here* full of

procellis: procella, *f.*
  hurricane, whirlwind

(ventus) Africus the African
  wind

vastos: vastus *here* huge,
  immense

volvunt: volvo roll, turn

litora: litus, -oris, *n.* shore

fluctus: fluctus, -us, *m.* wave

insequitur: insequor follow,
  press on

clamor, -oris, *m.* shouting, cry

-que ... -que both ... and

virum = virorum

stridor, -oris, *m.* creaking,
  scream, screech

rudentum: rudens, -entis, *m.*
  rope, *pl.* rigging

eripiunt: eripio seize, snatch
  away

nubes: nubes, -is, *f.* cloud

Teucrorum: Teucri, *m. pl.*
  Trojans

oculis: oculus, *m.* eye

subito nubes caelumque diemque
  eripiunt ex oculis Teucrorum

ponto: pontus, *m.* sea, wave

incubat: incubo brood over,
  settle on

atra: ater black

10 **intonuere = intonuerunt:**
  intono thunder, resound (with
  thunder)

poli: polus, *m.* pole, heavens

micat: mico dart, flash

ignibus: ignis, -is, *m.* *here*
  lightning

aether, -eris, *m.* upper ether,
  heaven

praesentem: praesens present,
  close at hand, before their eyes

intentant: intento + *dat. here*
  threaten with

extemplo immediately

solvuntur: solvo loose, *pass.*
  here become numb

frigore: frigus, -oris, *n.* cold,
  chill

membra: membrum, *n.* limb

ingemit: ingemo groan

duplices: duplex two, both

tendens: tendo hold out,
  stretch out

sidera: sidus, -eris, *n.* star

palmas: palma, *f.* palm, hand

refert: refero *here* speak

beati: beatus blessed

O ... beati O you who are blessed
  three and four times over

15 **quis = quibus**

ora: os, oris, *n.* face

moenibus: moenia, -ium, *n.*
  pl. walls

altis: altus high

contigit oppetere! o Danaum fortissime gentis
Tydide! mene Iliacis occumbere campis
non potuisse tuaque animam hanc effundere dextra,
saevus ubi Aeacidae telo iacet Hector, ubi ingens
20   Sarpedon, ubi tot Simois correpta sub undis
scuta virum galeasque et fortia corpora volvit!'

3. How does Aeneas react to the storm?

4. Why do you think Aeneas would have preferred to die on the battle field?

The fate of the ships

talia iactanti stridens Aquilone procella
velum adversa ferit, fluctusque ad sidera tollit.
franguntur remi, tum prora avertit et undis
25   dat latus, insequitur cumulo praeruptus aquae mons.
hi summo in fluctu pendent; his unda dehiscens
terram inter fluctus aperit, furit aestus harenis.
tres Notus abreptas in saxa latentia torquet
(saxa vocant Itali mediis quae in fluctibus Aras,
30   dorsum immane mari summo), tres Eurus ab alto
in brevia et Syrtes urget, miserabile visu,
inliditque vadis atque aggere cingit harenae.

5. Pick out the words for sea, waves, water etc.

6. In line 25, how does 'insequitur ... mons' gain its effect?

Aeneas sees his companions shipwrecked.

unam, quae Lycios fidumque vehebat Oronten,
ipsius ante oculos ingens a vertice pontus
35   in puppim ferit: excutitur pronusque magister
volvitur in caput, ast illam ter fluctus ibidem
torquet agens circum et rapidus vorat aequore vertex.
apparent rari nantes in gurgite vasto,
arma virum tabulaeque et Troia gaza per undas.
40   iam validam Ilionei navem, iam fortis Achatae,
et qua vectus Abas, et qua grandaevus Aletes,
vicit hiems; laxis laterum compagibus omnes
accipiunt inimicum imbrem rimisque fatiscunt.

Virgil *Aeneid* 1.81–123

7. What is the effect of the details in lines 38–39?

8. Why do you think Virgil names particular people at this point?

contigit: contingo + *inf.* befall, happen to, be the fate of

oppetere: oppeto (mortem) meet (death)

Danaum = Danaorum: Danai, *m. pl.* Greeks (descendants of Danaus, founder of Argos)

Tydide: Tydides, *m.* son of Tydides, Diomedes (Greek warrior)

Iliacis: Iliacus of Ilium, Trojan

campis: campus, *m.* field, battle field

occumbere: occumbo go down, set, die

mene ... occumbere ... potuisse ... Could I not have fallen ...?

animam: anima, *f.* soul, life

effundere: effundo pour out, give up

dextra: dextra, *f.* right hand

telo: telum, *n.* weapon, spear

Aeacidae: Aeacides, *m.* descendant of Aeacus, Achilles (Greek warrior)

20 **Simois, *m.*** Simois (one of the rivers of Troy)

correpta: corripio snatch away, carry off

scuta: scutum, *n.* shield

virum = virorum

galeas: galea, *f.* helmet

iactanti: iacto throw, hurl (words)

talia iactanti while he was hurling words like these

stridens screaming, creaking

Aquilone: Aquilo, *m.* north wind

velum: velum, *n.* sail

adversa: adversus *here* head on

ferit: ferio hit, strike

tollit: tollo lift, raise

remi: remus, *m.* oar

prora, *f.* prow, (bow of ship)

avertit: averto turn

undis: unda, *f.* wave, surge, billow

25 **dat: dare** *here* expose

latus: latus, -eris, *n. here* beam/hull (of a ship)

cumulo: cumulus, *m.* mass

praeruptus steep

insequitur ... mons a steep mountain of water presses on in a mass

pendent: pendeo hang, dangle

dehiscens opening up, gaping wide

terram: terra, *f. here* sea bed

aperit: aperio open, lay bare

furit: furo rage, seethe

aestus, -us, *m.* swell, current

harenis: harena, *f.* sand

abreptas: abripio carry off

saxa: saxum, *n.* rock

latentia: lateo lie hidden

torquet: torqueo whirl around, fling

aras: ara, *f.* altar

Itali, *m. pl.* Italians

saxa in mediis fluctibus, quae Itali aras vocant

30 **dorsum: dorsum, *n.*** back, *here* ridge

immane: immanis *here* savage, dangerous

mari summo *lit.* on top of the sea, *here* breaking the surface of the sea

alto: altum, *n.* the deep, the open sea

brevia: brevia, -ium, *n. pl.* shallows

Syrtes: Syrtis, -is, *f.* the Syrtes (sand-banks off the African coast)

urget: urgeo press, drive force

miserabile visu a miserable sight to see

(naves) inlidit: inlido + *dat.* dash against

vadis: vadum, *n.* shallow water

cingit: cingere surround

aggere: agger, -eris, *m.* wall, mound

fidum: fidus loyal, trusty

vehebat: veho carry

ipsius ante oculos before the eyes of (Aeneas) himself

a vertice from above, from a great height

35 **puppim: puppis, -is, *f.*** stern, ship

ingens ... pontus ... unam (navem)... ferit

excutitur: excutio shake out, *passive: here* fall overboard

pronus forward, face down

magister, *m. here* helmsman

in caput headlong

ast = at

ibidem in the same place

rapidus swift, devouring

vorat: voro swallow, gulp down

aequore: aequor, -oris, *n.* surface of the sea, sea

vertex, -icis, *m.* whirlpool

apparent: appareo appear, be seen

rari: rarus scattered, few and far between, here and there

nantes: no swim

in gurgite vasto in the watery waste

virum = virorum

tabulae: tabula, *f. here* board, plank

gaza, *f.* riches, treasures

40 **validam: validus** strong, sturdy

Achatae: Achates, -tae, *m.* Achates (companion of Aeneas)

grandaevus aged, full of years

hiems, hiemis, *f.* winter, storm, tempest

iam (navem) ... Achatae, et (navem) qua vectus (est) Abas, et (navem) qua ... Aletes (vectus est) ...

laxis: laxus opened up, loose

compagibus: compages, -is, *f.* joint

omnes (naves)

inimicum: inimicus hostile, hateful

imbrem: imber, -bris, *m.* rain, *here* water

rimis: rima, *f.* hole, chink, crack

fatiscunt: fatisco gape open, break open

The whole passage

1. Do you find this description terrifying, unnatural or exaggerated?
2. Compare this description with other accounts or films of storms you have come across.

6. The ship of state in troubled waters

Horace expresses his anxiety for the state in a poem addressed to a ship in trouble at sea

> O navis, referent in mare te novi
> fluctus! o quid agis? fortiter occupa
>   portum! nonne vides ut
>   nudum remigio latus,
>
> 5 et malus celeri saucius Africo,
> antennaeque gemant, ac sine funibus
>   vix durare carinae
>   possint imperiosius
>
> aequor? non tibi sunt integra lintea,
> 10 non di, quos iterum pressa voces malo.
>   quamvis Pontica pinus,
>   silvae filia nobilis,
>
> iactes et genus et nomen inutile,
> nil pictis timidus navita puppibus
> 15   fidit. tu, nisi ventis
>   debes ludibrium, cave.
>
> nuper sollicitum quae mihi taedium,
> nunc desiderium curaque non levis,
>   interfusa nitentes
> 20   vites aequora Cycladas.

Horace *Odes* 1.14

1. How does Horace make the ship seem like a person?
2. How does Horace show that his concern is for something more than a ship?
3. Why do you think Horace avoids mentioning the crew of the ship?
4. Discuss reasons why our word 'government' comes from the Latin word for helmsman (*gubernator*).

referent: refero carry back
fluctus, -us, m. wave
fortiter boldly
occupa: occupo seize, gain,
  reach
portum: portus, -us, m.
  harbour
ut *here* how
nudum: nudus + *abl.* stripped
  of
remigio: remigium, n. oars
latus, -eris, n. side, hull, beam
nudum (sit)
5 **malus, m.** mast
saucius wounded, injured
celeri ... (vento) Africo by the
  gale from Africa, *lit.* by the swift
  African wind
antenna, f. sail-yard, spar
  (supporting head of sail)
gemant: gemo groan, creak
funibus: funis, -is, m. rope
vix scarcely, with difficulty
durare: duro endure, put up
  with
carinae: carina, f. keel, ship
possint: possum be able
imperiosius (*comparative*):
  imperiosior *here* too
  domineering, too masterful
aequor: aequor, -oris, n. sea
integra: integer whole, in one
  piece
lintea, n. pl. *here* sails
10 **di = dei**
non di (tibi sunt)
pressa: pressus hard-pressed,
  overwhelmed
malo: malum, n. danger,
  disaster
quamvis although
Pontica: Ponticus from Pontus
  (province bordering Black Sea)
pinus, f. pine tree
iactes: iacto boast of
genus: genus, -eris, n. birth,
  pedigree
inutile: inutilis useless,
  worthless
pictis: pictus ornate,
  embellished
navita = nauta
puppibus: puppis, -is, f. stern,
  here ship
15 **fidit: fido** + *dat.* trust
nisi ... debes ... if it is not your
  destiny to be ...
ludibrium, n. plaything, sport
cave: caveo beware, take care

nuper recently, not long ago
sollicitum: sollicitus
  anxious, *here* causing anxiety,
  distressing
taedium, n. weariness, burden
desiderium, n. love, object of
  love
levis light
interfusa: interfusus flowing
  between
nitentes: nitens shining,
  sparkling
20 **vites: vito** avoid, *here* steer clear
  of
(tu) quae nuper (eras) mihi
  taedium sollicitum, nunc (es)
  desiderium ...

CONFLICT AND CONQUEST

Caesar's clear and detailed description of his actions in Gaul allows us an insight not only into various characters but also his own abilities during conflict. Tacitus shows the vehemence of the two sides when conquest is being resisted, whilst Cicero's letters to Atticus tell of a domestic conflict. The size of opposing armies may matter – but does it all come down to opposing, conflicting personalities? In the tale of Atalanta, we see subtle methods at work for a young man making his conquest and acquiring his heart's desire. Ovid's idea of personal conquest is much to the fore in the *Ars Amatoria*, and here his suggestions are more direct. Is conflict the only way to conquest and so true love?!

Augustus as a triumphant general

1. Bravery and strategy in battle

Caesar tells of the bravery and heroism of two of his centurions at the very heart of battle, whilst dealing with revolt in Gaul.

> erant in ea legione fortissimi viri, centuriones, qui primis ordinibus
> appropinquarent, Titus Pullo et Lucius Vorenus. hi perpetuas inter se
> controversias habebant, quinam anteferretur, omnibusque annis de
> locis summis simultatibus contendebant. ex his Pullo, cum
> 5   acerrime ad munitiones pugnaretur, 'quid dubitas,' inquit,
> 'Vorene? aut quem locum tuae pro laude virtutis spectas? hic dies
> de nostris controversiis iudicabit.' haec cum dixisset, procedit extra
> munitiones, quaeque pars hostium confertissima est visa irrumpit.
> ne Vorenus quidem sese vallo continet sed omnium veritus
> 10 existimationem subsequitur. tum mediocri spatio relicto Pullo
> pilum in hostes immittit atque unum ex multitudine procurrentem
> traicit; quo percusso et exanimato, hunc scutis protegunt, in hostem
> tela universi coiciunt neque dant regrediendi facultatem.
> transfigitur scutum Pulloni et verutum in balteo defigitur. avertit
> 15 hic casus vaginam et gladium educere conanti dextram moratur
> manum, impeditumque hostes circumsistunt. succurrit inimicus illi
> Vorenus et laboranti subvenit. ad hunc se confestim a Pullone
> omnis multitudo convertit; illum veruto arbitrantur occisum. gladio
> comminus rem gerit Vorenus atque uno interfecto reliquos paulum
> 20 propellit: dum cupidius instat, in locum deiectus inferiorem
> concidit. huic rursus circumvento fert subsidium Pullo, atque ambo
> incolumes compluribus interfectis summa cum laude sese intra
> munitiones recipiunt. sic fortuna in contentione et certamine
> utrumque versavit, ut alter alteri inimicus auxilio salutique esset
> 25 neque diiudicari posset, uter utri virtute anteferendus videretur.

1. **Describe in detail how both of these men show their bravery in their actions towards each other.**
2. **How, through word order and choice of words, does Caesar make his description of the fighting particularly vivid?**

Caesar plans to come to the aid of Cicero.

> quanto erat in dies gravior atque asperior oppugnatio, et maxime
> quod magna parte militum confecta vulneribus res ad paucitatem
> defensorum pervenerat, tanto crebriores litterae nuntiique ad
> Caesarem mittebantur; quorum pars deprehensa in conspectu

ordinibus: ordo, -inis, *m.* rank
perpetuas: perpetuus
continual, ongoing
controversias: controversia, *f.*
dispute
quinam 'as to which'
anteferretur: antefero prefer
simultatibus: simultas, -atis, *f.*
quarrel
contendebant: contendo
contend
5 **acerrime: acer** fierce
munitiones: munitio, -onis, *f.*
fortification
quid? why?
dubitas: dubito hesitate
laude: laus, laudis, *f.* praise
iudicabit: iudico decide, judge
extra + *acc.* outside
quaeque pars: 'and in that area
which'
confertissima: confertus
thick, crowded
irrumpit: irrumpo rush into
ne ... quidem not even
sese = se
vallo: vallum, *n.* rampart
continet: contineo keep
veritus: vereor fear
10 **existimationem: existimatio,**
-onis, *f.* opinion
subsequitur: subsequor follow
mediocri: mediocris moderate
spatio: spatium, *n.* distance
pilum: pilum, *n.* spear, javelin
procurrentem: procurro run
forward
traicit: traicio thrust through,
pierce
percusso: percutio hit
exanimato: exanimo exhaust,
knock unconscious
scutis: scutum, *n.* shield
protegunt: protego protect,
cover
tela: telum, *n.* weapon, spear
universi 'all together'
coiciunt: coicio throw
facultatem: facultas, -atis, *f.*
opportunity
transfigitur: transfigo pierce
through
verutum, *n.* short throwing
spear
balteo: balteus, *m.* belt, baldric
defigitur: defigo fix, thrust into
avertit: averto turn aside,
knock out of position
15 **hic casus** 'this event'
vaginam: vagina, *f.* scabbard

educere: educo draw out
dextram: dextra, *f.* right hand
moratur: moror delay
impeditum: impedio impede,
hinder
circumsistunt: circumsisto
surround
succurrit: succurro + *dat.* run
to the aid of
inimicus, *m.* enemy
subvenit: subvenio + *dat.* help
confestim speedily
convertit: converto turn
arbitrantur: arbitror think
comminus 'at close quarters'
paulum a little
20 **propellit: propello** drive away,
drive back
cupidius 'too greedily'
instat: insto press on
deiectus: deicio throw down
inferiorem: inferior lower
concidit: concido slip, fall
rursus again
circumvento: circumvenio
surround
subsidium: subsidium, *n.*
help, relief
ambo both
incolumes: incolumis safe,
unharmed
compluribus: complures
several

sese = se
intra + *acc.* inside
sese recipiunt: me recipio
retreat
contentione: contentio,
-onis, *f.* rivalry
certamine: certamen, -inis, *n.*
conflict
utrumque: uterque each of two
versavit: verso deal with
saluti: salus, -utis, *f.* safety
25 **diiudicari: diiudico** decide,
determine
uter which of two

quanto ... tanto ... as much
as ..., so .../the more ...,
the more ...
in dies daily
asperior: asper rough
oppugnatio, -onis, *f.* attack
confecta: conficio exhaust,
wear out
paucitatem: paucitas, -atis, *f.*
shortage, small number
defensorum: defensor, -oris,
m. defender
pervenerat: pervenio reach
crebriores: creber frequent
litterae, *f. pl.* letter
deprehensa: deprehendo
catch, seize
conspectu: conspectus, -us,
m. sight, view

Roman soldiers in action (Trajan's column)

30 nostrorum militum cum cruciatu necabatur. erat unus intus Nervius
nomine Vertico, loco natus honesto, qui a prima obsidione ad
Ciceronem perfugerat, suamque ei fidem praestiterat. hic servo spe
libertatis magnisque persuadet praemiis ut litteras ad Caesarem
deferat. has ille in iaculo inligatas effert et Gallus inter Gallos sine
35 ulla suspicione versatus ad Caesarem pervenit. ab eo de periculis
Ciceronis legionisque cognoscitur.
...

3. How does Caesar convey that the situation is becoming more difficult?
4. What strategy does Cicero use to get his message through?

venit magnis itineribus in Nerviorum fines. ibi ex captivis
cognoscit quae apud Ciceronem gerantur, quantoque in periculo
res sit. tum cuidam ex equitibus Gallis magnis praemiis persuadet
40 uti ad Ciceronem epistolam deferat. hanc Graecis conscriptam
litteris mittit, ne intercepta epistola nostra ab hostibus consilia
cognoscantur. si adire non possit, monet ut tragulam cum epistola
ad ammentum deligata intra munitionem castrorum abiciat. in
litteris scribit se cum legionibus profectum celeriter adfore;
45 hortatur ut pristinam virtutem retineat. Gallus periculum veritus, ut
erat praeceptum, tragulam mittit. haec casu ad turrim adhaesit
neque ab nostris biduo animadversa tertio die a quodam milite
conspicitur, dempta ad Ciceronem defertur. ille perlectam in
conventu militum recitat, maximaque omnes laetitia adficit. tum
50 fumi incendiorum procul videbantur, quae res omnem
dubitationem adventus legionum expulit.

Caesar *Gallic War* 5.44–48 (abridged)

5. Describe how Caesar manages to reply to Cicero.

2. Caesar at the heart of battle against the Belgae

Caesari omnia uno tempore erant agenda: vexillum proponendum,
quod erat insigne cum ad arma concurri oporteret; signum tuba
dandum; ab opere revocandi milites; qui paulo longius aggeris
petendi causa processerant arcessendi; acies instruenda; milites
5 cohortandi; signum dandum. quarum rerum magnam partem
temporis brevitas et incursus hostium impediebat. his
difficultatibus duae res erant subsidio, scientia atque usus militum,
quod superioribus proeliis exercitati quid fieri oporteret non minus
commode ipsi sibi praescribere quam ab aliis doceri poterant, et

30 **cruciatu: cruciatus, -us, _m._**
  torture
intus inside (the camp)
Nervius a Nervian
loco natus honesto 'born in a
  high-ranking position'
obsidione: obsidio, -onis, _f._
  siege
fidem: fides, _f._ loyalty
praestiterat: praesto show
libertatis: libertas, -atis, _f._
  freedom
iaculo: iaculum, _n._ javelin
inligatas: inligo tie on
35 **suspicione: suspicio, -onis, _f._**
  suspicion
versatus: versor come and go
  frequently

fines: fines, _m. pl._ territory
captivis: captivus, _m._ prisoner
40 **uti = ut**
litteris: littera, _f._ letter (of the
  alphabet)
intercepta: intercipio
  intercept
tragulam: tragula, _f._ spear
  fitted with a throwing strap
ammentum: ammentum, _n._
  strap, thong
deligata: deligo tie, fasten
adfore: adsum be present
45 **pristinam: pristinus** former,
  ancient
retineat: retineo maintain
veritus: vereor fear
ut erat praeceptum 'as had
  been ordered'
casu 'by chance'
turrim: turris, -is, _f._ tower
adhaesit: adhaereo stick to
biduo: biduum, _n._ period of
  two days
animadversa: animadverto
  notice, spot
dempta: demo take down
perlectam: perlego read
  through
conventu: conventus, -us, _m._
  assembly
recltat: recito read out, recite
laetitia: laetitia, _f._ happiness,
  joy
adficit: adficio move, affect, fill
fumi: fumus, _m._ smoke
50 **incendiorum: incendium, _n._**
  fire
**dubitationem: dubitatio,
  -onis, _m._** doubt

adventus: adventus, -us, _m._
  arrival

agenda: ago do
vexillum: vexillum, _n._
  standard, banner
proponendum: propono
  display
insigne 'the signal (for)'
concurri: concurro run,
  assemble together
oporteret: oportet it is
  necessary
tuba: tuba, _f._ trumpet
opere: opus, -eris, _n._ work,
  task
revocandi: revoco call back
paulo by a little
aggeris: agger, -eris, _m._
  rampart
arcessendi: arcesso summon
acies, _f._ battle-line
instruenda: instruo draw up
5 **cohortandi: cohortor**
  encourage
brevitas, -atis, _f._ brevity,
  shortness
incursus: incursus, -us, _m._
  attack
impediebat: impedio impede,
  hinder
**difficultatibus: difficultas,
  -atis, _f._** difficulty
subsidio: subsidium, _n._ help
scientia, _f._ knowledge, skill
usus, -us, _m._ experience
superioribus: superior
  previous
exercitati: exercito train
fieri: fio happen
**non minus commode ...
  quam ...** no less conveniently
  than ...
praescribere: praescribo
  suggest

10   quod ab opere singulisque legionibus singulos legatos Caesar
discedere nisi munitis castris vetuerat. hi propter propinquitatem et
celeritatem hostium nihil iam Caesaris imperium exspectabant, sed
per se quae videbantur administrabant.

Caesar Gallic War 2.20

1. How does Caesar portray that he has to do everything at once in this passage?
2. What picture of Caesar as a leader emerges in this passage? What qualities do you think a leader should have? How far does Caesar display these qualities?

3. Inspiration for the fight

In AD 60–61, Suetonius and Boudicca meet in battle. They both make speeches to inspire their forces (you should be aware, therefore, that Tacitus writes the first two of these three passages as reported speech).

Boudicca curru filias prae se vehens, ut quamque nationem
accesserat, solitum quidem Britannis feminarum ductu bellare
testabatur, sed tunc non ut tantis maioribus ortam regnum et opes,
verum ut unam e vulgo libertatem amissam, confectum verberibus
5   corpus, contrectatam filiarum pudicitiam ulcisci. eo provectas
Romanorum cupidines ut non corpora, ne senectam quidem aut
virginitatem impollutam relinquant. adesse tamen deos iustae
vindictae: cecidisse legionem, quae proelium ausa sit; ceteros
castris occultari aut fugam circumspicere. ne strepitum quidem
10   et clamorem tot milium, nedum impetus et manus perlaturos: si
copias armatorum, si causas belli secum expenderent, vincendum
illa acie vel cadendum esse. id mulieri destinatum: viverent viri et
servirent.

1. What does Boudicca give as her reason for fighting?
2. How does her speech emphasise the extent of the outrageous Roman behaviour?
3. What stark alternative does she give to the tribes?

ne Suetonius quidem in tanto discrimine silebat. quamquam
15   confideret virtuti, tamen exhortationes et preces miscebat ut
spernerent sonores barbarorum et inanes minas: plus illic
feminarum quam iuventutis aspici. imbelles inermes cessuros
statim ubi ferrum virtutemque vincentium toties fusi adgnovissent.
etiam in multis legionibus paucos qui proelia profligarent;
20   gloriaeque eorum accessurum quod modica manus universi
exercitus famam adipiscerentur. conferti tantum et pilis emissis

10 **singulis: singuli** every single, respective
munitis: munio fortify
vetuerat: veto forbid
propinquitatem: propinquitas, -atis, *f.* closeness, proximity
celeritatem: celeritas, -atis, *f.* speed
quae videbantur 'what seemed right'
administrabant: administro perform, carry out

curru: currus, -us, *m.* chariot
prae + *abl.* in front of
vehens: veho carry
ut as
quamque nationem 'each tribe'
accesserat: accedo approach
solitum 'it was usual'
quidem indeed
ductu: ductus, -us, *m.* leadership
bellare: bello fight war
testabatur: testor declare
tunc = tum
maioribus: maiores, *m. pl.* ancestors
ortam: orior arise, be born
opes: opes, *f. pl.* wealth
vulgo: vulgus, *n.* crowd, the common people
libertatem: libertas, -atis, *f.* freedom, liberty
amissam: amitto lose
confectum: conficio exhaust, finish
verberibus: verber, -eris, *n.* scourging
5 **contrectatam: contrecto** outrage, manhandle
pudicitiam: pudicitia, *f.* chastity
ulcisci: ulciscor avenge
eo so much
provectas: provectus advanced
cupidines: cupido, -inis, *f.* desire, lust
ne ... quidem not even ...
senectam: senecta, *f.* old age
virginitatem: virginitas, -atis, *f.* virginity
impollutam: impollutus unpolluted
vindictae: vindicta, *f.* vengeance
cecidisse: cado fall, be slain

ausa sit: audeo dare
occultari: occulto conceal
circumspicere: circumspicio look around for
strepitum: strepitus, -us, *m.* din, noise
10 **nedum** still less
impetus: impetus, -us, *m.* attack, charge
perlaturos: perfero bear
copias: copiae, *f. pl.* forces, troops
armatorum: armati, *m. pl.* armed men
expenderent: expendo weigh, judge, consider
acie: acies, *f.* battle-line
mulieri: mulier, -eris, *f.* woman
destinatum: destino determine, resolve
viverent: vivo live
servirent: servio be a slave

ne ... quidem nor indeed
discrimine: discrimen, -inis, *n.* crisis
silebat: sileo be silent
15 **confideret: confido** + *dat.* trust
exhortationes: exhortatio, -onis, *f.* encouragement
preces: prex, precis, *f.* prayer, pleading
miscebat: misceo mix
spernerent: sperno disdain, scorn
sonores: sonor, -oris, *m.* sound, noise, din
inanes: inanis empty
minas: minae, *f. pl.* threats
iuventutis: iuventus, -utis, *f.* youth
adspici = aspici: aspicio consider, look at, see
imbelles: imbellis unwarlike
inermes: inermis unarmed
cessuros: cedo yield, give way
ferrum: ferrum, *n.* sword
toties so often
fusi: fundo rout
adgnovissent: agnosco recognise
profligarent: profligo decide (battle)
20 **gloriaeque eorum accessurum quod** 'it will be more to their glory that'
modica manus 'a small band of men'

universi: universus whole
adipiscerentur: adipiscor obtain, earn
conferti: confertus crowded, densely packed
tantum only
pilis: pilum, *n.* javelin

post umbonibus et gladiis stragem caedemque continuarent,
praedae immemores: parta victoria cuncta ipsis cessura. is ardor
verba ducis sequebatur, ita se ad intorquenda pila expedierat vetus
25   miles et multa proeliorum experientia ut certus eventus Suetonius
daret pugnae signum.

4. How in this speech does Suetonius emphasise his enemy's weakness?

5. Pick out and translate two Latin phrases which are forceful and appropriate for the situation in which the Romans find themselves.

ac primum legio gradu immota et angustias loci pro munimento
retinens, postquam in propius suggressos hostes certo iactu tela
exhauserat, velut cuneo erupit. idem auxiliarium impetus; et eques
30   protentis hastis perfringit quod obvium et validum erat. ceteri terga
praebuere, difficili effugio, quia circumiecta vehicula saepserant
abitus. et miles ne mulierum quidem neci temperabat, confixaque
telis etiam iumenta corporum cumulum auxerant. clara et antiquis
victoriis par ea die laus parta: quippe sunt qui paulo minus quam
35   octoginta milia Britannorum cecidisse tradant, militum
quadringentis ferme interfectis nec multo amplius vulneratis.
Boudicca vitam veneno finivit. et Poenius Postumus, praefectus
castrorum secundae legionis, cognitis quartadecimanorum
vicesimanorumque prosperis rebus, quia pari gloria legionem suam
40   fraudaverat abnueratque contra ritum militiae iussa ducis, se ipse
gladio transegit.

Tacitus Annals 14.35–37

6. Pick out and translate three Latin phrases which make this battle scene vivid.

7. How was that day's victory special?

8. Why does Poenius Postumus kill himself?

4. Marital Conflict

Cicero writes to Atticus telling him of the problems his brother Quintus is having in his marriage to Pomponia (the sister of Atticus).

quod ad me scribis de sorore tua, testis erit tibi ipsa quantae mihi
curae fuerit ut Quinti fratris animus in eam esset is qui esse
deberet. quem cum esse offensiorem arbitrarer, eas litteras ad eum
misi quibus et placarem ut fratrem et monerem ut minorem et
5   obiurgarem ut errantem. itaque ex iis quae postea saepe ab eo ad
me scripta sunt confido ita esse omnia ut et oporteat et velimus.

Cicero Ad Atticum 1.5.2

umbonibus: umbo, -onis, *m.* shield

stragem: strages, -is, *f.* destruction

caedem: caedes, -is, *f.* slaughter

continuarent: continuo continue

praedae: praeda, *f.* booty

immemores: immemor without thinking of

parta: pario procure

cessura: cedo yield

cuncta: cunctus all

is ardor 'such desired enthusiasm'

is ardor ... , ita se ... ut ...

intorquenda: intorqueo hurl

expedierat: expedio act, prepare

vetus miles 'veteran soldiers'

25 **experientia, *f.*** experience

certus eventus 'confident in the outcome'

gradu immota 'in their unmoved position'

angustias: angustiae, *f. pl.* narrow places

pro munimento for, as a defence

retinens: retineo keep to

propius more closely

suggressos 'approaching'

iactu: iactus, -us, *m.* throw

tela: telum, *n.* weapon

exhauserat: exhaurio discharge

velut cuneo 'in wedge formation'

erupit: erumpo break out

auxiliarium: auxiliaris auxiliary soldier

impetus, -us, *m.* attack

eques, -itis, *m.* 'the cavalry'

30 **protentis: protendo** stretch out

perfringit: perfringo break through, smash

obvium: obvius hostile, in the way

validum: validus strong

terga: tergum, *n.* back

praebuere: praebeo provide, show ('turned their backs in flight')

effugio: effugium, *n.* flight

quia because

circumiecta: circumicio place around

vehicula: vehiculum, *n.* cart, waggon

saepserant: saepio block

abitus: abitus, -us, *m.* retreat

neci: nex, necis, *f.* death, murder

temperabat: tempero exercise restraint

confixa: configo pierce through

iumenta: iumentum, *n.* beast of burden

cumulum: cumulus, *m.* heap, pile

auxerant: augeo increase

clara: clarus famous, illustrious

antiquis: antiquus of old

par equal

ea die 'that day'

laus, laudis, *f.* glory, praise

quippe for

35 **octoginta** eighty

tradant: trado say, tell

quadringentis: quadringenti four hundred

ferme about

amplius more

finivit: finio end

praefectus, *m.* commander

quartadecimanorum: quartadecimani, *m. pl.* the men of the Fourteenth Legion

vicesimanorum: vicesimani, *m. pl.* the men of the Twentieth Legion

prosperis rebus 'the success'

quia because

40 **fraudaverat: fraudo** cheat

abnuerat: abnuo reject, refuse

contra ritum militiae contrary to military practice *or* observance

transegit: transigo pierce through

sorore: soror, -oris, *f.* sister

testis, -is, *m.f.* witness

animus, *m.* spirit, attitude

offensiorem: offensus offensive, odious

arbitrarer: arbitror think

litteras: litterae, *f. pl.* letter

placarem: placo appease

5 **obiurgarem: obiurgo** chide, rebuke

errantem: erro do wrong, make a mistake

confido trust

et oporteat et velimus 'both as it should be and as we would wish'

1. How and why has Cicero written to his brother Quintus?

Some years later, Cicero again writes to Atticus to tell of an incident which shows how bad things have become between Quintus and Pomponia.

> postridie ex Arpinati profecti sumus ... prandimus in Arcano (nosti
> hunc fundum). quo ut venimus, humanissime Quintus, 'Pomponia,'
> inquit, 'tu invita mulieres, ego vero accivero pueros'; nihil potuit,
> mihi quidem ut visum est, dulcius idque cum verbis tum etiam
> 5   animo ac vultu. at illa audientibus nobis 'ego ipsa sum' inquit, 'hic
> hospita'; id autem ex eo, ut opinor, quod antecesserat Statius ut
> prandium nobis videret. tum Quintus, 'en,' inquit mihi, 'haec ego
> patior cotidie.' dices 'quid quaeso istuc erat?' magnum; idque me
> ipsum commoverat; sic absurde et aspere verbis vultuque
> 10 responderat. dissimulavi dolens. discubuimus omnes praeter illam,
> cui tamen Quintus de mensa misit; illa reiecit. quid multa? nihil
> meo fratre lenius, nihil asperius tua sorore mihi visum est ... ego
> inde Aquinum. Quintus in Arcano remansit et in Aquinum ad me
> postridie mane venit mihique narravit nec secum illam dormire
> 15 voluisse et cum discessura esset fuisse eius modi qualem ego
> vidissem.

Cicero Ad Atticum 5.1.3–4

2. What picture do we gain of both Quintus and Pomponia from this extract?

3. How does Cicero make his writing very personal?

5. Atalanta meets her match

Within Ovid's *Metamorphoses*, Venus tells Adonis the tale of Atalanta, the renowned runner.

> forsitan audieris aliquam certamine cursus
> veloces superasse viros; non fabula rumor
> ille fuit (superabat enim). nec dicere posses
> laude pedum formaene bono praestantior esset.
> 5 scitanti deus huic de coniuge 'coniuge' dixit
> 'nil opus est, Atalanta, tibi; fuge coniugis usum.
> nec tamen effugies teque ipsa viva carebis.'
> territa sorte dei per opacas innuba silvas
> vivit et instantem turbam violenta procorum
> 10 condicione fugat 'nec sum potienda nisi' inquit
> 'victa prius cursu. pedibus contendite mecum;

prandimus: prandeo have lunch
in Arcano 'at Arcanum'
nosti = novisti: novi know
fundum: fundus, *m.* farm
quo there
ut when
humanissime: humanus considerate, civilised
invita: invito invite, call
accivero: accio send for, summon
pueros: puer, *m.* *here* slave
quidem indeed
dulcius: dulcis sweet
cum ... tum ... both ... and...
5 **vultu: vultus, -us, *m.*** face, expression
hospita, *f.* 'a stranger'
id autem ex eo ... quod 'and this was because ...'
opinor think
antecesserat: antecedo go before
Statius Statius, a slave
prandium: prandium, *n.* lunch
videret: video see to
en! look!
patior suffer
quaeso ask
istuc: istic that
commoverat: commoveo move, affect
absurde: absurdus senseless, irrational
aspere: asper rough
10 **dissimulavi: dissimulo** hide
dolens: doleo be upset
discubuimus: discumbo recline
praeter + *acc.* except
reiecit: reicio reject, refuse
lenius: lenis gentle
ego inde Aquinum 'I went from there to Aquinum'
remansit: remaneo stay
15 **eius modi qualem** 'in the same mood as'

forsitan by chance
aliquam 'some girl'
certamine: certamen, -inis, *n.* contest
cursus: cursus, -us, *m.* running, race
veloces: velox speedy, fast
superasse = superavisse
rumor, -oris, *m.* rumour

formaene 'or of beauty'
bono: bonus 'by the excellence of ...'
praestantior: praestans outstanding
5 **scitanti: scitor** enquire, consult
deus, *m.* 'oracle'
huic 'to her'
coniuge: coniunx, -iugis, *m.f.* spouse, husband, wife
nil = nihil
opus est + *abl.* 'there is a need'
usum: usus, -us, *m.* experience
viva : vivus alive, living
carebis: careo lose
sorte: sors, -tis, *f.* fate, lot
opacas: opacus dark
innuba: innubus unmarried
vivit: vivo live
instantem: insto press
violenta: violentus violent, harsh
procorum: procus, *m.* suitor
10 **condicione: condicio, -onis, *f.*** condition
fugat: fugo chase away
potienda: potior win, take possession of
contendite: contendo compete, contest

praemia veloci coniunx thalamique dabuntur,
mors pretium tardis. ea lex certaminis esto.'
illa quidem inmitis; sed (tanta potentia formae est)
15   venit ad hanc legem temeraria turba procorum.
sederat Hippomenes cursus spectator iniqui
et 'petitur cuiquam per tanta pericula coniunx?'
dixerat ac nimios iuvenum damnarat amores;
ut faciem et posito corpus velamine vidit
20   (quale meum, vel quale tuum, si femina fias),
obstipuit tollensque manus 'ignoscite' dixit,
'quos modo culpavi; nondum mihi praemia nota,
quae peteretis, erant.' laudando concipit ignes
et ne quis iuvenum currat velocius optat
25   insidiasque timet. 'sed cur certaminis huius
intemptata mihi fortuna relinquitur?' inquit
'audentes deus ipse iuvat.' dum talia secum
exigit Hippomenes, passu volat alite virgo.

    ...

1. **How does Venus praise both Atalanta's speed and her beauty in lines 3 and 4?**
2. **Why is Atalanta terrified by the oracle of the god?**
3. **What rewards are on offer for both the speedy and the slow in this race?**
4. **How does Ovid make line 20 humorous?**
5. **Pick out and translate the phrase which implies that Hippomenes will race against Atalanta.**

Hippomenes watches Atalanta racing against several young men and is overcome by her beauty.

    dum notat haec hospes, decursa novissima meta est
30   et tegitur festa victrix Atalanta corona;
dant gemitum victi penduntque ex foedere poenas.
non tamen eventu iuvenis deterritus horum
constitit in medio vultuque in virgine fixo
'quid facilem titulum superando quaeris inertes?
35   mecum confer' ait. 'seu me fortuna potentem
fecerit, a tanto non indignabere vinci;

    ...

6. **Which words make Hippomenes' challenge particularly forceful and why?**

thalami: thalamus, _m._ marital bedchamber, marriage
pretium, _n._ reward
tardis: tardus slow
lex, legis, _f._ law
esto 'be it so!'
inmitis harsh, merciless
potentia, _f._ power
formae: forma, _f._ beauty
15 **temeraria: temerarius** rash
iniqui: iniquus unfair
cuiquam: quisquam anyone
nimios: nimius excessive
damnarat = damnaverat: damno condemn
ut when
faciem: facies, _f._ face, beauty
velamine: velamen, _n._ clothing
20 **quale meum** 'such as mine'
vel or
fias: fio become
obstipuit: obstipesco be astounded
tollens: tollo lift, raise
ignoscite: ignosco forgive, pardon

modo 'just now'
culpavi: culpo blame, find fault with
nondum not yet
concipit: concipio cause, produce
ne quis 'that no one'
optat: opto pray
25 **insidias: insidiae, _f. pl._** a plot
invidia: invidia, _f._ envy, jealousy
intemptata: intemptatus untried
exigit: exigo weigh, consider
passu: passus, -us, _m._ step
volat: volo fly
alite: ales, -itis swift

notat: noto note
hospes, _m._ visitor
decursa ... est: decurro run down, reach by running
novissima: novissimus final
meta, _f._ end, winning line
30 **tegitur: tego** cover, crown
festa: festus festal

victrix 'as victor'
corona: corona, _f._ garland, crown
gemitum: gemitus, -us, _m._ groan, sigh
pendunt: pendo pay
foedere: foedus, -eris, _n._ bond, agreement
poenas: poena, _f._ punishment, penalty
eventu: eventus, -us, _m._ outcome, result
constitit: consisto stand
quid? why?
titulum: titulus, _m._ honour, glory, distinction
inertes: iners, inertis feeble
35 **confer: confero** compete, contest
seu if
potentem: potens powerful, able
indignabere: indignor be ashamed, be shamed

Girl with a victor's wreath

Hippomenes tells of his pedigree, and Atalanta's heart begins to soften on seeing his boyish looks.

<blockquote>

iam solitos poscunt cursus populusque paterque,
cum me sollicita proles Neptunia voce
invocat Hippomenes 'Cytherea' que 'conprecor ausis
40 adsit' ait 'nostris et quos dedit adiuvet ignes.'
detulit aura preces ad me non invida blandas;
motaque sum, fateor, nec opis mora longa dabatur.
est ager, indigenae Tamasenum nomine dicunt,
telluris Cypriae pars optima, quem mihi prisci
45 sacravere senes templisque accedere dotem
hanc iussere meis; medio nitet arbor in arvo,
fulva comas, fulvo ramis crepitantibus auro.
hinc tria forte mea veniens decerpta ferebam
aurea poma manu; nullique videnda nisi ipsi
50 Hippomenen adii docuique quis usus in illis.
signa tubae dederant, cum carcere pronus uterque
emicat et summam celeri pede libat harenam;
posse putes illos sicco freta radere passu
et segetis canae stantes percurrere aristas.
55 adiciunt animos iuveni clamorque favorque
verbaque dicentum 'nunc, nunc incumbere tempus;
Hippomene, propera! nunc viribus utere totis;
pelle moram, vinces!' dubium, Megareius heros
gaudeat an virgo magis his Schoeneia dictis.

</blockquote>

7. **What is Venus' reaction to Hippomenes' plea?**
8. **Describe the special tree which Venus mentions.**
9. **What does the phrase 'quis usus in illis' (line 50) mean?**
10. **What imagery does Venus use to illustrate the speed of both Hippomenes and Atalanta?**
11. **How are the words of the crowd particularly encouraging?**

<blockquote>

60 o quotiens, cum iam posset transire, morata est
spectatosque diu vultus invita reliquit!
aridus e lasso veniebat anhelitus ore,
metaque erat longe; tum denique de tribus unum
fetibus arboreis proles Neptunia misit.
65 obstipuit virgo nitidique cupidine pomi
declinat cursus aurumque volubile tollit.

</blockquote>

solitos: soleo be accustomed
poscunt: posco demand
populus, m. people
sollicita: sollicitus anxious
proles Neptunia 'offspring of
  Neptune' i.e. Hippomenes
invocat: invoco call upon
Cytherea 'Cytherean one' i.e.
  Venus
conprecor pray that, supplicate
ausis: audeo dare
40 **ignes** 'fires of love'
aura, f. breeze
preces: prex, precis, f. prayer
invida: invidus envious
blandas: blandus flattering,
  kind
fateor admit, confess
opis: ops, opis, f. help
mora, f. delay
indigenae: indigena, m. native
Tamasenum 'Tamasenus'
telluris Cypriae 'of the land of
  Cyprus'
prisci: priscus ancient, of old
45 **sacravere = sacraverunt**
senes 'elders'
accedere: accedo 'to be added'
dotem: dos dotis, f. dowry, gift,
  enrichment
iussere = iusserunt
medio ... in arvo
nitet: niteo shine, gleam
arvo: arvum, n. field
fulva: fulvus golden, yellow
comas: coma, f. foliage
ramis: ramus, m. branch
crepitantibus: crepito rustle
decerpta: decerpo pluck, pull
  off
poma: pomum, n. apple
nullique videnda 'invisible to
  all'
50 **usus, -us, m.** use
tubae: tuba, f. trumpet
carcere: carcer, -eris, m.
  starting-gate
pronus crouching
uterque each of two
emicat: emico spring forth
libat: libo skim
harenam: harena, f. sand
putes: puto think, imagine
sicco: siccus dry, unwet
freta: fretum, n. sea
radere: rado graze
segetis: seges, -etis, f. corn,
  grain
canae: canus ripened

percurrere: percurro pass
  quickly over
aristas: arista, f. ear of corn
55 **adiciunt: adicio** add
animos: animus, m. spirit
favor, -oris, m. support
incumbere: incumbo apply
  oneself
propera: propero hurry
utere: utor *with abl.* use
pelle: pello be rid of
moram: mora, f. delay
dubium = dubium est
Megareius son of Megareus
  (Hippomenes)
heros, -oos, m. hero
gaudeat: gaudeo rejoice
an or
Schoeneia daughter of
  Schoeneus (Atalanta)

60 **quotiens** how often
morata est: moror delay
invita: invitus unwilling
aridus dry
lasso: lassus tired
anhelitus, -us, m. panting
denique finally
fetibus: fetus, -us, m. fruit,
  produce
arboreis: arboreus of a tree
65 **nitidi: nitidus** shining
cupidine: cupido, -inis, f.
  desire
declinat: declino turn aside,
  avoid
volubile: volubilis rolling

praeterit Hippomenes; resonant spectacula plausu.
illa moram celeri cessataque tempora cursu
corrigit atque iterum iuvenem post terga relinquit;
70 et rursus pomi iactu remorata secundi
consequitur transitque virum. pars ultima cursus
restabat; 'nunc' inquit 'ades, dea muneris auctor'
inque latus campi, quo tardius illa rediret,
iecit ab obliquo nitidum iuvenaliter aurum.
75 an peteret, virgo visa est dubitare; coegi
tollere et adieci sublato pondera malo
inpediique oneris pariter gravitate moraque.
neve meus sermo cursu sit tardior ipso,
praeterita est virgo, duxit sua praemia victor.

Ovid Metamorphoses 10.560–587, 597–604, 638–680

12. From line 68, what indications do we have that Hippomenes is tiring?

13. How does Ovid create a picture that is dramatic and exciting in these lines?

14. In what two ways is Atalanta referred to in the last line of this extract?

15. Which is the more appealing character – Atalanta or Hippomenes? Why?

As a result of Hippomenes' lack of gratitude to Venus, both he and Atalanta are turned into lions.

6. Advice for would-be lovers

Ovid suggests where and how to acquire a suitable girlfriend or boyfriend.

quaerenda est oculis apta puella tuis.
scit bene venator, cervis ubi retia tendat;
    scit bene, qua frendens valle moretur aper.
aucupibus noti frutices; qui sustinet hamos,
5   novit quae multo pisce natentur aquae.
tu quoque, materiam longo qui quaeris amori,
    ante frequens quo sit disce puella loco.
non ego quaerentem vento dare vela iubebo,
    nec tibi, ut invenias, longa terenda via est.
10 Andromedan Perseus nigris portarit ab Indis,
    raptaque sit Phrygio Graia puella viro:
tot tibi tamque dabit formosas Roma puellas,
    'haec habet' ut dicas 'quicquid in orbe fuit.'
Gargara quot segetes, quot habet Methymna racemos,

praeterit: praetereo go past
plausu: plausus, -us, _m._ applause
cessataque tempora 'time lost'
corrigit: corrigo make up for
terga: tergum, _n._ back
70 **iactu: iactus, -us, _m._** throwing
remorata: remoror delay again
transit: transeo go past
ultima: ultimus last
restabat: resto remain
muneris: munus, -eris, _n._ gift
auctor, -oris, _c._ cause, creator, maker
ab obliquo 'at an angle to the side'
iuvenaliter youthfully
75 **an** whether
coegi: cogo compel
adieci: adicio add
sublato: tollo pick up
pondera: pondus, -eris, _n._ weight
malo: malum, _n._ apple
inpedii: impedio impede
gravitate: gravitas, -atis, _f._ weight

neve 'and so that not'
sermo, -onis, _m._ tale

quaerenda est: quaero seek, search for
oculis: oculus, _m._ eye
apta: aptus suitable
venator, -oris, _m._ hunter
cervis: cervus, _m._ stag
retia: rete, -is, _n._ net
tendat: tendo stretch out
qua ... valle
frendens: frendeo gnash the teeth
valle: vallis, -is, _f._ valley
moretur: moror delay, wait
aper, _m._ boar
aucupibus: auceps, -cupis, _m._ bird-catcher
noti: notus well known
frutices: frutex, -icis, _m._ bush, shrub
sustinet: sustineo hold
hamos: hamus, _m._ fish-hook
5 **novit: novi** know
quae aquae
pisce: piscis, -is, _m._ fish

natentur 'teem'
materiam: materia, _f._ subject-matter
ante first
frequens numerous
quo ... loco
vento: ventus, _m._ wind
dare vela: do vela expose one's sails to the wind
terenda: tero tread
10 **portarit = portaverit**
ab Indis 'from India'
rapta sit: rapio snatch
Phrygio: Phrygius Phrygian, Trojan
Graia: Graius Greek
formosas: formosus beautiful
quicquid whatever
orbe: orbis, -is, _m._ world
Gargara, _n. pl._ Gargara
quot ... tot ... as many as ... so many...
Methymna, _f._ Methymna
racemos: racemus, _m._ bunch of grapes

Hunters with their prize

15   aequore quot pisces, fronde teguntur aves,
        quot caelum stellas, tot habet tua Roma puellas:
           mater in Aeneae constitit urbe sui.
        seu caperis primis et adhuc crescentibus annis,
           ante oculos veniet vera puella tuos:
20   sive cupis iuvenem, iuvenes tibi mille placebunt.

        ...

1. In the first five lines, with which group of people does Ovid compare lovers? What similarities are there between the two groups?
2. Ovid suggests would-be lovers will not have to make long journeys. Why does he mention Perseus and Andromeda?
3. How does Ovid emphasise that Rome has a great deal to offer to those in search of love?
4. Who is the 'mater' referred to?

Ovid goes on to describe the particular hunting ground of the theatre and tells the story of the rape of the Sabine women.

      sed tu praecipue curvis venare theatris;
        haec loca sunt voto fertiliora tuo.
      illic invenies quod ames, quod ludere possis,
        quodque semel tangas, quodque tenere velis.
25   ut redit itque frequens longum formica per agmen,
        granifero solitum cum vehit ore cibum,
      aut ut apes saltusque suos et olentia nactae
        pascua per flores et thyma summa volant,
      sic ruit ad celebres cultissima femina ludos;
30   copia iudicium saepe morata meum est.
      spectatum veniunt, veniunt spectentur ut ipsae:
        ille locus casti damna pudoris habet.
      primus sollicitos fecisti, Romule, ludos,
        cum iuvit viduos rapta Sabina viros.
35   tunc neque marmoreo pendebant vela theatro,
        nec fuerant liquido pulpita rubra croco;
      illic quas tulerant nemorosa Palatia frondes
        simpliciter positae scaena sine arte fuit;
      in gradibus sedit populus de caespite factis,
40   qualibet hirsutas fronde tegente comas.
      respiciunt oculisque notant sibi quisque puellam
        quam velit, et tacito pectore multa movent.

15 **aequore: aequor, -oris, n.** sea
fronde: frons, -dis, f. foliage
teguntur: tego cover, hide
aves: avis, -is, f. bird
stellas: stella, f. star
constitit: consisto settle, stop
adhuc still
crescentibus: cresco grow
vera: verus true

20 **praecipue** especially
venare: venor go hunting
voto: votum, n. prayer
fertiliora: fertilis fertile
semel once
tangas: tango touch
ut as
25 **frequens** in crowds, in large numbers
formica, f. ant
granifero: graniferus grain-carrying
solitum: soleo be accustomed
vehit: veho carry
ore: os, oris, n. mouth
apes: apis, -is, f. bee
saltus: saltus, -us, m. glade
olentia: oleo smell, be fragrant
nactae: nanciscor obtain
pascua: pascuum, n. pasture
thyma: thymum, n. thyme
volant: volo fly
celebres: celeber crowded, famous
cultissima: cultus elegant, civilised
30 **copia, f.** abundance
iudicium: iudicium, n. judgement
spectatum *supine* 'to watch'
casti: castus chaste, pure
damna: damnum, n. loss
pudoris: pudor, -oris, m. modesty
sollicitos: sollicitus troubled
ludos: ludi, m. pl. games
iuvit: iuvo delight
viduos: viduus single, without partners
35 **tunc = tum**
marmoreo: marmoreus of marble
pendebant: pendeo hang
vela: velum, n. curtain, awning
liquido: liquidus liquid
pulpita: pulpitum, n. stage
rubra: ruber red, reddish-orange

croco: crocus, m. *or* **crocum, n.** saffron
nemorosa: nemorosus well-wooded
Palatia: Palatium, n. the Palatine Hill
scaena, f. stage
caespite: caespes, -itis, m. turf
40 **qualibet** everywhere
hirsutas: hirsutus rough, shaggy
comas: coma, f. foliage
notant: noto mark out
quisque each man
tacito: tacitus silent
pectore: pectus, -oris, n. heart

dumque rudem praebente modum tibicine Tusco
   ludius aequatam ter pede pulsat humum,
45   in medio plausu (plausus tunc arte carebant)
      rex populo praedae signa petenda dedit.
   protinus exsiliunt animum clamore fatentes,
      virginibus cupidas iniciuntque manus.
   ut fugiunt aquilas, timidissima turba, columbae,
50   utque fugit visos agna novella lupos,
   sic illae timuere viros sine lege ruentes;
      constitit in nulla qui fuit ante color.
   nam timor unus erat, facies non una timoris:
      pars laniat crines, pars sine mente sedet;
55   altera maesta silet, frustra vocat altera matrem;
      haec queritur, stupet haec; haec manet, illa fugit;
   ducuntur raptae, genialis praeda, puellae,
      et potuit multas ipse decere timor.

Ovid *Ars Amatoria* 1.44–63, 89–126

5. **What 'categories of lover' does Ovid suggest you can find in the theatre?**
6. **Why is Ovid's simile using ants and bees appropriate?**
7. **How does Ovid successfully depict a primitive theatre?**
8. **How does Ovid highlight the differing reactions of the Sabine women?**
9. **In what ways is Ovid's advice useful for the modern world?**

rudem: rudis rough
praebente: praebeo provide
modum: modus, *m.* tune,
   rhythm
tibicine: tibicen, -inis, *m.*
   flute-player, piper
Tusco: Tuscus Tuscan,
   Etruscan
ludius, *m.* stage-player,
   pantomimist
aequatam: aequatus levelled
ter three times
pede: pes, pedis, *m.* foot
pulsat: pulso beat
humum: humus, *f.* ground,
   earth
45 **carebant: careo** + *abl.* lack
praedae: praeda, *f.* booty
protinus straightaway
exsiliunt: exsilio leap up
animum: animus, *m.* intention
fatentes: fateor admit,
   proclaim
cupidas: cupidus desirous
iniciunt: inicio lay (hands)
aquilas: aquila, *f.* eagle
columbae: columba, *f.* dove
50 **agna, *f.*** ewe lamb
novella: novellus young,
   tender
lupos: lupus, *m.* wolf
timuere = timuerunt
lege: lex, legis, *f.* law
ruentes: ruo rush
constitit: consisto stay, remain
laniat: lanio tear at
crines: crinis, -is, *m.* hair
mente: mens, -tis, *f.* mind
55 **maesta: maestus** sad,
   mournful, sorrowful
queritur: queror complain,
   protest
stupet: stupeo be dumbstruck,
   be stunned
genialis merry, festive
decere: decet it is fitting, proper

PROPHECIES AND PORTENTS

This section illustrates the Romans' fascination with the supernatural. The writers describe sudden light or darkness, thunder or stars appearing with these prophecies and portents, and the people who see them are overcome by awe or terror.

Caesar on the Ides of March

Pliny tells of visions, dreams and prophecies, as well as a ghost story. Lucan describes Caesar horror-struck by a vision of Rome that warns against war, but in the end he takes no notice, just as he ignores warnings of his murder, according to Suetonius. A freak thunderbolt gives Horace a sense of the power of the gods over the whole earth and its inhabitants, and Persius makes fun of superstition. Where the destiny of the individual affects the destiny of Rome, prophecies and portents can be powerful instruments of propaganda, demonstrating that particular people are rightful rulers, or, like Romulus and Caesar, that they are to be worshipped as gods. Virgil's description of Aeneas' shield makes it a supernatural work of art, as its pictures of Rome's future come alive. But as prophecies of events in the history of Rome, these pictures are the poet's celebration of a dynasty that claims to go back to Aeneas and to reach a climax in the triumphs of Augustus.

In these passages, some people express doubt, others seem quick to believe in a convenient prophecy; but the writers make full use of the supernatural as the basis of their stories and descriptions.

1. Do you believe in ghosts?

GAIUS PLINIUS SURAE SUO S.

et mihi discendi et tibi docendi facultatem otium praebet. igitur
perquam velim scire, esse phantasmata et habere propriam
figuram numenque aliquod putes an inania et vana ex metu nostro
imaginem accipere. ego ut esse credam in primis eo ducor, quod
audio accidisse Curtio Rufo. tenuis adhuc et obscurus, obtinenti
Africam comes haeserat. inclinato die spatiabatur in porticu;
offertur ei mulieris figura humana grandior pulchriorque.
perterrito Africam se futurorum praenuntiam dixit: iturum enim
Romam honoresque gesturum, atque etiam cum summo imperio in
eandem provinciam reversurum, ibique moriturum. facta sunt
omnia. praeterea accedenti Carthaginem egredientique nave
eadem figura in litore occurrisse narratur. ipse certe implicitus
morbo futura praeteritis, adversa secundis auguratus, spem salutis
nullo suorum desperante proiecit.

1. How does Pliny suggest that Curtius Rufus' career was surprising?
2. What does the fact that no one else expected Curtius Rufus to die suggest about
   the apparition?

Pliny

GAIUS PLINIUS SURAE SUO

S. 'Pliny sends greetings to his [friend] Sura'

S. = salutem (dicit) greets

discendi: disco learn

docendi: doceo teach

facultatem: facultas, -atis, *f.* opportunity

otium: otium, *n.* leisure

praebet: praebeo offer, provide

perquam very much

esse *here* exist

phantasmata, -atum, *n. pl.* ghosts

propriam: proprius own

figuram: figura, *f.* shape, form

numen: numen, -inis, *n.* divine/supernatural power

aliquod: aliqui some, any

putes: puto think

inania: inanis empty

vana: vanus of no substance

metu: metus, -us, *m.* fear

5 **imaginem: imago, -inis, *f.*** image, form, likeness

credam: credo believe

in primis especially, in particular

eo ... quod audio accidisse ... 'by what I heard befell/ happened to'

tenuis thin, slight, *here* of low rank

adhuc still, as yet

obscurus unknown

obtinenti: obtineo hold, possess, *here* have as his province

haeserat: haereo *here* be attached

comes, -itis, *m.f.* *here* member of provincial governor's retinue

inclinato die in the afternoon

spatiabatur: spatior walk

porticu: porticus, -us, *m.* colonnade

offertur: offero pass. show oneself, appear

mulieris: mulier, -eris, *f.* woman

humana grandior pulchriorque of more than human size and beauty

Africam: Africa, *f.* *here* the spirit of Africa

perterrito: perterritus terrified

praenuntiam: praenuntius foretelling

futurorum praenuntiam 'telling him in advance what would happen to him'

iturum: eo (*fut. part.*) go

10 **Romam** to Rome

honores: honor, -oris, *m.* honour, public office

honores gesturum: honorem gero hold office

cum summo imperio with the highest authority, i.e. as governor

eandem: idem the same

reversurum: reverto return

moriturum: morior die

(dixit eum) iturum esse ... gesturum esse ... reversurum esse ... moriturum esse

praeterea moreover, and what is more

accedenti: accedo approach

egredienti: egredior leave, disembark

litore: litus, -oris, *n.* shore

occurrisse: occurro + *dat.* come to meet

narratur: narro tell, relate, *here* the story goes

certe certainly, for sure

morbo: morbus, *m.* disease, sickness

implicitus: implico seize with, entangled in

implicitus morbo on falling ill

praeteritis: praeterita, *n. pl.* the past

adversa: adversa, *n. pl.* setbacks

secundis: secunda, *n. pl.* successes, good fortune

auguratus: auguror predict, interpret

salutis: salus, -utis, *f.* health, recovery

15 **desperante: despero** despair

proiecit: proicio throw away, give up

iam illud nonne et magis terribile et non minus mirum est quod
exponam ut accepi? erat Athenis spatiosa et capax domus sed
infamis et pestilens. per silentium noctis sonus ferri, et si
attenderes acrius, strepitus vinculorum longius primo, deinde
20   e proximo reddebatur: mox adparebat idolon, senex macie et
squalore confectus, promissa barba horrenti capillo; cruribus
compedes, manibus catenas gerebat quatiebatque. inde
inhabitantibus tristes diraeque noctes per metum vigilabantur;
vigiliam morbus et crescente formidine mors sequebatur. nam
25   interdiu quoque, quamquam abscesserat imago, memoria imaginis
oculis inerrabat, longiorque causis timoris timor erat. deserta inde
et damnata solitudine domus totaque illi monstro relicta;
proscribebatur tamen, seu quis emere seu quis conducere ignarus
tanti mali vellet. venit Athenas philosophus Athenodorus, legit
30   titulum auditoque pretio, quia suspecta vilitas, percunctatus omnia
docetur ac nihilo minus, immo tanto magis conducit. ubi coepit
advesperascere, iubet sterni sibi in prima domus parte, poscit
pugillares stilum lumen, suos omnes in interiora dimittit; ipse ad
scribendum animum oculos manum intendit, ne vacua mens audita
35   simulacra et inanes sibi metus fingeret. initio, quale ubique,
silentium noctis; dein concuti ferrum, vincula moveri. ille non

magis more
mirum: mirus amazing, astonishing
exponam: expono set out, tell, relate
accepi: accipio *here* hear
iam non est illud quod exponam ut accepi et magis terribile et non minus mirum?
Athenis at Athens
spatiosa: spatiosus large, spacious
capax roomy
infamis notorious, with a bad reputation
pestilens dangerous
sonus, m. sound
ferri: ferrum, n. iron
attenderes: attendo concentrate, listen
acrius: acer *here* closely, acutely
strepitus, -us, m. loud noise, rattle, jangle
vinculorum: vincula, n. pl. shackles
longius: longus at a distance, far away
20 **e proximo** *here* very close by
reddebatur: reddo give back, *here* echo
mox soon
adparebat: adpareo appear
idolon = idolum, n. spectre, apparition
squalore: squalor, -oris, m. dirt, filth
confectus: conficio finish, *here* consume
macie: macies, f. leanness, thinness, wasting
promissa: promissus *here* long (of hair/beard)
barba: barba, f. beard
horrenti: horrens bristling, standing on end
capillo: capillus, m. hair
cruribus: crus, cruris, n. leg
compedes: compes, -edis, f. fetters, leg-irons
catenas: catena, f. chain
gerebat: gero *here* wear
quatiebat: quatio shake
inde then, therefore, *here* as a result
inhabitantibus: inhabito, inhabit, occupy
tristes: tristis sad, grim
dirae: dirus terrible

metum: metus, -us, m. fear
vigilabantur: vigilo stay awake, (*pass.*) *here* be spent awake
vigiliam: vigilia, f. wakefulness, sleeplessness
crescente: crescens increasing
formidine: formido, -inis, f. fear
sequebatur: sequor follow
25 **interdiu** during the day
abscesserat: abscedo depart
oculis: oculus, m. eye
inerrabat: inerro stray into, drift before
longior *here* longer-lasting
causis: causa, f. cause
timoris: timor, -oris, m. fear
deserta: desero desert, leave alone
damnata: damno *here + abl.* condemn
solitudine: solitudo, -inis, f. loneliness, isolation
monstro: monstrum, n. monster
tota ... relicta totally abandoned
proscribebatur: proscribo *here* advertise
emere: emo buy
conducere: conduco rent
seu quis ... seu quis ... vellet in case anyone should want to ... or to ...
ignarus ignorant
ignarus tanti mali not knowing there was so much wrong with it
Athenas to Athens
30 **titulum: titulus, m.** notice
pretio: pretium, n. price
quia because
suspecta: suspectus suspect
vilitas, -atis, f. cheapness, low price
percunctatus: percunctor investigate, make a full enquiry
omnia docetur he is told everything
nihilo minus, ... magis conducit he was no less willing to rent but actually more keen to do so
advesperascere: advesperascit (*impers.*) it gets dark, evening falls

coepit: coepi began
sterni: sternere spread, *here* prepare a couch/bed
prima domus parte in the front part of the house
poscit: posco ask for
pugillares: pugillares, -ium, m. pl. writing tablets
stilum: stilus, m. implement for writing on wax tablets, pen
lumen: lumen, -inis, n. light, lamp
interiora, n. pl. *here* the inner rooms
scribendum: scribo write
dimittit: dimitto send away, abandon
intendit: intendo apply, concentrate
vacua: vacuus empty
mens, mentis, f. mind
35 **simulacra: simulacrum, n.** vision, apparition
fingeret: fingo create, make up, invent
initio: initium, n. beginning
quale ubique as everywhere
dein = deinde
concuti = concutiebantur: concutio shake, jangle
moveri = movebantur

tollere oculos, non remittere stilum, sed offirmare animum
auribusque praetendere. tum crebrescere fragor, adventare et iam
ut in limine, iam ut intra limen audiri. respicit, videt agnoscitque
40 narratam sibi effigiem. stabat innuebatque digito similis vocanti.
hic contra ut paulum exspectaret manu significat rursusque ceris et
stilo incumbit. illa scribentis capiti catenis insonabat. respicit
rursus idem quod prius innuentem, nec moratus tollit lumen et
sequitur. ibat illa lento gradu quasi gravis vinculis. postquam
45 deflexit in aream domus, repente dilapsa deserit comitem. desertus
herbas et folia concerpta signum loco ponit. postero die adit
magistratus, monet ut illum locum effodi iubeant. inveniuntur ossa
inserta catenis et implicita, quae corpus aevo terraque putrefactum
nuda et exesa reliquerat vinculis; collecta publice sepeliuntur.
50 domus postea rite conditis manibus caruit.

3. What do you think makes the ghost more frightening, his appearance or the effect
    he has on people who see him (lines 20–26)?
4. How does Pliny's description of Athenodorus and his actions in the house
    encourage us to see Athenodorus as a reliable witness (lines 29–35)?
5. Why do you think Pliny does not explain who the ghost was and what had
    happened to him in the past?

tollere = tollebat raise
remittere = remittebat:
remitto let go, *here* put down
offirmare = offirmabat:
offirmo keep firm/steadfast
praetendere = praetendebat:
praetendo put in front of, *here*
obstruct
sed offirmare ... praetendere
but kept his mind firm as a
way of stopping his ears
crebrescere = crebrescebat:
crebresco increase, grow
loud
fragor, -oris, *m.* noise,
clashing
adventare = adventabat:
advento advance, come
closer
limine: limen, -inis, *n.*
threshold
intra + *acc.* within
audiri = audiebatur
respicit: respicio look back/
behind, look round
agnoscit: agnosco recognise
40 **narratam sibi** that he has
been told about
effigiem; effigies, *f.* ghost
innuebat: innuo make a sign,
beckon
digito: digitus, *m.* finger
similis + *dat.* like, similar to
similis vocanti as if calling
him
contra (*adv.*) *here* in turn
paulum for a little while
significat: significo make a
sign
rursus again
ceris: cera, *f.* wax, wax tablet
incumbit: incumbo + *dat.*
bend over, concentrate on
illa (effigies)
insonabat: insono make a
loud noise, *here* rattle
prius: prior earlier, former
idem quod prius in the same
way as before
moratus: moror delay
tollit: tollo lift, raise, pick up
lento: lentus slow
gradu: gradus, -us, *m.* step
quasi as if
gravis heavy, weighted down
45 **deflexit: deflecto** turn
aside/away
aream: area, *f.* courtyard

dilapsa: dilabor melt away,
vanish
herbas: herba, *f.* grass, plant
folia: folium, *n.* leaf
concerpta: concerpo pick
postero die on the next day
adit: adeo go to
magistratus: magistratus,
-us, *m.* magistrate
effodi: effodere dig up
ossa: os, ossis, *n.* bone
inserta: insero put in/among,
mix up with
implicita: implicitus
entwined, entangled
putrefactum: putreficio
make rotten, (*pass.*) decompose
aevo: aevum, *n.* age, time
exesa: exedo eat up, consume,
corrode
ossa ... quae corpus ...
putrefactum ... reliquerat nuda
et exesa vinculis
publice at public expense
collecta: colligo collect
sepeliuntur: sepelio bury,
inter
50 **rite** duly, properly
conditis: condo hide, *here*
bury, lay to rest
manibus: manes, -ium, *m.*
pl. spirits of the dead, shades
caruit: careo + *abl.* be
without, be free from

et haec quidem adfirmantibus credo; illud adfirmare aliis possum.
est libertus mihi non inlitteratus. cum hoc minor frater eodem
lecto quiescebat. is visus est sibi cernere quendam in toro
residentem, admoventemque capiti suo cultros, atque etiam ex
55 ipso vertice amputantem capillos. ubi inluxit, ipse circa verticem
tonsus, capilli iacentes reperiuntur. exiguum temporis medium, et
rursus simile aliud priori fidem fecit. puer in paedagogio mixtus
pluribus dormiebat. venerunt per fenestras (ita narrat) in tunicis
albis duo cubantemque detonderunt et qua venerant recesserunt.
60 hunc quoque tonsum sparsosque circa capillos dies ostendit. nihil
notabile secutum, nisi forte quod non fui reus, futurus, si
Domitianus sub quo haec acciderunt diutius vixisset. nam in
scrinio eius datus a Caro de me libellus inventus est; ex quo
coniectari potest, quia reis moris est summittere capillum, recisos
65 meorum capillos depulsi quod imminebat periculi signum fuisse.

6. **Apart from his interest in the supernatural, why might Pliny have wanted to tell this story?**
7. **Pliny describes his freedman as 'non inlitteratus' (line 52). Do you think this makes him more reliable as a witness or less?**
8. **Why do you think Pliny adds the words 'ita narrat' (line 58) when he tells the slave's story?**

proinde rogo, eruditionem tuam intendas. digna res est quam diu
multumque consideres; ne ego quidem indignus, cui copiam
scientiae tuae facias. licet etiam utramque in partem (ut soles)
disputes, ex altera tamen fortius, ne me suspensum incertumque
70 dimittas, cum mihi consulendi causa fuerit, ut dubitare desinerem.
vale

Pliny *Letters* 7.27

9. **Pliny tells Sura he is worth taking seriously. Does the evidence he offers in the letter justify this claim?**
10. **Is Pliny's request that Sura should come down on one side or the other reasonable?**

The whole letter
1. **Is Pliny interested in a scientific explanation for the supernatural, or in telling a good story, or both?**
2. **Do you find any of the stories more interesting or convincing than the others?**
3. **Write a brief reply from Sura to Pliny.**

haec *here* these stories
adfirmantibus: adfirmo declare, vouch for the truth of
illud *here* the following story
inlitteratus unlearned, uneducated
cum hoc (liberto)
minor younger
lecto: lectus, *m.* bed
quiescebat: quiesco be at rest, rest, sleep
visus est sibi seemed to himself, imagined, dreamt
cernere: cerno see
quendam: quidam someone
toro: torus, *m.* couch
residentem: residens sitting
admoveo + *dat.* move (something) towards, apply (something) to
cultros: culter, *m.* knife, scissors
55 **vertice: vertex, -icis, *m.*** head, top of the head
amputantem: amputo cut around/off
capillos: capilli, *m. pl.* hair, hairs
inluxit it grew light, day dawned
circa + *acc.* around
tonsus shorn, shaved
tonsus (est)
iacentes: iaceo lying
reperiuntur: reperio find
exiguum: exiguus slight, small
exiguum temporis medium after a short interval
fidem: fides, *f.* faith, credibility
fidem fecit priori added credibility to the earlier one
puer, *m.* *here* slave
mixtus *here* together with, sharing
paedagogio: paedagogium, *n.* paedagogium, sleeping-quarters of young slaves
fenestras: fenestra, *f.* window
tunicis: tunica, *f.* tunic
albis: albus white
ita narrat so he says
cubantem: cubo lie in bed
detonderunt: detondeo shave/cut off
qua venerant by the way they had come
recesserunt: recedo go away, depart, leave

60 **sparsos: sparsus** scattered
ostendit: ostendo reveal
notabile: notabilis remarkable, out of the ordinary
forte perhaps
reus, *m.* a person accused/committed for trial
futurus (essem) I would have been
sub quo haec acciderunt in whose reign these events took place
vixisset: vivo live
scrinio: scrinium, *n.* book-box, file
libellus, *m.* little book, *here* accusation
coniectari: coniecto guess, infer
moris est it is the custom
summittere: summitto allow to grow
recisos: recido cut short
65 **meorum: mei** *here* my men
depulsi: depello remove
imminebat: immineo threaten
coniectari potest ... recisos capillos meorum signum fuisse periculi depulsi quod imminebat

proinde and so, therefore
eruditionem: eruditio, -onis, *f.* learning
digna: dignus worthy, fit, suitable
consideres: considero look closely at, consider carefully
digna res ... consideres the matter is worthy of your long and full consideration
indignus unworthy, unsuitable
ne ... quidem not even, nor indeed
ne ego quidem (sim) indignus
copiam: copia, *f.* supply, wealth, riches
scientiae: scientia, *f.* knowledge, expertise
facias: facio *here* provide, make available
licet it is allowed, *here* although
utramque in partem for each side
disputes: disputo speak, put/make the case
(ut soles) as you usually do

ex altera on one side
fortius (disputa) *here* make a stronger case
suspensum: suspensus in doubt
incertum uncertain
70 **ne ... dimittas** so that you do not abandon me to a state of doubt and uncertainty
consulendi: consulo + *dat.* consult
dubitare: dubito doubt, be in doubt
desinerem: desino stop

2. The mysterious death of Romulus

Romulus, believed to be the son of Mars, founded the city of Rome, and as king secured her position through war and peace.

his immortalibus editis operibus cum ad exercitum recensendum contionem in campo ad Caprae paludem haberet, subito coorta tempestas cum magno fragore tonitribusque tam denso regem operuit nimbo ut conspectum eius contioni abstulerit; nec deinde
5   in terris Romulus fuit. Romana pubes sedato tandem pavore postquam ex tam turbido die serena et tranquilla lux rediit, ubi vacuam sedem regiam vidit, etsi satis credebat patribus qui proximi steterant sublimem raptum procella, tamen velut orbitatis metu icta maestum aliquamdiu silentium obtinuit. deinde a paucis
10 initio facto, deum deo natum, regem parentemque urbis Romanae salvere universi Romulum iubent; pacem precibus exposcunt, uti volens propitius suam semper sospitet progeniem. fuisse credo tum quoque aliquos qui discerptum regem patrum manibus taciti arguerent; manavit enim haec quoque sed perobscura fama; illam
15 alteram admiratio viri et pavor praesens nobilitavit. et consilio etiam unius hominis addita rei dicitur fides. namque Proculus Iulius, sollicita civitate desiderio regis et infensa patribus, gravis, ut traditur, quamvis magnae rei auctor in contionem prodit. 'Romulus' inquit, 'Quirites, parens urbis huius, prima hodierna
20 luce caelo repente delapsus se mihi obvium dedit. cum perfusus horrore venerabundusque adstitissem petens precibus ut contra

editis: edo bring about, perform

immortalibus: immortalis immortal, deathless

operibus: opus, -eris, *n.* work, achievement

exercitum: exercitus, -us, *m.* army

recensendum: recenseo survey, review

contionem: contio, -onis, *f.* assembly

campo: campus, *m.* field

ad *here* at, by

Caprae paludem: Caprae palus, -udis, *f.* the marsh of Capra (in Rome)

coorta: coorior arise

tempestas, -atis, *f.* storm

fragore: fragor, -oris, *m.* crashing, noise

tonitribus: tonitrus, -us, *m.* thunder

denso: densus thick

operuit: operio cover, hide

nimbo: nimbus, *m.* cloud

conspectum: conspectus, -us, *m.* sight

abstulerit: aufero remove

ut ... abstulerit that it removed him from the sight of the assembly, *lit.* that it removed the sight of him from the assembly, i.e. he was out of their sight

deinde *here* after that

5 **pubes, pubis, *f.*** young men, men

sedato: sedo calm, allay

pavore: pavor, -oris, *m.* fear, alarm

ex + *abl.* *here* after

turbido: turbidus disturbed, violent

**die: dies, *m.* *here* part of day, period, spell

serena: serenus clear, bright

tranquilla: tranquillus calm, settled

lux, lucis, *f.* daylight, day

vacuam: vacuus empty

sedem: sedes, -is, *f.* seat

regiam: regius of the king, royal

ubi (Romana pubes) vidit sedem regiam (esse) vacuam

etsi although

**patribus: patres, -um, *m. pl.* *here* senators

proximi: proximus + *acc.* close by, next to

sublimem: sublimis lifted up, on high

raptum: rapio carry, snatch

procella: procella, *f.* gale, whirlwind

satis credebat ... procella they believed well enough the senators who had stood next to him (and said that) he was carried on high by a whirlwind

velut as if

orbitatis: orbitas, -tatis, *f.* bereavement, state of being orphaned

metu: metus, -us, *f.* fear

ictus struck

maestum: maestus sad, sorrowful

aliquamdiu for some time

silentium: silentium, *n.* silence

10 **initio: initium, *n.*** beginning

natum: natus born

parentem: parens, -tis, *m.f.* parent

universi, *m. pl.* the whole body, *here* the whole assembly

salvere iubent: salvere iubeo greet, welcome, *here* hail

exposcunt: exposco ask for, beg for

precibus: prex, precis, *f.* prayer

volens propitius favourably and kindly

semper always

sospitet: sospito preserve, protect

progeniem: progenies, *f.* descendants

tum *here* at that time

discerptum: discerpo tear apart, tear to pieces

taciti: tacitus silent, in secret

arguerent: arguo claim, assert

qui arguerent regem discerptum (esse) manibus patrum

manavit: mano flow, spread abroad

fama, *f.* story, rumour

perobscura: perobscurus very obscure, under cover

haec fama quoque manavit, sed perobscura

15 **alteram: alter** the other

illam alteram (famam) i.e. that he had been taken up to heaven

admiratio, -onis, *f.* admiration

viri *(gen.) here* for the man

praesens present, current

nobilitavit: nobilito make famous, render superior

fides, *f.* faith, credibility

addita: addo add

et dicitur etiam fides rei addita (esse) consilio unius hominis

namque for

sollicita: sollicitus disturbed, unsettled

desiderio: desiderium, *n.* loss, longing

infensa: infensus hostile

gravis *here* respected

ut traditur according to tradition. *lit.* as it is handed down

quamvis magnae rei however serious the matter

auctor, -oris, *m.* a man of influence

prodit: prodeo go forward, come before

Quirites, *m. pl.* Quirites (title of Romans when addressed as citizens)

prima hodierna luce today at dawn

20 **repente** suddenly

delapsus: delabor descend

se mihi obvium dedit met me, appeared to me

perfusus: perfundo pour over, fill with

horrore: horror, -oris, *m.* trembling, fear, awe

venerabundus reverent, in reverence

adstitissem: adsto stand, stand by

contra *here* face to face

intueri fas esset, "abi, nuntia" inquit "Romanis, caelestes ita velle
ut mea Roma caput orbis terrarum sit; proinde rem militarem
colant sciantque et ita posteris tradant nullas opes humanas armis
25   Romanis resistere posse." 'haec' inquit 'locutus sublimis abiit.'
mirum quantum illi viro nuntianti haec fidei fuerit, quamque
desiderium Romuli apud plebem exercitumque facta fide
immortalitatis lenitum sit.

Livy *A History of Rome* 1.16

1. How does the way in which Romulus disappeared lead to his being hailed as a god
   so soon?
2. How popular was Romulus?
3. Why would Proculus' use of the term 'parens urbis huius' (line 19) appeal to
   troops at this time?

3. Omens, portents and the murder of Julius Caesar

Caesar ignores omens warning that he would be assassinated,

proximis diebus equorum greges, quos in traiciendo Rubiconi
flumini consecrarat ac vagos et sine custode dimiserat, comperit
pertinacissime pabulo abstinere ubertimque flere. et immolantem
haruspex Spurinna monuit, caveret periculum, quod non ultra
5   Martias Idus proferretur. pridie autem easdem Idus avem
regaliolum cum laureo ramulo Pompeianae curiae se inferentem
volucres varii generis ex proximo nemore persecutae ibidem
discerpserunt. ea vero nocte, cui inluxit dies caedis, et ipse sibi
visus est per quietem interdum supra nubes volitare, alias cum
10   Iove dextram iungere; et Calpurnia uxor imaginata est conlabi
fastigium domus maritumque in gremio suo confodi; ac subito
cubiculi fores sponte patuerunt. ob haec simul et ob infirmam
valitudinem diu cunctatus an se contineret et quae apud senatum

intueri: intueor look upon
fas *(indecl.)* right, lawful
abi go!
caelestes, m. pl. gods
caelestes ita velle ut that the
  will of the gods is that …
caput, -itis, n. *here* capital
orbis terrarum, m. world
proinde therefore
rem militarem: res militaris,
  f. military art, art of wars
colant: colo cultivate, practise
posteris: posteri, m. pl.
  descendants
tradant: trado pass on, hand
  down
opes: opes, opum, f. pl. might,
  strength
25 **locutus: loquor** speak
mirum: mirus wonderful,
  amazing
quantum how much
quam how
apud + *acc.* among
plebem: plebs, plebis, f.
  people
facta fide immortalitatis by
  the creation of belief in his
  immortality
lenitum: lenio soften, soothe

proximis diebus in the days
  just before his death
greges: grex, gregis, m. herd
traiciendo: traicio cross
in traiciendo when he crossed
  (it)
Rubiconi: Rubico,
  Rubiconis, m. Rubicon
consecrarat =
  consecraverat: consecro
  dedicate, deify, place among
  gods
greges quos (Caesar)
  consecraverat flumini Rubiconi
  in traiciendo
vagos: vagus wandering *here*
  loose, free
sine + *abl.* without
custode: custos, custodis,
  m.f. guard, keeper, herdsman
dimiserat: dimitto send away,
  let go
comperit: comperio find out,
  learn
proximis diebus (Caesar)
  comperit …
pertinacissime most
  stubbornly, very obstinately

pabulo: pabulum, n. fodder,
  grazing
abstinere: abstineo stay away
  from, refuse
ubertim copiously, in floods
flere: fleo weep, shed tears
immolentem: immolo make
  an offering, sacrifice
(Caesarem) immolantem
haruspex, -spicis, m.
  haruspex (soothsayer who
  looked for omens in entrails of
  sacrificed animals)
Spurinna, m. Spurinna
  (a haruspex)
caveret: cavere beware, be on
  guard against
ultra + *acc.* beyond
5 **Martias Idus: Martiae Idus,**
  f. pl. the Ides of March
  (15 March)
proferretur: profero *here* put
  off, delay
pridie the day before
autem however
easdem: idem the same
avem: avis, avis, f. bird
regaliolus, m. small bird,
  wren, king-bird
laureo: laureus of laurel
ramulo: ramulus, m. little
  branch, sprig
Pompeaianae: Pompeianus of
  Pompey
curiae: curia, f. meeting-place
  of senate
se inferentem: me infero
  enter, rush into
volucres: volucris, -is, f. bird
varii generis of a different
  kind
nemore: nemus, -oris, n.
  grove
persecutae: persequor
  pursue
ibidem in the same place
discerpserunt: discerpo tear
  to pieces
volucres …, persecutae avem … se
  inferentem Pompeianae curiae,
  (eam) discerpserunt
vero in fact
inluxit it grew light
caedis: caedes, -is, f. murder
cui inluxit dies caedis when
  the day of the murder began
  to dawn
visus est: videor be seen, seem
per quietem in his sleep

supra + *acc.* above, over
nubes: nubes, -is, f. cloud
volitare: volito fly
interdum sometimes, at times
interdum … alias at one time
  … at another time, now …
  now …
10 **dextram iungere cum Iove:**
  to be shaking the right (hand)
  of Jupiter
Calpurnia, f. Calpurnia (wife of
  Caesar)
uxor, -oris, f. wife
imaginata: imaginor
  imagine, dream
conlabi: conlabor fall in ruins,
  collapse
fastigium, n. gable, pediment
maritum: maritus, m.
  husband
gremio: gremium, n. lap,
  arms, bosom
confodi: confodio *here* stab
cubiculi: cubiculum, n.
  bedroom
fores, forum, f. pl. door
sponte of its own accord
patuerunt: pateo be open
ob + *acc.* because of
simul et at the same time, also
infirmam: infirmus weak,
  poor (of health)
valitudinem: valetudo, -inis,
  f. health
cunctatus an: cunctor an +
  subj. hesitate/be in two minds
  whether
se contineret: se contineo
  remain (at home)
apud + *acc.* at
senatum: senatus, -us, m.
  senate

proposuerat agere differret, tandem Decimo Bruto adhortante, ne
15 frequentes ac iam dudum opperientes destitueret, quinta fere hora
progressus est libellumque insidiarum indicem ab obvio quodam
porrectum libellis ceteris, quos sinistra manu tenebat, quasi mox
lecturus commiscuit. dein pluribus hostiis caesis, cum litare non
posset, introiit curiam spreta religione Spurinnamque irridens et
20 ut falsum arguens, quod sine ulla sua noxa Idus Martiae adessent:
quamquam is venisse quidem eas diceret, sed non praeterisse
...

For the crossing of the Rubicon see Passage 4 (Lucan Civil War) below.

1. **What do you think the men plotting to kill Caesar might have thought about Spurinna's warnings?**

The conspirators immediately attacked Caesar, and he died of numerous stab wounds. In his will he left money and the use of his gardens to the people of Rome. The funeral reminded the people of his achievements and the loyalty they owed him, and they were stirred to a frenzy of anger and sorrow at this death.

A portent confirms Caesar's divinity

...
ludis, quos primos consecrato ei heres Augustus edebat, stella
crinita per septem continuos dies fulsit exoriens circa undecimam
horam, creditumque est animam esse Caesaris in caelum recepti;
25 et hac de causa simulacro eius in vertice additur stella.

Suetonius *Divine Julius* 81, 88

2. **How do you think the appearance of the comet helped Augustus?**

The whole passage
1. **How do the omens described in the passage add to Caesar's importance?**
2. **Why might Caesar have chosen to ignore the omens?**

proposuerat: propono propose, intend

differret: differo *here* put off, postpone

Decimo Bruto: Decimus Brutus, m. Decimus Brutus, one of the chief conspirators

adhortante: adhortor + ne + infin. urge not to

15 **frequentes, m. pl.** *here* those attending in large numbers

iam dudum now for a long time

opperientes: opperior wait

destitueret: destituo desert, *here* let down

quinta fere hora almost at the fifth hour

progressus est: progredior go out

libellum: libellus, m. little book, paper

insidiarum: insidiae, f. pl. conspiracy

indicem: index, -icis, m. f. summary

obvio: obvius on the way

porrectum: porrigo *here* hold out, offer

ab obvio quodam by someone who met him on the way

commiscuit: commisceo mix, put in with

sinistra manu in his left hand

quasi as if

dein = deinde then

pluribus: plures *here* many

hostiis: hostia, f. victim, sacrificed animal

caesis: caedo kill

litare: lito obtain favourable omens

introiit: introeo go into

spreta: sperno reject, make light of

religione: religio, -onis, f. religion, ritual

irridens: irrideo make fun of, pour scorn on

20 **ut falsum** as false, as a false seer

arguens: arguo prove, show up

ulla: ullus any

sua *here* to himself

noxa: noxa, f. harm, injury

adessent: adsum be here

is i.e. Spurinna

quidem indeed

Decimus Brutus

praeterisse = praeteriisse: praetereo pass, be gone

ludis: ludi, m. pl. gladiatorial games

heres, -edis, m. f. heir

Augustus, m. Caesar Augustus (who became the first Roman emperor)

edebat: edo *here* put on (show, games)

quos primos ... edebat the first that Augustus put on for him (Caesar) as a god

stella crinita, f. comet, *lit.* long-haired star

per septem continuos dies for seven days on end

fulsit: fulgeo shine

exoriens: exorior rise

circa undecimam horam about the eleventh hour

animam: anima, f. soul

recepti: recipio take, receive

25 **hac de causa** for this reason

simulacro: simulacrum, n. statue

vertice: vertex, -icis, m. *here* top of the head

additur: addo add

4. Caesar crosses the Rubicon

The river Rubicon was the boundary of Caesar's province. By crossing it with his army Caesar would be committing treason.

> iam gelidas Caesar cursu superaverat Alpes
> ingentesque animo motus bellumque futurum
> ceperat. ut ventum est parvi Rubiconis ad undas,
> ingens visa duci patriae trepidantis imago
> 5   clara per obscuram vultu maestissima noctem
> turrigero canos effundens vertice crines
> caesarie lacera nudisque adstare lacertis
> et gemitu permixta loqui: 'quo tenditis ultra?
> quo fertis mea signa, viri? si iure venitis,
> 10 si cives, huc usque licet.' tum perculit horror
> membra ducis, riguere comae gressumque coercens
> languor in extrema tenuit vestigia ripa.
> mox ait 'o magnae qui moenia prospicis urbis
> Tarpeia de rupe Tonans Phrygiique penates
> 15 gentis Iuleae et rapti secreta Quirini
> et residens celsa Latiaris Iuppiter Alba
> Vestalesque foci summique o numinis instar
> Roma, fave coeptis. non te furialibus armis
> persequor: en, adsum victor terraque marique
> 20 Caesar, ubique tuus (liceat modo, nunc quoque) miles.
> ille erit ille nocens, qui me tibi fecerit hostem.'
> inde moras solvit belli tumidumque per amnem
> signa tulit propere
>
> ...

1. How does the description of the image of Rome make it clear that she believes Caesar is acting wrongly?

gelidas: gelidus icy, freezing
Caesar, -is, m. *here* Julius Caesar
cursu: cursus, -us, m. journey
superaverat: supero overcome, defeat
Alpes: Alpes, -ium, f. pl. Alps
motus: motus, -us, m. movement
futurum: futurus future, to come
ceperat: capio form, conceive
ventum est he came
undas: unda, f. water, stream
Rubiconis: Rubico, -onis, m. the River Rubicon (boundary between Italy and Caesar's province of Gaul)
visa (est): videor + *dat.* be seen by, appear to
duci: dux, ducis, m. leader
patriae: patria, f. fatherland, native country
trepidantis: trepidans anxious, in distress
imago, -inis, f. image, vision
5 **clara: clarus** bright, clear
obscuram: obscurus dark
vultu: vultus, -us, m. face
maestissima: maestus sad, sorrowful
noctem: nox, noctis, f. night
vultu maestissima showing great sorrow in her face
duci visa (est) imago patriae trepidantis, clara per obscuram noctem, vultu maestissima, ...
turrigero: turriger turreted, crowned with turrets
canos: canus white
effundens: effundo pour out, let loose
vertice: vertex, -icis, m. top, *here* top of head, head
crines: crinis, -is, m. hair
caesarie: caesaries, f. hair, locks
lacera: lacer torn, rent
canos crines effundens turrigero vertice, caesarie lacera
lacertis: lacertus, m. shoulder, upper arm
nudis: nudus bare
adstare = adstabat: adsto stand near, stand before
gemitu: gemitus, -us, m. groan, sigh

permixta: permixtus mixed together, mingled
loqui = loquebatur: loquor speak
nudisque ... loqui and (she) stood before him, her shoulders bare, and spoke and groaned together
quo? whither? to what place?
tenditis: tendo reach out, go to
ultra further, beyond (this point)
signa: signum, n. sign, *here* military standards
iure lawfully
10 **huc usque** only as far as this
perculit: percello strike down
horror, -oris, m. shaking, trembling, dread
membra: membrum, n. limb
riguere = riguerunt: rigeo be stiff, stand on end
comae, f. pl. hair
gressum: gressus, -us, m. step, course
coercens: coerceo check, restrain
languor, -oris, m. weakness, faintness
vestigia: vestigium, n. footstep
ripa: ripa, f. river bank
in extrema ... ripa at the very edge of the river bank
ait he says
moenia: moenia, -ium, n. pl. walls
prospicis: prospicio look out at
Tarpeia de rupe from the Tarpeian Rock (from which traitors were thrown)
Tonans, m. the Thunderer (the god Jupiter)
o Tonans, qui prospicis moenia magnae urbis de Tarpeia rupe
Phrygii: Phrygius *here* Trojan, of Troy (city in Phrygia)
penates, -ium, m. pl. penates, household gods
15 **gentis Iuleae: gens Iulea, f.** clan of Iulus (Aeneas' son, claimed as ancestor by Caesar)
rapti: rapio carry off/away (*here* to heaven)
secreta: secretum, n. secret, mystery

Quirini: Quirinus, m. Quirinus (Romulus, founder of Rome, when worshipped as a god)
residens: resideo settle, remain
celsa: celsus high, lofty
Latiaris of Latium, Latin
Alba: Alba, f. Alba Longa, mother city of Rome built by Iulus
et Latiaris Juppiter, residens celsa Alba
Vestales: Vestalis of Vesta (goddess of hearth)
foci: focus, m. hearth
numinis: numen, -inis, n. divine power, god, deity
instar, n. (*indecl.*) image
o Roma, instar summi numinis
fave: faveo + *dat.* favour, look on with favour
coeptis: coeptum, n. what is begun, undertaking
furialibus: furialis of the Furies, furious, vengeful
armis: arma, n. pl. arms, weapons
persequor pursue
en see! behold!
adsum I am present/here
victor, -oris, m. victor, conqueror
20 **ubique** everywhere
liceat modo, nunc quoque at this time too, if I am only allowed
nocens guilty, at fault
ille qui me fecerit hostem tibi, ille erit nocens
inde then
mora, f. delay, hindrance
solvit: solvo loose, break down, remove
tumidum: tumidus swollen
amnem: amnis, -is, m. river
propere quickly, in haste

...
Caesar, ut adversam superato gurgite ripam
25   attigit, Hesperiae vetitis et constitit arvis,
'hic' ait 'hic pacem temerataque iura relinquo;
te, Fortuna, sequor. procul hinc iam foedera sunto;
credidimus satis his, utendum est iudice bello.'

Lucan Civil War 1.183–205, 223–227

2. How does Caesar's mood change as he approaches the Rubicon, then sees the image and finally decides to cross?
3. Comment on the way the poet describes Caesar as 'defeating' the Alps (line 1) and the river (line 24).

5. Praying for profit

The poet makes fun of the man who prays for wealth but loses it all in offerings.

rem struere exoptas caeso bove Mercuriumque
arcessis fibra: 'da fortunare Penates,
da pecus et gregibus fetum.' quo, pessime, pacto,
tot tibi cum in flamma iunicum omenta liquescant?
5   et tamen hic extis et opimo vincere ferto
intendit: 'iam crescit ager, iam crescit ovile,
iam dabitur, iam iam'; donec deceptus et exspes
nequiquam fundo suspiret nummus in imo.

Persius Satires 2.44–52

1. How does Persius bring out the irony of the situation with the use of the word 'iam'?

6. A sign from heaven

parcus deorum cultor et infrequens
insanientis dum sapientiae
    consultus erro, nunc retrorsum
    vela dare atque iterare cursus

5   cogor relictos: namque Diespiter,
igni corusco nubila dividens
    plerumque, per purum tonantes
    egit equos volucremque currum,

adversam: adversus opposite
gurgite: gurges, -itis, *m.*
whirlpool, *here* swirling
waters
25 **attigit: attingo** touch, reach
Hesperiae: Hesperia, *f.* Italy
vetitis: veto forbid
constitit: consisto stand
arvis: arvum, *n.* field
temerata: temero violate,
dishonour
iura: ius, iuris, *n.* law
Fortuna, *f.* Fortune (goddess)
sequor follow
procul far away
hinc from here
foedera: foedus, -eris, *n.*
treaty
sunto let ... be
utendum: utor + *abl.* use
utendum (nobis) est we must
use
iudice: iudex, -icis, *m.* judge

rem: res, *f.* thing, *here* wealth
struere: struo pile up
exoptas: exopto long for
caeso: caedo kill, slaughter
bove: bos, bovis, *m.* bull
Mercurium: Mercurius, *m.*
Mercury (god of wealth and
profit)
arcessis: accesso send for
fibra, *f.* entrails, *here* liver
da: do give, grant
fortunare: fortuno prosper,
make
Penates, -ium, *m. pl.*
household gods
da fortunare Penates grant
that the household gods
prosper me/make my fortune
pecus: pecus, -oris, *n.* cattle
gregibus: grex, gregis, *m.*
flock, herd
fetum: fetus, -us, *m.* offspring
quo ... pacto how
pessime you wretch, you fool
flamma: flamma, *f.* flame
omentum, *n.* fat, bowel, fatty
entrails
iunicum: iunix, -icis, *f.* young
cow, heifer
tot tibi ... iunicum omenta
the fat of so many heifers of
yours
liquescant: liquesco melt
5 **extis: exta, *n. pl.*** internal
organs, esp. heart, lungs and
liver used for divination

opimo: opimus rich, fat
vincere: vinco *here* get what
one wants
ferto: fertum, *n.* cake-offering
intendit: intendo *here*
concentrate on, be
determined to
iam now
crescit: cresco increase
ager, *m.* field
ovile, -is, *n.* sheepfold
donec until
deceptus: decipio deceive,
cheat
exspes without hope, in
despair
nequiquam in vain
fundo: fundus, *m.* bottom
suspiret: suspiro sigh
nummus, *m.* coin, *here* a
single/solitary coin
in fundo imo at the very
bottom (*here* of a purse,
money-box etc.)

parcus thrifty, frugal
cultor, -oris, *m. here*
worshipper
infrequens infrequent,
occasional
insanientis: insaniens *here*
without reason
sapientiae: sapientia, *f.*
wisdom, philosophy
consultus expert in
erro wander
retrorsum = retroversum
back, for the return
vela: velum, *n.* sail
vela dare: vela do set sail
iterare: itero repeat, *here* steer
again
cursus: cursus, -us, *m.*
course
nunc cogor vela dare retrorsum
atque iterare cursus relictos
5 **namque** for
Diespiter, *m.* = the god Jupiter
igni: ignis, ignis, *m.* fire, *here*
lightning
corusco: coruscus flashing
nubila: nubila, -orum, *n. pl.*
clouds
dividens: divido divide, part
plerumque for the most part,
usually
purum, *n.* clear, bright sky
tonantes thundering
egit: ago drive

volucrem: volucer winged,
flying
currum: currus, -us, *m.*
chariot

quo bruta tellus et vaga flumina,
10   quo Styx et invisi horrida Taenari
          sedes Atlanteusque finis
          concutitur. valet ima summis

mutare et insignem attenuat deus,
obscura promens; hinc apicem rapax
15   Fortuna cum stridore acuto
          sustulit, hic posuisse gaudet.

Horace *Odes* 1.34

1. How does the poet compare following his beliefs to making a journey?
2. How does the poet describe the impact of the thunder?
3. What is different about the mood of the poem at the end compared to the beginning?

7. The shield of Aeneas

Venus gives her son armour, made by the god Vulcan. The shield is covered in scenes showing Rome' future.

at Venus aetherios inter dea candida nimbos
dona ferens aderat; natumque in valle reducta
ut procul egelido secretum flumine vidit,
talibus adfata est dictis seque obtulit ultro:
5   'en perfecta mei promissa coniugis arte
munera. ne mox aut Laurentes, nate, superbos
aut acrem dubites in proelia poscere Turnum.'
dixit, et amplexus nati Cytherea petivit,
arma sub adversa posuit radiantia quercu.
10   ille deae donis et tanto laetus honore
expleri nequit atque oculos per singula volvit,
miraturque interque manus et bracchia versat
terribilem cristis galeam flammasque vomentem,
fatiferumque ensem, loricam ex aere rigentem,
15   sanguineam, ingentem, qualis cum caerula nubes
solis inardescit radiis longeque refulget;

quo by which (referring to the chariot)

bruta: brutus *here* immovable still

tellus, -uris, f. earth

vaga: vagus wandering

10 **Styx, f.** Styx (a river of the Underworld)

invisi: invisus hated

horrida: horridus *here* dreadful

Taenari: Taenarus, m. town believed to be entrance to Underworld

sedes, -is, f. seat, dwelling, *here* depth

Atlanteus of Atlas/of Mt Atlas in Libya

finis, -is, m. end, boundary

Atlanteus finis the boundary where Atlas stands/marked by Atlas

concutitur: concutio shake

valet: valeo has strength/ power

ima summis mutare to change the lowest for the highest

insignem: insignis prominent, well known

attenuat: attenuo decrease diminish

obscura: obscurus dark, hidden, *here* unknown, insignificant

promens: promo bring forward, promote

hinc from here, *here* from one man

apicem: apex, -icis, m. highest point, *here* crown

rapax grasping

15 **Fortuna, f.** Fortune (goddess)

stridore: stridor, -oris, m. scream, shriek (any harsh, shrill sound)

acuto: acutus sharp, *here* piercing

sustulit: tollo lift off, remove

hic here, *here* on this man

gaudet: gaudeo + *infin.* rejoices, takes pleasure

Venus, -eris, f. Venus, mother of Aeneas (Roman goddess of love and beauty)

aetherios: aetherius airy, ethereal, heavenly

candida: candidus white, *here* bright, shining

nimbos: nimbus, m. cloud

aderat: adsum be present, come

at Venus aderat, dona ferens, dea candida inter nimbos aetherios

natum: natus, m. son

valle: vallis, -is, f. valley

reducta: reductus remote, lonely, secluded

ut procul in the distance

egelido: egelidus chill, cold

secretum: secretus cut off

adfata est: adfor speak to, address

dictis: dictum, -eris, n. word

se obtulit appeared

ultro suddenly, of one's own accord

5 **en** Look! Behold!

perfecta: perficio finish

promissa: promitto promise

munera: munus, -eris, n. gift

perfecta mei promissa coniugis arte finished by the promised skill of my husband

mox soon, from now on

Laurentes, m. pl. Laurentines (tribe living on coast of Latium)

superbos: superbus proud

acrem: acer *here* violent

dubites: dubito hesitate

poscere: posco demand, *here* call up

Turnum: Turnus, m. Turnus, prince of the Rutulians

amplexus: amplexus, -us, m. embrace

Cytherea, f. Cytherea, Venus (worshipped at Cythera)

arma: arma, n. pl. armour

adversa: adversus in front of (him), facing (him)

radiantia: radians shining, gleaming

quercu: quercus, -us, f. oak tree

arma radiantia posuit sub quercu adversa

10 **deae donis et tanto laetus honore** delighted with the honour of his mother's gifts

expleri: expleo fill, satisfy

nequit: nequeo be unable to

expleri nequit *here* could not look enough

oculos: oculus, m. eye

singula: singuli *pl. adj.* each, single, every single

volvit: volvo roll

oculos per singula voluit gazes at every single piece, *lit.* rolls his eyes over every single object

miratur: miror wonder at, be amazed

bracchia: bracchium, n. arm

versat: verso turn, turn over

interque manus et bracchia versat ... and he takes into his hands and arms and turns over ...

cristis: crista, f. crest (of helmet)

galeam: galea, f. helmet

flammas: flamma, f. flame

vomentem: vomo vomit, *here* pour out

fatiferum: fatifer deadly, bringing death

ensem: ensis, -is, m. sword

loricam: lorica, f. *here* breastplate

aere: aes, aeris, m. bronze

rigentem: rigeo be stiff

15 **sanguineam: sanguineus** blood-red

qualis cum as when

caerula: caerulus dark, dark blue

nubes, -is, f. cloud

solis: sol, -is, m. sun

inardescit: inardesco burn, be set on fire, glow

radiis: radius, m. *here* beam, ray

longe a long way off, far away. in the distance

refulget: refulgeo reflect (light), flash back

tum leves ocreas electro auroque recocto,
hastamque et clipei non enarrabile textum.
illic res Italas Romanorumque triumphos
20   haud vatum ignarus venturique inscius aevi
fecerat ignipotens, illic genus omne futurae
stirpis ab Ascanio pugnataque in ordine bella.

1. In lines 10–12 how does Aeneas react to the gift of the armour?
2. Pick out words to do with brightness and shining in this passage, and discuss
   how they are used.
3. What makes the shield of particular interest to Aeneas?

The early history of Rome (omitted), and then events that happened in the poet's
lifetime, with the Battle of Actium shown in the middle of the shield.

The battle ships are lined up

haec inter tumidi late maris ibat imago
aurea, sed fluctu spumabant caerula cano,
25   et circum argento clari delphines in orbem
aequora verrebant caudis aestumque secabant.
in medio classes aeratas, Actia bella,
cernere erat, totumque instructo Marte videres
fervere Leucaten auroque effulgere fluctus.
30   hinc Augustus agens Italos in proelia Caesar
cum patribus populoque, penatibus et magnis dis,
stans celsa in puppi, geminas cui tempora flammas
laeta vomunt patriumque aperitur vertice sidus.
parte alia ventis et dis Agrippa secundis
35   arduus agmen agens, cui, belli insigne superbum,
tempora navali fulgent rostrata corona.

4. How does Virgil suggest movement in this scene from the shield?

leves: **levis** smooth

ocreas: ocrea, *f.* greave, leg armour

electro: electrum, *n.* amber, *here* metal alloy the colour of amber

recocto: recoquo cook, forge again

electro auroque recocto made of reforged amber and gold

hastam: hasta, *f.* spear

clipei: clipeus, *m.* shield

enarrabile: enarrabilis that can be described

textum: textum, *n.* fabric

tum leves ocreas (versat) ... hastamque et clipei ... textum

illic there, *here* on it

res Italas: res Italae, *f. pl.* the events in Italy, *lit.* the Italian things/matters

20 **haud ... ignarus** not unacquainted with, not unmindful of, fully aware of

vatum: vates, -is, *m.f.* seer, prophet, soothsayer

venturi: venturus that is to come, of the future

aevi: aevum, *n.* time, age

(haud) inscius (not) unknowing, knowing full well

ignipotens, -entis, *m.* master of fire, the god Vulcan

genus: genus, -eris, *n. here* race

stirpis: stirps, -pis, *f.* stem, offspring, descent

Ascanio: Ascanius, *m.* Ascanius (son of Aeneas)

pugnata: pugno fight

in ordine in order

haec inter = inter haec

tumidi: tumidus swelling

late widely, broadly, in its breadth

ibat: eo go, *here* pass, wind, flow

imago, -inis, *f.* image, picture

aurea: aureus golden, made of gold

fluctu; fluctus, -us, *m.* wave, surf

spumabant: spumo foam

caerula, caerulorum, *n. pl.* blue sea/surface of the sea

cano: canus white

25 **argento: argentum**, *n.* silver

clari: clarus bright, distinct, picked out

delphines: delphin, -inis, *m.* dolphin

circum ... in orbem around in a circle

aequora: aequor, -oris, *n.* sea, surface of the sea

verrebant: verro sweep

caudis: cauda, *f.* tail

aestum: aestus, -us, *m.* surge (of the sea)

secabant: seco cut, cut through

in medio in the middle (of the shield)

classes: classis, -is, *f.* fleet

aeratas: aeratus made of bronze, armed with bronze

Actia: Actius of/at Actium, where Octavian defeated Antony and Cleopatra

cernere: cerno see

erat *here* it was possible

totum ... instructo Marte with full battle order, *lit.* with Mars fully drawn up

videres you might see

fervere: fervo = ferveo boil, seethe

Leucaten (*Greek acc.*): **Leucate** Leucate (a promontory near Actium)

effulgere: effulgeo shine/blaze out

30 **hinc** on this side

Augustus ... Caesar Octavian (later Augustus, first Roman emperor)

hinc (est) Augustus ... Caesar ...

agens: ago lead

proelia: proelium, *n.* battle

patribus: patres, -um, *m. pl.* fathers, *here* Senate

penatibus: penates, -ium, *m. pl.* Penates, Roman household gods

dis = deis

celsa: celsus high, raised

puppi: puppis, *f.* poop, stern (of ship)

geminas: geminus twin, two, double

cui = cuius whose

tempora, -orum, *n. pl.* temples (of head)

patrium: patrius of a father, *here* his father's (referring to Julius Caesar)

aperitur: aperio (*pass.*) appear

vertice: vertex, -icis, *m. here* on his head

sidus: sidus, -eris, *n.* star

parte alia in another part (of the shield)

ventis: ventus, *m.* wind

Agrippa, Agrippae, *m.* Marcus Vipsanius Agrippa, Octavian's general

secundis: secundus favourable, on one's side

35 **arduus** high, elevated *here* at their head

agmen: agmen, -inis, *n.* battle line

insigne, -is, *n.* badge of honour, decoration

superbum: superbus proud, splendid

belli insigne superbum his proud decoration of war

fulgent: fulgeo shine

rostrata: rostratus adorned with the beaks (**rostra**) from ships' prows

navali ... corona: navalis corona, *f.* Naval Crown

cui tempora rostrata fulgent navali corona, belli insigne superbum

hinc ope barbarica variisque Antonius armis,
victor ab Aurorae populis et litore rubro,
Aegyptum viresque Orientis et ultima secum
40 Bactra vehit, sequiturque (nefas) Aegyptia coniunx.
una omnes ruere ac totum spumare reductis
convulsum remis rostrisque tridentibus aequor.
alta petunt; pelago credas innare revulsas
Cycladas aut montes concurrere montibus altos,
45 tanta mole viri turritis puppibus instant.
stuppea flamma manu telisque volatile ferrum
spargitur, arva nova Neptunia caede rubescunt.
regina in mediis patrio vocat agmina sistro,
necdum etiam geminos a tergo respicit angues.
50 omnigenumque deum monstra et latrator Anubis
contra Neptunum et Venerem contraque Minervam
tela tenent. saevit medio in certamine Mavors
caelatus ferro, tristesque ex aethere Dirae,
et scissa gaudens vadit Discordia palla,
55 quam cum sanguineo sequitur Bellona flagello.

Battle of Actium

hinc on the other side (see **hinc** line 30)

ope: ops, opis, f. power, wealth

barbarica: barbaricus barbaric, outlandish, exotic

variis: varius varied, different, motley

victor, -oris, m. victor

Aurorae: Aurora, f. Dawn, the east

populis: populus, m. people

litore rubro: litus rubrum the red shore, the shore of the Indian Ocean

Aegyptum: Aegyptus, f. Egypt

vires: vires, virium, f. pl. strength

Orientis: Oriens, -tis, m. the east

ultima: ultimus most remote, distant

40 **Bactra: Bactra, n. pl.** Bactra, the chief city in Bactria in central Asia

vehit: veho carry, bring

hinc ... Antonius ... victor ... Aegyptum ... vehit

sequitur: sequor follow

nefas, n. indecl. crime, impious/wicked action, *here* what a crime! how shameful/shocking!

Aegyptia coniunx, f. Egyptian wife (Cleopatra)

una together

ruere = ruebant: ruo rush

spumare = spumabant

reductis: reduco draw back

convulsum: convello break/tear up, split open

remis: remus, m. oar

rostris: rostrum, n. beak, curved end of ship's prow

tridentibus: tridens *lit.* with three teeth, three-pronged, triple

totum aequor spumare, convulsum remis reductis rostrisque tridentibus

alta: alta, n. pl. *here* deep water, open sea

pelago: pelagus, n. sea

credas: credo *here* you might think/believe

innare: inno swim/float in/on

revulsas: revello tear out, uproot

Cycladas: Cyclades, f. pl. the Cyclades (islands in Aegean Sea)

concurrere: concurro collide, clash

45 **mole: moles, -is, f.** mass. bulk

turritis: turritus towered, turreted

instant: insto stand on

tanta mole ... instant so great is the mass in which the men stand on the towered poops, *lit.* the men stand in so great mass on the towered poops

stuppea: stuppeus made of tow (coarse, fibrous part of flax)

stuppea flamma weapons of flaming tow

telis: telum, n. missile, weapon

volatile: volatilis winged, flying, given wings/flight

ferrum, n. iron

spargitur: spargo throw about, scatter, shower

arva: arvum, n. pl. fields, *here* water

nova: novus new, fresh

Neptunia: Neptunius of/belonging to Neptune

caede: caedes, -is, f. slaughter, bloodshed

rubescunt: rubesco grow red

arva Neptunia rubescunt nova caede

regina, f. queen (Cleopatra)

in mediis in the middle, in the midst

patrio: patrius of the native land

sistro: sistrum, n. sistrum (Egyptian rattle used in worship of Isis)

respicit: respicio look back at, have thought of

necdum etiam ... respicit as yet had no thought of

angues: anguis, -is, m.f. snake

tergo: tergum, n. back

a tergo behind

50 **omnigenum = omnigenorum: omnigenus** of all kinds

deum = deorum

monstra: monstrum, n. monster

deum monstra *here* monstrous forms of gods

latrator, -oris, m. barker, *here* the barking god

Anubis, m. Egyptian god with head of a jackal

contra + *acc.* against

Neptunum: Neptunus, m. Neptune (Roman god of the sea)

Minervam: Minerva, f. Minerva (Roman equivalent of Athene, goddess of wisdom and warfare)

saevit: saevio rage

certamine: certamen, -inis, n. contest, conflict, battle

Mavors, m. = Mars, m. Mars (Roman god of war)

caelatus engraved, shaped

tristes: tristis sad, stern, harsh

aethere: aether, -eris, m. upper air, sky

Dirae, Dirarum, f. pl. Dread Goddesses, Furies

tristesque ... Dirae (saeviunt)

scissa: scissus torn

gaudens: gaudeo + *abl.* delight/rejoice/take pleasure in

vadit: vado go, rush in

Discordia, f. Discord, Strife (goddess who causes civil war)

palla: palla, f. robe, mantle

55 **sanguineo: sanguineus** blood-stained

Bellona, f. Bellona, (goddess of war, sister of Mars)

flagello: flagellum, n. whip, scourge

Actius haec cernens arcum intendebat Apollo
desuper; omnis eo terrore Aegyptus et Indi,
omnis Arabs, omnes vertebant terga Sabaei.
ipsa videbatur ventis regina vocatis
60   vela dare et laxos iam iamque immittere funes.
illam inter caedes pallentem morte futura
fecerat ignipotens undis et Iapyge ferri,
contra autem magno maerentem corpore Nilum
pandentemque sinus et tota veste vocantem
65   caeruleum in gremium latebrosaque flumina victos.

5. **How do the forces of Augustus contrast with those of Antony?**
6. **What part do the gods play in the battle?**
7. **In lines 61–65, does the poet arouse sympathy for the Egyptian queen (Cleopatra)?**

Caesar celebrates his triumph in Rome. The nations shown reveal the extent of the future empire.

at Caesar, triplici invectus Romana triumpho
moenia, dis Italis votum immortale sacrabat,
maxima ter centum totam delubra per urbem.
laetitia ludisque viae plausuque fremebant;
70   omnibus in templis matrum chorus, omnibus arae;
ante aras terram caesi stravere iuvenci.
ipse sedens niveo candentis limine Phoebi
dona recognoscit populorum aptatque superbis
postibus; incedunt victae longo ordine gentes,
75   quam variae linguis, habitu tam vestis et armis.

Coin celebrating Augustus' victory at Actium

Actius of Actium

cernens: cerno see

intendebat: intendo stretch, bend (a bow)

arcum: arcus, -us, m. bow

Apollo, -inis, m. god of music and archery who protected the Trojans

desuper from above

eo terrore at that terror

Indi, m. pl. Indians

Arabs, m. Arab

vertebant: verto turn

Sabaei, m. pl. Sabaeans (people of Saba in Arabia)

videbatur *here* could be seen

60 **vela: velum, n.** sail

vela dare: vela do set sail

laxos: laxus loose

iam iamque at that very moment

immittere: immitto *here* let go, slacken

funes: funis, -is, m. rope, sheet (of sail)

laxos ... immittere funes let the ropes go slack (i.e to let the sails fill)

pallentem: pallens pale

morte: mors, -tis, f. death

futura: futurus future, impending

fecerat: facio *here* show, portray, represent

undis: unda, f. wave

Iapyge: Iapyx, m. north-west wind (favourable for sailing from Actium to Alexandria)

ferri *(pass. inf.)* **fero** *here* being carried

contra *(adv.)* opposite, facing (her)

autem but, however, yet

maerentem: maerens grieving, in sorrow

magno ... corpore in his mighty stream/waters

pandentem: pando open, spread out

sinus: sinus, -us, m. curve, hollow, fold (of clothing)

veste: vestis, -is, f. clothing, robe, mantle

65 **caeruleum: caeruleus** dark, blue, sea-green, azure (colour of water and sky)

gremium: gremium, n. lap, bosom

latebrosa: latebrosus hidden, secret

flumina: flumen, -inis, n. flow, river, current

contra (fecerat ignipotens) Nilum ... maerentem ... pandentemque ... vocantem

Caesar, -is, m. Caesar, *here* Augustus Caesar (see line 30)

triplici: triplex threefold, triple (referring to Augustus' triumphs in Illyricum, Actium and Egypt)

invectus: invehor be carried into, enter

triumpho: triumphus, m. triumph, triumphal procession

moenia, -ium, n. pl. city walls

votum: votum, n. vow

immortale: immortalis deathless

sacrabat: sacro *here* make (a vow), dedicate

ter centum three hundred

delubra: delubrum, n. shrine

laetitia: laetitia, f. joy, gladness

ludis: ludus, m. game, show, spectacle

fremebant: fremo roar, resound

plausu: plausus, -us, m. applause

70 **chorus, m.** dance, choral dance

(erat) chorus matrum mothers were singing and dancing

arae: ara, f. altar

ante + *acc.* before, in front of

terram: terra, f. *here* ground

caesi: caedo kill, slaughter

stravere = straverunt *(perf.)*: **sterno** stretch over, be spread over cover

iuvenci: iuvencus, m. bullock, young bull

ipse he himself, i.e. Caesar

niveo: niveus snowy, snow-white

candentis: candens shining, dazzling

limine: limen, -inis, n. threshold

Phoebi: Phoebus, m. Phoebus (the sun god Phoebus Apollo)

limine Phoebi on the threshold of Phoebus (marble temple of Apollo, dedicated by Augustus)

recognoscit: recognosco recognise, recall, *here* review, inspect

aptat: apto put on, fasten to

postibus: postis, -is, m. post, door-post

incedunt: incedo move, approach

longo ordine in a long line

gentes: gens, -tis, f. race, nation

linguis: lingua, f. tongue, language

habitu: habitus, -us, m. type, appearance, style

75 **quam variae ... et armis** just as varied in the appearance of their dress and weapons as in their languages

hic Nomadum genus et discinctos Mulciber Afros,
hic Lelegas Carasque sagittiferosque Gelonos
finxerat; Euphrates ibat iam mollior undis,
extremique hominum Morini, Rhenusque bicornis,
80   indomitique Dahae, et pontem indignatus Araxes.

8. How does the poet convey the scale of Augustus' triumph?
9. Euphrates, Rhenus, Araxes (lines 78–80): how are these rivers portrayed as
   people?

Aeneas takes up his shield

talia per clipeum Volcani, dona parentis,
miratur rerumque ignarus imagine gaudet
attollens umero famamque et fata nepotum.

Virgil *Aeneid* 8.608–629, 671–731

10. Comment on the symbolism of Aeneas' carrying the shield.

The whole passage
1. How does the description of the shield go beyond a series of pictures?
2. Is the prophecy of Rome's future greatness included to encourage Aeneas or to
   flatter the poet's readers?

Nomadum: Nomades, *m.* *pl.* nomadic tribes of Africa, Numidians

genus: genus, -eris, *n.* race, tribe

discinctos: discinctus in loose clothes

Mulciber, *m.* Vulcan, *lit.* the Softener (of metal)

Afros: Afri, *m. pl.* Africans *hic Mulciber ... (finxerat)*

Lelegas Carasque: Lelages Caresque, *m. pl.* Lelages and Carians (tribes of Asia Minor)

sagittiferos: sagittiferus carrying arrows

Gelonos: Geloni, *m. pl.* Gelonians (tribe of Scythia)

finxerat: fingo form, shape, fashion

Euphrates, *m.* the river Euphrates

ibat *here* flowed

mollior: mollis soft, gentle, calm

undis: unda, *f.* *here* stream, movement of its waters

extremi: extremus furthermost, most remote

Morini, *m. pl.* Morini (tribe on the Channel coast of northern Gaul)

Rhenus, *m.* the river Rhine

bicornis with two horns, *here* mouths

80 **indomiti: indomitus** unconquered

Dahae, *m. pl.* Dahae, Scythian tribe

pontem: pons, -tis, *m.* bridge

indignatus displeased at, resenting

Araxes, *m.* the river Araxes (in Armenia)

talia *here* such scenes as these

per + *acc. here* all over *(Aeneas) miratur*

rerum: res, *f.* thing, *here* event

imagine gaudet takes pleasure in the picture of them

attollens: attollo lift up

umero: umerus, *m.* shoulder

famam: fama, *f.* fame

fata: fatum, *n.* fate, destiny

nepotum: nepos, -otis, *m.* descendant, *pl.* children's children

APPENDIX: THE LATIN WRITERS

CAESAR – **Gaius Iulius Caesar (100–44 BC).** One of the great figures of the ancient world, both as a general and a statesman. He wrote his *Commentaries*, seven books on his campaign in Gaul and Britain (58–52 BC) and three on the Civil War, between himself and Pompey (49–48 BC). Cicero remarked that only a fool would try to improve on his accounts (*Brutus* 262).

CATULLUS – **Gaius Valerius Catullus (*c*.84–*c*.54 BC).** Born in Verona, he wrote poetry on a number of themes but is most famous for his passionate love poems addressed to 'Lesbia', who may have been a historical person, and if so, probably the notorious aristocrat Clodia.

CICERO – **Marcus Tullius Cicero (106–43 BC).** Born at Arpinum some 70 miles southeast of Rome, this celebrated Roman orator and statesman was a prolific writer on many themes. Among his 58 surviving speeches are the 6 against Verres (*In Verrem*), the 4 against Catiline (*In Catilinam*), the 14 *Philippics* against Mark Antony, and the speech in defence of Milo (*Pro Milone*). Two works on oratory are *De Oratore (On the Orator)* and *Brutus*. We have more than 800 letters, including the collections *Ad Familiares (To his Friends)* and *Ad Atticum (To Atticus)*. Among his philosophical works are *De Republica* ('On the republic'), the theological *De Natura Deorum (On the Nature of the Gods)*, and the ethical *De Finibus (On Objectives)*, *De Senectute (On Old Age)*, and *De Officiis* ('On duties').

HORACE – **Quintus Horatius Flaccus (65–8 BC).** Born the son of a freedman in Venusia (Venosa) in Apulia, south Italy, he later became part of the circle of Maecenas, Augustus' patron of the arts, and rubbed shoulders with the most powerful politicians and the leading poets of his day. His published works consist of the *Epodes* and *Satires* (published in 30 BC), the *Epistles* – which include the *Art of Poetry* – and his major achievement, the *Odes* (published in 23 and 13 BC).

LIVY – **Titus Livius (59 BC–AD 17).** Born in Patavium (Padua) in northeast Italy, he became the friend of the emperor Augustus. He wrote a history of Rome from its foundation to 9 BC in 142 books. Only books 1–10 (dealing with 753–293 BC), 21–45 (dealing with 219–167 BC), and a fragment of book 91 survive.

LUCAN – **Marcus Annaeus Lucanus (AD 39–65).** Born at Corduba (Cordoba) in Spain, he was educated at Rome. After joining a conspiracy against the emperor Nero, he was forced to commit suicide. His incomplete poem (10 books), the *Civil War (Bellum Civile)*, deals with the war between Caesar and Pompey. Also known as *Pharsalia* after Caesar's victory over Pompey at Pharsalus in 48 BC, it promotes the republican cause, a bold stance under Nero.

OVID – **Publius Ovidius Naso (43 BC–AD 17).** Born at Sulmo in the Appenines about 90 miles east of Rome, he was educated and based there until about AD 8 when he was banished by the emperor Augustus for involvement in an imperial scandal and banished to Tomis (Constantza) on the Black Sea where he died.

A prolific poet, he wrote *Loves (Amores), Heroines (Heroides), The Technique of Love (Ars Amatoria)* and *How to Fall out of Love (Remedia Amoris)*. More politically correct works are *Calendar Days* and *Metamorphoses*, the latter proving to be his masterpiece. Other works include the two great poems of his exile, *Sad Poems (Tristia)* and *Letters from the Black Sea (Epistulae ex Ponto)*. The cheerful immorality of much of his verse belies the fact that alone of the Augustan poets he was a happily married man.

PERSIUS – **Aulus Persius Flaccus (AD 34–62).** Born in an equestrian family at Volaterrae in Etruria, he fell under the influence of the Stoics at Rome. He wrote one book of six *Satires*, modelled on Lucilius and Horace.

PLAUTUS – **Titus Maccius Plautus (*c*.250–184 BC).** Born at Sarsina in Umbria, he was the writer of up to 130 comedies, 20 of which survive. The plays are all adapted from Greek originals.

PLINY – **Gaius Plinius Caecilius Secundus (AD 61/2–*c*.113).** Known as Pliny the Younger, he had a highly successful political career which culminated in his admirable service as governor of Bithynia. His fame is due to his ten books of letters.

SUETONIUS – **Gaius Suetonius Tranquillus (born *c*.69 AD).** He became a secretary at the imperial palace. This gave him access to the imperial archives, but he was dismissed by Hadrian in 121/2 apparently for some indiscretion involving the emperor's wife. His surviving works include the *Lives of the Caesars (De Vita Caesarum)*.

SULPICIA – **Sulpicia** is the only known woman from Ancient Rome whose poetry survives in quantity to this day. She lived in the reign of Augustus, and was probably the daughter of Servius Sulpicius Rufus and a niece of Messalla, a politician and patron of literature. Her verses were preserved with those of Tibullus, and were for a long time attributed to him. They consist of six elegiac poems addressed to a lover called Cerinthus.

TACITUS – **Publius (or Gaius) Cornelius Tacitus (AD 56/57–after 117).** Possibly born in Narbonese Gaul, Tacitus had a successful political career. His historical writings include his monograph about his father-in-law, the general Agricola, and his major works, the *Histories* (covering the years AD 69–96) and *Annals* (covering AD 14–68). Much of these works is lost. The historian Edward Gibbon thought more highly of Tacitus than of any other ancient historian.

VIRGIL – **Publius Vergilius Maro (70–19 BC).** Born at Mantua in Cisalpine Gaul, Virgil was educated at Cremona, Milan and Rome. He became part of the circle of Maecenas, the great Augustan patron, and a friend and supporter of Augustus. His pastoral poems, the *Eclogues*, were perhaps published in 37 BC, the *Georgics*, his four-book didactic poem on farming, in 29, and his great twelve-book epic, the *Aeneid*, after his death. He was buried near Naples. The mediaeval Italian poet Dante regarded Virgil as 'our greatest poet'.

GENERAL VOCABULARY

a, ab + *abl.* from, away from, by, on the side of

ab oblīquō from the side

abdō, -ere, abdidī, abditum hide, conceal

abdūcō, -ere, abdūxī, abductum lead away, abduct

abeō, abīre, abiī, abitum go away, pass

abiciō, -ere, abiēcī, abiectum throw away

abigō, -ere, abēgī, abāctum drive away, dispel

abitus, -ūs, m. retreat

abnuō, -ere, abnuī, abnūtum reject, refuse

abripiō, -ere, abripuī, abreptum carry off

abrumpō, -ere, abrūpī, abruptum break off, tear away from

abscēdō, -ere, abscessī, abscessum depart, disappear

abstineō, -ere, abstinuī, abstentum stay away from, refuse

absum, abesse, afuī be out, be absent, be away

absūmptus removed, destroyed

absurdus senseless, irrational

abūtor, -utī, abūsus sum + *abl.* abuse, make use of

ac, atque and

accēdō, -ere, accessī, accessum approach, come near, *pass.* be added to

accendō, -ere, accendī, accēnsum blaze, set alight

accidō, -ere, accidī fall upon, happen

accingō, -ere, accīnxī, accīnctum prepare

acciō, -īre, accīvī, accītum send for, summon

accipiō, -ere, accēpī, acceptum accept, take in, receive, hear, welcome

accipiter, -tris, m. hawk

accola, m.f. dweller, inhabitant

accurrō, -ere, accurrī, accursum run up

accūsātor, -ōris, m. accuser, prosecutor

accūsō (1) accuse

ācer eager, acute, passionate, fierce violent

acerbus bitter, grievous

acētum, n. sour wine, vinegar

acies, -iēī, f. battle-line

Actius of/at Actium

actūtum quickly, instantly

acūtus sharp

ad + *acc.* to, towards, at, by the side of

ad usque + *acc.* all the way to, right up to

addō, -ere, addidī, additum add

adeō, adīre, adiī, aditum go to/into, approach

adeō so much, so greatly

adferō, -ferre, attulī, adlātum bring to, carry

adficiō, -ere, adfēcī, adfectum move, affect, fill

adfirmō (1) declare, vouch for the truth of

adflīctus struck, deprived of

adfor, adfārī, adfātus sum speak to, address

adhaereō, -ēre, adhaesī, adhaesum stick to

adhibeō, -ēre, adhibuī, adhibitum use, make use of

adhortor (1) encourage, urge

adhūc still, as yet, so far

adiciō, -ere, adiēcī, adiectum add to, bring to

adimō, -ere, adēmī, ademptum take away

adipiscor, adipīscī, adeptus sum achieve, bring about

aditus, -ūs, m. entrance, point of access

adiuvō, -āre, adiuvī, adiutum help

adlābor, -lābī, adlāpsus sum come in, flow in

administrō (1) perform, do, carry out

admirātiō, -ōnis, f. wonder, admiration

admittō, -ere, admīsī, admissum let in, allow; commit (a crime)

admodum fully, to the full

admoveō, -ēre, admōvī, admōtum move to, move (something) towards

adolescō, -ere, adolēvī, adultum grow up

adōrō (1) worship

adpāreō = appāreō

adprobō (1) approve

adscēnsus, -ūs, m. ascent

adsiduus constant, incessant

adspiciō = aspiciō

adsternō, -ere, adstrāvī, adstrātum prostrate oneself

adstō, -stāre, adstiti stand by/near/before

adsum, adesse, adfuī be here, be present; + *dat.* help

adulēscēns, -entis m. young man

adulter, m. adulterer, lover

adurō, -ere, adussī, adustum burn

adveniō, -venīre, -vēnī, -ventum arrive

adventō (1) advance, come closer, arrive

adventus, -ūs, m. arrival

adversor (1) oppose, be against, resist

adversus opposite, unfavourable, contrary

adversa, n. pl. setbacks, misfortunes

advertō, -ere, advertī, adversum turn

advesperāscit *impers.* it gets dark, evening falls

Aeacidēs, m. Achilles, descendant of Aeacus

aedīlis, -is, m. aedile

aegrē with difficulty, hardly

aegrōtō (1) be sick

Aegyptius Egyptian

Aegyptus, f. Egypt

aemulor (1) rival, emulate

aequālis equal

aequātus levelled

aequinoctium, n. equinox

aequor, -oris, n. sea, surface of the sea

aequus equal, even, favourable, reasonable, patient, calm

aerātus made of bronze, armed with bronze

aes, aeris, n. bronze, money

aestus, -ūs, m. tide, heat, current

aetās, -ātis, f. age, youth, life

aeternitās, -ātis, f. immortality, eternity

aethēr, -eris, m. sky, upper air

aetherius airy, ethereal, heavenly

aevum, n. age, time

Āfrī, m. pl. Africans

Āfricus African

ager, m. field

agger, -eris, m. rampart, wall, mound

agmen, -inis, n. column, group, force

agna, *f.* ewe lamb
agnōscō, -ere, agnōvī, agnitum recognise
agō, -ere, ēgī, āctum do, act, drive, lead
agrestis wild, rustic
aiō say
alacritās, -ātis, *f.* eagerness, keenness, spirit
albus white
ales, -itis swift
aliēnō (1) alienate
aliēnus of another
alii ... alii ... some ... others ...
aliquamdiū for some time
aliquandō sometimes
aliquantō somewhat, rather
aliquī, aliqua, aliquod some, any
aliquis, aliquid someone, something
aliquot some
aliter otherwise, other
alius, alia, aliud other, another, else
alloquor, -loquī, allocutus sum address
alō, -ere, aluī, alitum nourish
altāria, -ium, *n. pl.* altars
alter the other, another, the second of two
altitūdō, -inis, *f.* height, depth
altus high, deep
  altum, *n.* the sea, deep water
alvus, *f.* belly, bowels
amābilis pleasant
amārus bitter
ambigō, -ere go about, wander, doubt
ambō both
āmentia, *f.* madness
amīca, *f.* girlfriend, female friend
amīcus, *m.* friend
āmittō, -ere, āmīsī, āmissum lose
ammentum, *n.* strap, thong
amnis, -is, *m.* river
amō (1) love, like
amoenus pleasant
amor, -ōris, *m.* love
āmoveō, -ere, āmōvī, āmōtum remove
amplector, amplectī, amplexus sum embrace
amplexus, -ūs, *m.* embrace
amplius more
amputō cut around/off
an or, whether
ancora, *f.* anchor
ānfrāctus, -ūs, *m.* bend, zigzag
angō, -ere, ānxī, ānctum vex, trouble
anguis, -is, *m.f.* snake
angulus, *m.* corner

angustus narrow
  angustiae, *f. pl.* narrow places
anhēlitus, -ūs, *m.* panting
anīlis of an old woman
anima, *f.* soul, breath, life
animadvertō, -ere, animadvertī, animadversum notice, spot
animōsus strong, proud
animus, *m.* spirit, soul, mind
annus, *m.* year
ante + *acc.* before, in front of
ante first, before
antecēdō, -ere, antecessī, antecessum go before
anteferō, -ferre, antetulī, antelātum prefer
antenna, *f.* sail-yard, spar (supporting head of sail)
antepōnō, -ere, anteposuī, antepositum prefer
antequam before
antīquus ancient, of old
aper, *m.* boar
aperiō, -īre, aperuī, apertum open, reveal, lay bare
apertus open
apex, apicis, *m.* highest point
apis, -is, *f.* bee
Apollōniēnsis from Apollonia
appāreō, -ere, appāruī, appāritum appear, be seen
1 appellō (1) speak to, call
2 appellō, -ere, appulī, appulsum drive towards, bring in, put to land
appropinquō (1) + *dat.* approach, come near to
aprīcus sunny
aptō (1) put on, fasten to
aptus + *dat.* fit for, good for, suitable
apud + *acc.* at, among, with, at the house of
aqua, *f.* water
aquila, *f.* eagle
Aquilō, -ōnis, *m.* north wind
āra, *f.* altar
arbitror (1) think, consider
arbor, -ōris, *f.* tree
arboreus of a tree
arceō, -ēre, arcuī prevent, keep from
accessō, -ere, accessīvī, accessitum summon, send for
arcus, -ūs, *m.* bow
ardeō, -ere, arsī, arsum catch fire, blaze, burn
ardor, -ōris, *m.* heat, flame of passion
arduus high, elevated
ārea, *f.* courtyard

argentum, *n.* silver
arguō, -ere, arguī, argūtum claim, assert, prove
āridus dry
ariēs, -ietis *m.* ram
arista, *f.* ear of corn
arma, *n. pl.* weapons, armour
armātī, *m. pl.* armed men
arō (1) plough
Arpīnās, -ātis *(adj.)* of the town of Arpinum
arrēctus steep
arripiō, -ere, arripuī, arreptum seize, snatch
ars, artis, *f.* art, skill
artifex skilful
artus narrow
artūs, *m. pl.* limbs
arvum, *n.* field
arx, arcis, *f.* citadel
ascendō, -ere, ascendī, ascēnsum climb
asper rough
aspernor (1) despise
aspiciō, -ere, aspexī, aspectum consider, look at, see
ast/at but
āter black
Atlantēus of Atlas
atque and
attāctus, -ūs *m.* touch
attendō, -ere, attendī, attentum concentrate, listen
attentus attentive, careful
attenuō (1) lessen, reduce, diminish
attineō, -ēre, attinuī, attentum delay, detain
attingō, -ere, attigī, attāctum touch, reach
attollō, -ere lift up
attonitus astonished
attribuō, -ere, attribuī, attribūtum allot, assign
auceps, -cupis, *m.* bird-catcher
auctor, -ōris, *m.f.* creator, maker, father, prime mover, person with influence
audācia, *f.* boldness
audācter boldly, confidently
audāx, audācis bold, daring
audeō, -ēre, ausus sum dare
audiō, -īre, audīvī, audītum hear, listen to
auferō, -ferre, abstulī, ablātum take away, carry off, steal, remove
augeō, -ēre, auxī, auctum increase
auguror (1) predict, interpret
aura, *f.* air, breeze
aureus golden, made of gold

auris, -is, f. ear
Aurōra, f. Dawn, the East
aurum, n. gold
auspex, -icis, m. supporter
auspicātus fortunate, auspicious
aut or
    aut ... aut ... either ... or ...
autem but, however, yet, moreover
auxiliāris, m. auxiliary soldier
auxilium, n. help
avāritia, f. greed
avārus stingy, greedy
avē atque valē hail and farewell
āvellō, -ere, āvelli/āvulsī,
    āvulsum tear from, separate
    by force
āvertō, -ere, āvertī, āversum turn
    aside, drive away, knock out of
    position
avidus greedy, hungry, starving
avis, -is, f. bird
avītus ancestral, of a grandfather
avus, m. grandfather
axis, -is, m. vault of heaven, sky

balteus, m. belt, baldric
barba, f. beard
barbaricus barbaric, outlandish,
    exotic
barbarus, m./(adj.) foreigner,
    barbarian, enemy
bāsiō (1) kiss
beātus blessed, fortunate
bellō (1) fight war
bellum, n. war
bellus beautiful, pretty
bene well
benefacta, n. pl. good deeds
beneficium, n. kindness
bibō, bibere, bibī drink
bicornis with two horns
biduum, n. period of two days
biennium, n. period of two years
bifōrmis two-shaped
blandus flattering, kind
bōlētus, m. mushroom
bonus, bona, bonum good
    bona, n. pl. advantages
bōs, bovis, m. bull
bracchium, n. arm
brevis short, brief
    brevia, n. pl. shallows
brevitās, -ātis, f. brevity, shortness
Britannī, m. pl. the Britons
brūtus immovable, still, dull

cacūmen, -inis, n. peak
cadō, -ere, cecidī, cāsum fall, be
    slain
caedēs, -is, f. slaughter, murder

caedō, -ere, cecīdī, caesum cut,
    split, strike, kill
caelātus engraved, shaped
caelestis heavenly, divine
    caelestēs, -ium, m. pl. gods
caelum, n. sky, heaven
caeruleus dark, blue, sea-green
caerulus dark, dark blue
    caerula, n. pl. blue sea/sea surface
caesariēs, -iēī, f. hair, locks
caespes, -itis, m. turf
calamitās, -ātis, f. calamity
calciō (1) put shoes on
callidus experienced, canny
Camēna, f. Muse
camīnus, m. fire, furnace
campus, m. field, plain, battle field
candēns white, shining
candidus white, bright, shining
canis, canis, m.f. dog, bitch
canō, -ere, cecinī, cantum sing
cantō (1) sing
cantus, -ūs, m. spell, incantation
cānus white, ripened (of corn)
capāx, capācis spacious, roomy
capillī, m. pl. hair
capiō, -ere, cēpī, captum take,
    catch, capture, form
Capitōlium, n. the Capitoline hill
captīvus, m. captive, prisoner
caput, -itis, n. head, life, capital
carcer, -eris, m. prison; starting-gate
careō, -ēre, caruī, caritum + abl.
    lack, lose, be without/free from
carīna, f. keel, ship
carmen, -inis, n. song, poem
carnifex, -icis, m. executioner
carpō, -ere, carpsī, carptum pluck,
    take, make use of
    carpō iter make one's way, make
    a journey
cārus dear
castra, n. pl. camp
castus chaste, pure
cāsus, -ūs, m. fall, chance, leaving to
    chance
catēna, f. chain
caterva, f. crowd, squadron, troop
cathedra, f. chair
cauda, f. tail
caupō, -ōnis, m. tradesman, inn-
    keeper
caupōna, f. inn
causa, f. cause, reason, case
cautus cautious
caveō, -ēre, cāvī, cautum beware,
    be on guard against
cavus hollow
cedō, -ere, cessī, cessum yield, give
    way

celeber crowded, famous
celebrō (1) celebrate
celer quick, fast
celeritās, -ātis, f. speed
celerō (1) hasten, quicken
cella, f. chamber, room
celsus high, lofty, raised
cēna, f, dinner, meal
cēnō (1) dine, have dinner
centum a hundred
centuriō, -ōnis, m. centurion
Centuripīnus of Centuripa
cēra, f. wax, wax tablet
cerebrōsus hot-headed, hot-
    tempered
cernō, -ere, crēvī, crētum see, look
    at, determine, make out
certāmen, -inis, n. conflict, contest,
    battle
certātim in competition
certē certainly, at least
certus sure, certain
    certior sum be informed
cervīx, -īcis, f. neck
cervus, m. stag
cessō (1) delay, 'lose time'
cēterī the rest, the others
cēterum but, however
Chaldaeī, m. pl. a people of Assyria,
    astrologers
charta, f. leaf, paper, account
chorēa, f. dance
chorus, m. choir, chorus, dance,
cibus, m. food
cingō, -ere, cīnxī, cīnctum
    surround
cinis, -eris, m. ashes
circā adv., prep. + acc. around, about
circiter around, about
circumdō, -dare, -dedī, -datum
    surround
circumferō, -ferre, -tulī, -lātum
    carry round, carry about, spread
    abroad
circumiciō, -ere, -iēcī, -iectum
    place around
circumsideō, -ēre, -sēdī, -sessum
    besiege
circumsistō, –ere, -stetī
    surround
circumspiciō, -ere, -spexī,
    -spectum look around for
circumveniō, –īre, -vēnī, -ventum
    surround
civīlis civil
cīvis, -is, m.f. citizen
clam secretly
clāmō (1) shout
clāmor, -ōris, m. shouting, cry,
    noise

clārus bright, clear, famous, illustrious
classis, -is, *f.* fleet
claudō, -ere, clausī, clausum close
clipeus, *m.* shield
clītellae, *f. pl.* saddle-bags
clīvus, *m.* slope, gradient
Clōdiānus of Clodius and his supporters
Cocles, -itis of Horatius Cocles
coepī, coepisse, coeptum began
coeptum, *n.* what is begun, undertaking
coerceō, -ēre, coercuī, coercitum confine, check, restrain
cogitō (1) think, consider
cōgnātiō, -ōnis, *f.* family, relatives
cognoscō, -ere, cognōvī, cognitum get to know, find out
cogō, -ere, coēgī, coactum force, compel
cohibeō, -ere, cohibuī, cohibitum restrain
cohors, cohortis, *f.* cohort
cohortor (1) encourage, urge, exhort
coiciō, -ere, coiēcī, coiectum throw
Colchis, Colchidis, *f.* Colchis, a city on the Black Sea
Colchus, *m.* a Colchian, an inhabitant of Colchis
colligō, -ere, collēgī, collēctum collect, gather
collis, -is, *m.* upland, hill
collum, *n.* neck
collyrium, *n.* ointment
colō, -ere, coluī, cultum worship, honour, cultivate, practise
color, -ōris, *m.* colour
coluber, *m.* snake, serpent
colubra, *f.* snake, serpent
columba, *f.* dove
colus, *f.* distaff
coma, *f.* hair, foliage
comes, comitis, *m.f.* companion, comrade, fellow traveller
comitor (1) accompany
commereō, -ēre, commeruī, commeritum merit
comminus at close quarters
commisceō, -ēre, commiscuī, commixtum mix, put in with
committō, -ere, commīsī, commissum entrust
commodus well, healthy, advantageous
commoveō, -ēre, commōvī, commōtum move, affect
commūnis common, shared

compāgēs, -is, *f.* joint
comparo (1) gain
comperiō, -īre, comperī, compertum find out, learn
compēs, compedis, *f.* fetters, leg-irons
complector, complectī, complexus sum embrace
complexus, -ūs, *m.* embrace
complūrēs several
compōnō, -ere, composuī, compositum compose, arrange, settle, bring together, reconcile
comprehendō, -ere, comprehendī, comprehēnsum seize
concēdō, -ere, concessī, concessum grant
concerpō, -ere, concerpsī, concerptum pick
concidō, -ere, concidī slip, fall
concipiō, -ere, concēpī, conceptum cause, produce
concordia, *f.* harmony
concurrō, -ere, concurrī, concursum run, assemble together, collide, clash
concursus, -ūs, *m.* rush
concutiō, -ere, concussī, concussum shake, jangle
condemnō (1) condemn
condiciō, -ōnis, *f.* condition
condō, -ere, condidī, conditum hide, bury
condūcō, -ere, condūxī, conductum hire, rent
cōnferō, -ferre, -tulī, collātum collect, compete, contest, compare
cōnfertus crowded, densely packed
cōnfestim speedily
cōnficiō, -ere, cōnfēcī, cōnfectum finish, wear out, exhaust, consume
cōnfīdō, -ere, cōnfīsus sum + *dat.* trust, be confident
cōnfigō, -ere, cōnfīxī, cōnfīxum pierce through
cōnflō (1) bring about
cōnfodiō, -ere, cōnfōdī, cōnfossum dig, strike, stab
congelō (1) harden, congeal
congruēns fitting, appropriate, consistent
coniciō, -ere, coniēcī, coniectum throw, fling, hurl
coniectō (1) guess, infer
coniungō, -ere, coniūnxī, coniūnctum connect, associate
coniūnx, coniugis, *m.f.* spouse, husband, wife

coniūrō (1) swear
conlābor, -lābī, collāpsus sum fall, slip, fall in ruins, collapse
cōnor (1) try
conpōnō = compōnō
conprecor (1) pray that, supplicate
cōnquīrō, -ere, conquīsīvī, conquīsītum seek
cōnsalūtō (1) hail
cōnsanguineus related by blood
cōnscientia, *f.* complicity
cōnscius guilty
cōnscrībō, -ere, cōnscrīpsī, conscrīptum compose, write, enlist
cōnsecrō (1) dedicate, place among the gods
cōnsenēscō, -ere, cōnsenuī grow old
cōnsequor, cōnsequī, cōnsecūtus sum follow, pursue, catch up, overtake
cōnsīderō (1) look closely at, consider carefully
cōnsilium, *n.* plan, idea, advice
cōnsistō, -ere, cōnstitī, cōnstitum settle, stop, stand, stand still
cōnsobrīnus, *m.* cousin
cōnspectus, -ūs, *m.* sight, view
cōnspiciō, -ere, cōnspexī, cōnspectum observe, see, notice, catch sight of
cōnstantia, *f.* constancy, perseverance
cōnstituō, -ere, cōnstituī, cōnstitūtum position, decide, draw up, moor
cōnstringō, -ere, cōnstrīnxī, cōnstrictum check, restrain
cōnsuescō, -ere, cōnsuēvī, cōnsuetum be accustomed, be in the habit of
cōnsul, -is, *m.* consul
cōnsularis of consular rank
cōnsulātus, -ūs, *m.* consulship
cōnsulō, -ere, cōnsuluī, cōnsultum + *dat.* consult, consult the interest of, consider
cōnsultō (1) consult, deliberate
cōnsultum, *n.* decree
cōnsultus expert in
cōnsūmō, cōnsūmere, cōnsūmpsi cōnsūmptum eat, use up
contendō, -ere, contendī, contentum compete, contest, hurry, make an effort to reach
contentiō, -ōnis, *f.* rivalry
contentus happy; tense, tight
conterreō, -ēre, conterruī, conterritum terrify

contestor (1) call to witness, call on

contineō, -ēre, continuī, contentum contain, keep, hold

mē contineō stay, remain (at home)

contingō, -ere, contigī, contāctum touch, befall, happen to

continuō (1) continue

continuus continuous, uninterrupted

contiō, -ōnis, f. assembly

contrā *adv.* opposite, in turn, in return

contrā + *acc.* against, opposite to

contrārius opposite, opposing

contrectō (1) outrage, manhandle

contrōversia, f. dispute

convalēscō, -ere, convalui grow strong, rally, recover

convellō, -ere, convellī, convulsum overthrow, upturn, break/tear up, split open

conveniō, -īre, convēnī, conventum come together, assemble

conventus, -ūs, m. assembly

convertō, -ere, convertī, conversum turn, swing round

convīcium, n. abuse, insult

convincō, -ere, convīcī, convictum convict

convīva, m.f. guest, diner

convīvium, n. banquet, feast

convocō (1) call together

coorior, -īrī, coortus sum rise

cōpia, f. abundance, supply, wealth, riches

cōpiae, f. pl. forces, troops

coquō, -ere, coxī, coctum cook, stir up

cor, cordis, n. heart

coram *adv.* in the presence of, before

cōram + *abl.* in the presence of

corōna, f. garland, crown

corpus, -oris, n. body

corrigō, -ere, corrēxī, corrēctum make up for

corripiō, corripere, corripuī, correptum seize, snatch away, carry off

corruō, -ere, corruī fall to the ground

corruptus broken up, bad, in a bad condition

coruscus flashing

cōtīdiānus daily

cōtīdiē daily

crēber frequent, full of

crēbrēscō, -ere, crēbruī increase, grow strong/loud

crēdō, -ere, credidī, creditum + *dāt.* believe, trust, have faith in

creō (1) create, produce

crepitō (1) rustle

crēscō, -ere, crēvī, crētum grow, increase

crīmen, -inis, n. charge

crīnis, -is, m. hair

crista, f. crest (of helmet)

crocus, m. or crocum, n. saffron

cruciātus, -ūs, m. torture

cruciō (1) torture

crūdēlis cruel

crūdēlitās, -ātis, f. cruelty

crūdus raw, unripe, suffering from indigestion

cruentus bloody

crūs, crūris, n. leg

cubiculum, n. bedroom

cubīle, -is n. bed

cubō, -āre, cubuī, cubitum lie in bed

culex, culicis, m. gnat, mosquito

culīna, f. kitchen

culpa, f. blame

culpō (1) blame

culter, m. knife, scissors

cultor, -ōris, m. cultivator, farmer, worshipper

cultus elegant, civilised

cultus, -ūs, m. cultivation, dress, way of life, worship

cum + *abl.* with

cum + *subj.* when, since

cum ... tum ... both ... and ...

cumulō (1) accumulate

cumulus, m. heap, pile, mass

cūnctor (1) delay, hesitate

cūnctus every, all

cuneus, m. wedge

cupiditās, -ātis, f. desire

cupīdō, -inis, f. desire, lust

cupidus + *gen.* eager, desirous

cupiō, -ere, cupīvī, cupītum want, desire

cūr? why?

cūria, f. meeting-place of Senate

cūrō (1) look after, care for, supervise

curriculum, n. course, track

currō, currere, cucurrī, cursum run

currus, -ūs, m. chariot

cursus, -ūs, m. running, race, course, journey

curvus curved

cuspis, cuspidis, f. spear

custōdia, f. guard, protection

custōdiō, -īre, custōdīvī, custōdītum watch, guard

custōs, custōdis, m.f. guard, keeper, herdsman

Cytherea, f. Cytherea, Venus (worshpped at Cythera)

damnō (1) condemn

Danaī, m. pl. Greeks (descendants of Danaus, founder of Argos)

dē + *abl.* from, down from; about

dea, f. goddess

dēbeō, -ēre, dēbuī, dēbitum owe, ought, should, must

dēbitor, -ōris, m. debtor

dēcēdō, -ere, dēcessī, dēcessum die

dēcernō, -ere, dēcrēvī, dēcrētum decree

dēcerpō, -ere, dēcerpsī, dēcerptum pluck, pull off

decet, decuit it is fitting, proper

decimus tenth

dēcipiō, -ere, dēcēpī, dēceptum deceive, cheat

dēclinō (1) turn aside, avoid

decōrus graceful, noble

dēcurrō, -ere, dēcurrī, dēcursum run down, reach by running

decus, -oris, n. glory, reputation

dēdecus, -oris, n. disgrace, infamy

dēdō, -ere, dēdidī, dēditum surrender, devote

dēdūcō, -ere, deduxī, deductum lead out/down

dēfensor, -ōris, m. defender

dēferō, dēferre, dētulī, dēlātum carry down, report

dēfigō, -ere, defixī, defixum fix, thrust into

dēflectō, -ere, dēflēxī, dēflexum turn aside/away

dēfungor, dēfungī, dēfūnctus sum die

dēhīscēns opening up, gaping wide

dēiciō, -ere, dēiēcī, dēiectum throw down, fell

dein = deinde then, next

dēlābor, -labī, dēlāpsus sum descend

dēlectābilis delightful, favourite

dēlēniō, -īre, dēlēnīvī, dēlēnītum bewitch

dēligō (1) tie, fasten

deligō, -ere, dēlēgī, dēlectum choose

delphīn, -īnis, m. dolphin

dēlūbrum, n. shrine

dēmānō (1) spread down, pour down

dēminuō, -ere, dēminuī, dēminūtum diminish, reduce

dēmittō, -ere, dēmīsī, dēmissum lower, send down, let down

dēmō, -ere, dempsī, demptum take away from

dēmoror (1) delay

dēmum at last

dēnique finally

dēnsus thick

dēpellō, -ere, dēpulī, dēpulsum drive out, remove

dēplorō (1) lament for, mourn for

dēpōnō, -ere, dēposuī, dēpositum drop

dēposcō, -ere, dēpoposcī require, demand

dēprecor (1) beg

dēprehendō, -ere, dēprehendī, dēprehēnsum catch, seize

dērigescō, -ere, dēriguī become stiff, motionless

dēscendō, -ere, dēscendī, dēscēnsum descend, go down, come down

dēscīscō, -ere, dēsciī, dēscītum diminish, decline

dēserō, -ere, dēseruī, dēsertum desert, leave alone

dēsīderium, n. longing, regret, object of love

dēsidia, f. laziness

dēsiliō, -ere, dēsiluī, dēsultum jump down

dēsinō, -ere, dēsīvī, dēsitum stop, leave off, cease, desist

dēsistō, -ere, dēstitī, dēstitum stop, cease

dēspērātiō, -ōnis, f. hopelessness, desperation

dēspērō (1) despair

dēstinō (1) decide, determine, resolve

dēstituō, -ere, dēstituī, dēstitūtum leave, abandon

dēsum + dat. fail, be lacking

dēsuper from above

dēterior worse

dēterreō, -ēre, dēterruī, dēterritum frighten off, deter

dēterrimus worst

dētineō, -ere, dētinuī, dētentum to keep back, restrain

detondeō, -ēre, dētondī, dētōnsum shave, cut off

detorqueō, -ēre, dētorsī, dētortum twist, turn aside

dētruncō (1) lop

deus, m. god

deveniō, -īre, dēvēnī, dēventum arrive at

dexter right

dext(e)ra, f. right hand, pledge

dicō, -ere, dīxī, dictum say

dictitō (1) say often

dictū 'to say'

dictum, n. word

dīdūcō, -ere, dīdūxī, dīductum throw open

diēs, diēi, m.f. day, part of day, period

Diespiter, m. = the god Jupiter

differō, -ferre, distulī, dīlātum scatter, delay, put off, postpone, differ from, distract

differtus + abl. stuffed with, full of

difficilis difficult

difficultās, -ātis, f. difficulty

diffundō, -ere, diffūdī, diffūsum pour over, scatter

digitus, m. finger

dignitās, -ātis, f. position, dignity

dignus + abl. worthy of, fit

dīiūdicō (1) decide, determine

dīlābor, -lābī, dīlāpsus sum disperse, decay, fall apart, vanish, melt away

dīligēns careful, diligent, hard-working

dīligō, -ere, dīlēxī, dīlēctum love

dīmicō (1) fight

dīmissiō, -ōnis, f. dismissal, discharge

dīmittō, -ere, dimīsī, dīmissum send away, let go

Dīrae, Dīrārum, f. pl. Dread Goddesses, Furies

dīrus dreadful, terrible

discēdō, -ere, discessī, discessum depart, leave

discernō, -ere, discrevī, discrētum separate, distinguish

discerpō, -ere, discerpsī, discerptum tear to pieces

discīnctus in loose clothes

disciplīna, f. training, discipline

discō, -ere, didicī learn

discordia, f. discord, strife (also **Discordia**, personified as goddess)

discrīmen, -inis, n. crisis, struggle; distinction, difference

discumbō, -ere, discubuī, discubitum recline

discus, m. discus

disiciō, -ere, disiēcī, disiectum scatter

dispēnsō (1) dispense

disputō (1) speak, put/make the case

dissideō, -ere, dissēdī, dissessum be separated

dissimulō (1) hide

distō (1) be distant

diū for a long time

diūtius longer

dīva, f. goddess

dīversus different, separate

dīves, divitis + gen. rich in, well off for

dīvidō, -ere, dīvīsī, dīvīsum divide, separate, part

dīvīnus divine

dīvortium, n. divorce

dīvus, m. god

dō, dare, dedī, datum give, grant

doceō, -ēre, docuī, doctum teach

doctus clever, learned

doleō, -ēre, doluī, dolitum grieve, suffer, hurt

dolō (1) cut at, beat, shape

dolor, -ōris, m. grief, pain

dolus, m. trick, treachery

domina, f. mistress

dominus, m. master

domitor, -ōris, m. controller, tamer

domus, -ūs, f. home

domī at home

dōnātīvum, n. a gift

dōnec until

dōnō (1) give, present with

dōnum, n. gift, present

dormiō, -īre, dormīvī, dormītum sleep

dorsum, n. back

dōs, dōtis, f. dowry, gift, enrichment

dracō, -ōnis, m. serpent, snake, dragon

dubitātiō, -ōnis, m. doubt

dubitō (1) doubt, hesitate

dubius uncertain, doubting, doubtful

ducō, -ere, dūxī, ductum lead, take, consider, reckon

ductus, -ūs, m. leadership

dulcis sweet

dum + subj. until

dum while

duo, duae, duo two

duplex two, both

dūrō (1) endure, last, put up with

dūrus hard, tough

dux, ducis, m. leader

ē, ex + abl. from, out of

ēbrius drunk

eburnus of ivory

ēcastor by Castor!

ecce! see! look!

ecquis? anyone?

ēdō, -ere, ēdidī, ēditum give, bring about, perform, produce, publish, proclaim, raise up

ēditus high, lofty

ēducātiō, -ōnis, f. upbringing

ēducō (1) rear, educate, bring up

ēdūcō, -ere, edūxī, ēductum draw out, rear, educate

efferō, -ferre, extulī, ēlātum carry out

efficiō, -ere, effēcī, effectum effect, bring it about that

effigiēs, -iei, f. image, likeness, ghost

effodiō, -ere, effōdī, effossum dig up

effrēnō (1) unbridle, let loose

effugiō, -ere, effūgi escape

effugium, n. flight

effulgeō, -ēre, effulsī shine/blaze out

effundō, -ere, effūdī, effūsum pour out, let loose

ēgelidus chill, cold

egeō, -ēre, uī lack

ēgerō, -ere, ēgessī, ēgestum bring out, carry away

egō, meī I, me

ēgredior, -ī, ēgressus sum go out, leave, disembark

ēgregius excellent, eminent

ēlectrum, n. amber, metal alloy the colour of amber

elephantus, m. elephant

ēligō, -ere, ēlēgī, ēlēctum choose

ēloquentia, f. eloquence, rhetoric

ēluō, -ere, ēluī, ēlūtum wash out

ēmicō, -āre, ēmicuī, ēmicātum spring forth

ēmineō, -ēre, ēminuī stand out, be clearly seen

ēmittō, -ere, ēmīsī, ēmissum send out

emō, -ere, ēmī, ēmptum buy, hire

ēn behold! see! look!

ēnārrābilis that can be described

enim for

ēnītor, ēnītī, ēnīsus/ēnīxus sum strive to, force one's way up

ēnsis, -is, m. sword

eō so much; there, to that place

eō, īre, i(v)ī, itum go

eōdem to the same place

epistola/epistula, f. letter

epulae, f. pl. banquet, dishes

eques, equitis, m. horseman, pl. cavalry

equester of a horse

equidem indeed

equitātus, -ūs, m. cavalry

equitō (1) ride

equus, m. horse

ērepō, -ere, ērēpsī crawl out, climb over

ergā + acc. towards

ergō therefore

ēripiō, ēripere, ēripuī, ēreptum seize, snatch away

ērogō (1) spend, pay out

errō (1) make a mistake, wander

ērudītiō, -ōnis, f. learning

ērudītus learned

ērumpō, -ere, ērūpī, ēruptum break out

essedārius, m. fighter in a war-chariot

ēsuriō, -īre, ēsurīvī, ēsurītum be hungry

et and

et ... et ... both ... and ...

etēsiae, m. pl. northerly Etesian/trade winds

etiam also, even

etiamnum even now

etsi although, even if

Eurus, m. the east wind

ēveniō, -īre, ēvēnī, ēventum happen, turn out

ēventus, -ūs, m. outcome, result

ēvomō, -ere, ēvomuī, ēvomitum vomit out

exāmen, -inis, n. swarm

exanimis = exanimus dead, lifeless

exanimō (1) exhaust, knock unconscious

excēdō, -ere, excessī, excessum exceed

excipiō, -ere, excēpī, exceptum receive, take hold of

excitō (1) rouse

exclūdō, -ere, exclūsī, exclūsum shut out from

excolō, -ere, excoluī, excultum improve

excruciō (1) torment, torture

excubiae, f. pl. guard duty

excutiō, -ere, excussī, excussum shake off/out, drive out, examine

exedō, exēsse, exēdī, exēsum eat up, consume, corrode

exemplum, n. example

exerceō, -ēre, exercuī, exercitum administer, manage, exercise

exercitātiō, -ōnis, f. practice, opportunity to practise

exercitō (1) train

exercitus, -ūs, m. army

exhauriō, -īre, exhausī, exhaustum discharge

exhibeō, -ēre, exhibuī, exhibitum display

exhortātiō, -ōnis, f. encouragement

exigō, -ere, exēgī, exāctum drive out; complete; weigh, consider; demand, collect

exiguus slight, small

eximius extraordinary

exinde then

exīstimātiō, -ōnis, f. opinion, reputation

exitium, n. end, death

exoptō (1) long for

exorior, -īrī, exortus sum arise

exōrō (1) win over

expediō, -īre, expedīvī, expedītum act, prepare, hurl, send forth

expedītus lightly armed, unencumbered

expellō, -ere, expulī, expulsum drive out

expendō, -ere, expendī, expēnsum weigh, judge, consider

experientia, f. experience

experior, -īrī, expertus sum try, put to the test, undergo, experience

expleō, -ēre, explēvī, explētum fill, fill out, complete, satisfy

explorō (1) test

expōnō, -ere, exposuī, expositum set out, tell, relate

exposcō, -ere, expoposcī ask for, beg for

exprimō, -ere, expressī, expressum express

exquīsītus carefully sought out

exsanguis bloodless

exsequiae, f. pl. funeral procession

exsiliō, -īre, exsiluī leap up

exsolvō, -ere, exsolvī, exsolūtum perform, fulfil

exspectō (1) wait for

exspēs without hope, in despair

exstinguō, -ere, exstīnxī, exstīnctum extinguish

exstō (1) stand out, be visible

exstrūctus built on

exsul, -ulis, m.f. exile

exsultō (1) exult, rejoice

exta, n. pl. internal organs, esp. heart, lungs and liver used for divination

extemplō immediately

externus foreign

exterreō, -ēre, exterruī, exterritum scare, terrify

extrā + acc. outside

extrahō, -ere, extrāxī, extractum pull out

extrēmus final, furthest, last, most remote
exturbō (1) throw out

fabrīlis of *or* belonging to a metal worker
fābula, *f.* story
faciēs, iēī, *f.* face, appearance, shape
facilis easy
facinus, -oris, *n.* deed, crime
faciō, -ere, fēcī, factum do, make, give, provide
factu 'to do'
facultās, -ātis, *f.* opportunity
fallō, -ere, fefellī, falsum deceive, cheat, escape notice
falsus false, deceptive
fāma, *f.* rumour, fame, report
famēs, -is, *f.* hunger, starvation
familia, *f.* household
famula, *f.* female slave, maid-servant
fās (*indecl.*) right, lawful, proper
fastīgium, *n.* gable, pediment, summit
fātālis destined, fated
fateor, -ērī, fassus sum admit, confess
fātifer deadly, bringing death
fatīgātus worn out, exhausted
fatīscō, -ere gape open, break open
fātum, *n.* fate, destiny
faucēs, -ium *f. pl.* throat
faustus favourable, joyful
faveō, -ēre, fāvī, fautum + *dat.* favour, look on with favour, support
favor, -ōris, *m.* support
fax, facis, *f.* torch
febrīcula, *f.* slight fever
fēlīciter favourably
fēlix, fēlīcis fortunate, lucky, happy,
fēmina, *f.* woman
fēmineus womanly
fenestra, *f.* window
fera, *f.* wild beast
ferē = fermē about, almost, nearly, quite
feriō, -īre hit, strike
ferō, ferre, tulī, lātum bear, carry; obtain; tell, say
ferreus iron-hearted, of iron
ferrum, *n.* iron, sword, weapon
fertilis fertile
fertum, *n.* cake-offering
ferus wild, savage
ferveō, -ēre, ferbui boil, seethe
fessus tired
festivus agreeable, pretty
festus festal

fētus, -ūs, *m.* offspring, young, produce
fibra, *f.* fibre, entrails, liver
fidēlis faithful, loyal
fidēs, -iēī, *f.* faith, trust, credibility, loyalty, trustworthiness, promise
fīdō, -ere, fīsus sum + *dat.* trust
fīdus loyal, trusty
figō, -ere, fixī, fixum fix
figūra, *f.* shape, form
fīlia, *f.* daughter
fīlius, *m.* son
fingō, -ere, finxī, fictum fashion, create, form, invent; imagine
fīniō, -īre, fīnīvī, fīnītum end, finish
fīnis, -is, *m.f.* end, limit, boundary, marker
fīō, fierī, factus sum become, be made, happen
firmō (1) strengthen
fīxus fixed
flagellum, *n.* whip
flāgitiōsus disgraceful, infamous
flāgitium, *n.* crime
flagrō (1) blaze, flame, be excited
flamma, *f.* flame
flāvus yellowish
flectō, -ere, flexī, flexum turn, bend
fleō, -ēre, flēvī, flētum weep, shed tears
flētus, -ūs, *m.* tears, weeping
flōs, -ōris, *m.* flower
fluctus, -ūs, *m.* wave, surf, current
flūmen, -inis, *n.* flow, river, current
focilō (1) revive, resuscitate
foculus, *m.* fire, brazier
focus, *m.* hearth, ashes, fireplace
fodiō, -ere, fōdī, fossum dig
foedus, -eris, *n.* treaty, agreement
folium, *n.* leaf
fōmentum, *n.* poultice
fōns, -tis, *m.* fount, spring, fountain
forās out of doors
forēs, -um, *f. pl.* door, doors
forīs outside
fōrma, *f.* beauty
formīca, *f.* ant
formīdō, -inis, *f.* fear
fōrmō (1) shape, fashion
fōrmōsus beautiful
forsitan by chance, perhaps
fortasse perhaps
forte by chance, perhaps
fortis brave
fortiter bravely, boldly
fortūna, *f.* fortune, luck (also **Fortūna**, personified as goddess)
fortūnātus blessed

fortūnō (1) prosper, make happy/fortunate, make one's fortune
forum, *n.* forum, market place
fragor, -ōris, *m.* crashing, noise
frangō, -ere, frēgī, frāctum break, repress
frāter, frātris, *m.* brother
frāternus brotherly, of a brother
fraudō (1) cheat
fremō, -ēre, fremuī, fremitum roar, resound
frendeō, -ēre, frenduī, frēsum gnash the teeth
frēnum, *n.* bridle, bit
frequēns frequent, numerous, common
fretum, *n.* strait (of sea), sea, wave
frīgidus cold
frīgus, -oris, *n.* cold, chill
frōns, -dis, *f.* foliage
frūctus, -ūs, *m.* profit, fruit
frūstrā in vain
frūstror (1) deceive
frutex, -icis, *m.* bush, shrub
fuga, *f.* flight
fugiō, -ere, fūgī, fugitum run away, flee
fugō (1) chase away
fulgeō, -ēre, fulsī, fulsum shine
fulvus golden, yellow, tawny
fūmō (1) smoke
fūmus, *m.* smoke
fundō, -ere, fūdī, fūsum rout; spread
fundus, *m.* bottom; piece of land, farm
fūnestus fatal, destructive
fūnis, -is, *m.* rope, sheet (of sail)
fūnus, -eris, *n.* death; funeral
furiālis of the Furies, vengeful
furibundus raging, maddened, furious
furō, -ere, furuī rage, seethe
furor, -ōris, *m.* madness
fūrtum, *n.* theft, raid, robbery
fūstis, -is, *m.* stick
futūrus future, coming

galea, *f.* helmet
Gallicus Gallic
gaudeō, -ēre, gāvīsus sum be pleased, delight in, rejoice
gaudium, *n.* joy, pleasure
gāza, *f.* riches, treasures
gelidus cold, icy, freezing
geminus two, both, twin, double
gemitus, -ūs, *m.* groan, sigh
gemma, *f.* jewel
gemō, -ere, gemuī, gemitum groan, creak
gena, *f.* cheek

gener, *m.* son-in-law
genetrīx, -īcis, *f.* mother
genialis marital; festive
genitor, -ōris, *m.* father
gēns, -tis, *f.* family, tribe, race, nation
genus, -eris, *n.* type, sort, race, birth,
gerō, -ere, gessī, gestum wear (clothes), wage (war), bear, manage, conduct
   gesta, *n. pl.* deeds. achievements
gestō (1) carry, wear, display
gladius, *m.* sword
glōria, *f.* glory
glōrior (1) boast in
gnātos = nātos children
Gorgoneus of the Gorgons
gradus, -ūs, *m.* stage, step
Grāius Greek
grāmineus grassy
grandaevus aged, full of years
grandis big, grown-up
grāniferus grain-carrying
grassor (1) attack
grātia, *f.* grace, goodwill, kindness
grātus pleasing, joyful
gravis heavy, weighty, serious
gravitās, -ātis, *f.* seriousness, authority
gremium, *n.* lap, arms, bosom
gressus, -ūs, *m.* step, course
grex, gregis, *m.* flock, herd
gurges, gurgitis, *m.* whirlpool, current
gustus, -ūs, *m.* tasting
gutta, *f.* drop, tear

habeō, -ēre, habuī, habitum have
habitō (1) live
habitus, -ūs, *m.* type, appearance, style
haereō, -ēre, haesī, haesum cling, stick
Haluntīnus from Haluntium
hāmus, *m.* fish-hook
harēna, *f.* sand
haruspex, -spicis, *m.* haruspex, soothsayer
hasta, *f.* spear
haud not
hauriō, -īre, hausī, haustum drink in, consume, swallow
Hēracliensis from Heraclia
herba, *f.* grass, herb, plant
Herbitēnsis from Herbita
hērēs, hērēdis, *m.f.* heir
hērōs, -ōos, *m.* hero
Hesperia, *f.* Italy
heu alas
hīc here

hic, haec, hoc this
hiems, -is, *f.* winter, storm, tempest
hinc from here, next
hirsūtus rough, shaggy
Hister, *m.* the River Danube
hodiernus today's, of today
homō, -inis, *m.* man, human being
honestus noble, respectable, worthy
honor/honōs, -ōris, *m.* honour, regard, public office
honōrō (1) honour, respect
hōra, *f.* hour
horrēns bristling, standing on end
horridus standing on end, dreadful
horror, -ōris, *m.* trembling, dread, awe
hortātus, -ūs, *m.* encouragement
hortor (1) encourage, urge
hospes, -itis, *m.* host, visitor
hospita, *f.* stranger, host
hospitium, *n.* inn, accommodation
hostia, *f.* victim, sacrificed animal
hostīlis of an enemy, hostile
hostis, -is, *m.f.* enemy
hūc to this place, here
   hūc ūsque only as far as this
hūmānus human, considerate, civilised
humus, *f.* ground, earth
hymenaeus, *m.* marriage

iaceō, -ēre, iacuī, iacitum lie
iaciō, -ere, iēcī, iactum throw, utter
iactō (1) throw, toss, hurl (words/ threats), boast of
iactor (1) boast
iactus, -ūs, *m.* throw
iaculum, *n.* javelin
iam now, already
   iam dūdum now for a long time
ianitor, -ōris, *m.* doorkeeper
Iāpyx, Iāpygis, *m.* north-west wind
Iāzyges, *m. pl.* the Iazyges, a tribe from the Black Sea coast
ibi there
ibidem in the same place
ic(i)ō, -ere, icī, ictum strike, hit
ictus, -ūs, *m.* blow
idem, eadem, idem the same
identidem repeatedly
īdōlon, *n.* spectre, apparition
idōneus suitable
Īdus, -ūum, *f. pl.* Ides
igitur therefore, and so
ignārus + *gen.* ignorant of, not knowing, unaware
ignāvus lazy, cowardly
ignipotēns, -potentis, *m.* god/ master of fire, the god Vulcan

ignis, -is, *m.* fire, lightning
ignōrō (1) be unaware
ignōscō, -ere, ignōvī, ignotum + *dat.* forgive, pardon
ignōtus unknown
Īliacus of Ilium, Trojan
ille, illa, illud that, he, she, it
illīc there
illinō, -ere, illēvī, illitum smear with
imāginor (1) imagine, dream
imāgō, -inis, *f.* image, likeness, ghost
imbellis unwarlike
imber, -bris, *m.* rain; tears
immānis huge, dangerous
immānitās, -ātis, *f.* brutality
immemor + *gen.* without thinking of, unmindful
immēnsus boundless, immense
immineō, -ēre + *dat.* threaten
immittō, -ere, immīsī, immissum send; let down (hair), let go, slacken
immō rather
immolō (1) make an offering, sacrifice
immorior, -morī, immortuus sum die
immortālis immortal, deathless
immortālitās, -ātis, *f.* immortality
immōtus unmoved, motionless
impediō, -īre, impedīvī, impedītum impede, hinder
impedītus hindered, encumbered
impellō, -ere, impulī, impulsum strike
impendeō, -ēre impend, be imminent
impendium, *n.* expense
impendō, -ere, impendī, impēnsum devote, expend
impēnsus excessive
imperātor, -ōris, *m.* general, commander, emperor
imperiōsus commanding, powerful, domineering
imperitō (1) rule
imperītus + *gen.* inexperienced
imperium *n.* empire, power, command
imperō (1) + *dat.* order, command
impetrō (1) succeed, obtain by request
impetus, -ūs, *m.* attack
impingō, -ere, impēgī, impāctum drive into
impleō, -ēre, implēvī, implētum complete
implicitus seized with, entwined, entangled

implicō, -āre, implicāvī/implicuī, implicitum enfold, take hold of, entangle
implōrō (1) beg, beseech, beg for help
impollūtus unpolluted
impōnō, -ere, imposuī, impositum place upon, put on board
importūnus troublesome
impotēns powerless
improbus wicked
impudentia, f. shamelessness, nerve
impūne without punishment
impūnest = impūne est
īmus inmost, deepest, lowest
in prīmīs especially, in particular
in vicem in return
in + *abl.* in, on
in + *acc.* into, onto
inānis empty
inardēscō, -ere, inarsī burn, be set on fire, glow
inaudītus unheard of
incēdō, -ere, incessī, incessum go, walk, move, advance, approach
incendium, n. fire
incendō, -ere, incendī, incēnsum set on fire, kindle; excite
incertus uncertain
incipiō, -ere, incēpī, inceptum begin
incitō (1) urge/spur on
inclīnātus sunken, in decline
inclīnō (1) incline, turn towards
inclūdō, -ere, inclūsī, inclūsum shut in
incolumis safe, unharmed
incolumitās, -ātis, f. safety
incrēdibilis unbelievable
incubō, -āre, incubuī, incubitum + *dat.* brood over, settle on
incumbō, -ere, incubuī, incubitum lie on, press upon, apply oneself; bend over, concentrate on
incursus, -ūs, m. attack
inde from there, then
index, indicis, m.f. indicator, proof, summary
Indī, m. pl. the people of India
indicium, n. evidence
indicō (1) betray, reveal
indīcō, -ere, indīxī, indictum declare
indigena, m. native
indignātus displeased at, resenting
indignor (1) be ashamed, be indignant
indignus + *abl.* undeserving, undeserved, unworthy, unsuitable

indō, -ere, indidī, inditum put on
indomitus untamed, unconquered, unrestrained
inducō, -ere, indūxī, inductum bring into. draw/spread over
indulgēns kind
ineō, -īre, iniī, initum go in
ineptiō, -īre be silly
inermis unarmed
inerrō (1) stray into, drift before
iners, inertis feeble
īnfāmis notorious, with a bad reputation
infectus unfinished
īnfēnsus hostile
īnferiae, f. pl. funeral rites, offerings in honour of the dead
īnferior lower
īnferō, -ferre, intulī, illātum carry in, bear in, bring/throw into
īnficiō, -ere, īnfēcī, īnfectum infect, corrupt
īnfīdus treacherous, faithless
īnfirmus weak
īnflammō (1) inflame, excite
īnfrequēns infrequent, occasional
īnfringō, -ere, īnfrēgī, īnfrāctum break
īnfundō, -ere, īnfūdī, īnfūsum pour over, mix with
ingemō, -ere, ingemuī groan, mourn over
ingenium, n. skill, talent, nature, quality
ingens huge
ingerō, -ere, ingessī, ingestum throw into/onto, pile onto
inglorius shameful, inglorious
ingrātus ungrateful
ingredior, -gredī, ingressus sum enter
ingressus, -ūs, m. entrance, commencement
inhabitō (1) inhabit, occupy, reside
inhaereō, -ēre, inhaesī, inhaesum cling
inhonestus dishonourable, disgraceful
inhūmānus inhuman
iniciō, -ere, iniēcī, iniectum throw on, put on
inimīcus hostile, hateful
    inimīcus, m. enemy
inīquus unfair
initium, n. beginning
iniūria, f. injustice, injury
iniūstus unfair
inlīdō, -ere, inlīsī, inlīsum + *dat.* dash against
inligō (1) tie on

inlitam = illitam: illinō
inlitterātus unlearned, uneducated
inlūxit it grew light, day dawned
inmēnsus = immēnsus
inmītis harsh, merciless
innectō, -ere, innexuī, innexum fasten to, weave
innō (1) swim/float/sail upon
innocēns innocent, harmless
innubus unmarried
innuō, -ere, innuī, innūtum make a sign, beckon
inopia, f. shortage
inops needy, poor
inpediī = impediī
inpōnō, -ere, inposuī, inpositum put into, put on board, embark
inprobus = improbus
inprūdēns ignorant, thoughtless
inpulsus, -ūs, m. blow, onset
inquam, inquit, inquiunt I, he/she/it, they said
īnsāniēns mad, mindless
īnsānus mad, insane
īnscientia, f. lack of knowledge
īnscius unknowing
īnsequor, īnsequī, īnsecūtus sum pursue
īnserō, -ere, īnseruī, īnsertum put into/among, mix up with, cram in
īnserviō, -īre, īnservīvī, īnservītum + *dat.* devote oneself to
īnsideō, -ēre, īnsēdī, īnsessum sit on, settle on
īnsidiae, f. pl. ambush, plot, conspiracy
īnsignis clear, famous, distinguished, outstanding
īnsonō, -āre, īnsonuī make a loud noise
īnspīrō (1) blow into, inspire, instil
īnstābilis changeable
īnstar, n. (indecl.) image
īnstō, -stāre, īnstitī stand on, press
īnstrūmentum, n. tool
īnstruō, -ere, īnstrūxī, īnstrūctum draw up, set up, arrange
īnsuēfactus trained in/accustomed to
īnsuētus unaccustomed, not used to
īnsula, f. island, block of flats
īnsum, inesse, īnfuī be in
intāctus untouched, unharmed
integer whole, in one piece, untouched, virtuous
intellegenter intelligently
intellegō, -ere, intellēxī, intellēctum understand, realise

intemptātus untried

intendō, -ere, intendī, intentum apply, concentrate on, bend

intentō (1) stretch/turn towards, threaten with

inter + *acc.* among, between

intercipiō, -ere, intercēpī, interceptum intercept

interdiū during the day, by day

interdum sometimes, at times

intereā meanwhile

interest + *gen.* it is important to, it is to the advantage of

interfector, -ōris, m. killer

interficiō, -ere, interfēcī, interfectum kill

interfluō, -ere, interflūxi flow between, float among

interfūsus flowing between

interim meanwhile, in the meantime

interior inner

interius inside

interrogō (1) ask, question

intexō, -ere, intexuī, intextum weave into

intimus inmost

intolerandus not to be tolerated

intonō, -āre, intonuī thunder, resound (with thunder)

intorqueō, -ēre, intorsī, intortum hurl

intrā + *acc.* within, inside

introō *adv.* inside

introō (1) enter

introeō, -īre, introiī (-īvī), introitum go into, enter

intueor, -ērī, intuitus sum look upon

intus inside, within

inultus unavenged, unpunished

inūtilis useless, worthless

invehor, -vehī, invectus sum be carried into, enter

inveniō, -īre, invēnī, inventum find

invidia, f. envy, jealousy

invidus envious

inviolātus unviolated

invīsus hated

invitō (1) invite

invītus unwilling

invius impassable

invocō (1) call upon

involvō, -ere, involvī, involūtum envelop, cover, overwhelm

iocōsus pleasant, humorous

iocus, m. joke, fun

ipse, ipsa, ipsum himself, herself, itself, themselves

īra, f. anger

īrātus angry

irrīdeō, -ēre, irrīsī, irrīsum make fun of, pour scorn on

irrumpō, -ere, irrūpī, irruptum burst/break into, rush into

is, ea, id this, that, he, she, it, them

iste that

istic that

istinc from here

ita so, in this way

itaque and so, therefore

item in the same way

iter, itineris, n. journey, stage

iterō (1) repeat, do/make again

iterum again

itidem in the same way

iubeō, -ēre, iussī, iussum order, command

iūcundus pleasant, agreeable

iūdex, -icis, m. judge, member of jury

iūdicium, n. judgement

iūdicō (1) decide, judge

iugum, n. yoke, ridge, summit

iūmentum, n. baggage animal, beast of burden

iūnctus joined, united

iungō, -ere, iūnxī, iūnctum join

iūnīx, iunīcis, f. young cow, heifer

Iuppiter, Iovis, m. Jupiter

iūs, iūris, n. law
  iūre lawfully, with justification

iūstus just

iuvat it pleases

iuvenāliter youthfully

iuvencus, m. bullock, young bull

iuvenis, -is, m. young man

iuventūs, -ūtis, f. youth

iuvō, -āre, iūvī, iūtum help, delight

Kalendae, f. pl. Kalends

labefactō (1) overthrow

labellum, n. lip

lābor, lābī, lāpsus sum slip, fall

labor, -ōris, m. work, effort

labōrō (1) work

Lacedaemōn, -onis, f. Lacedaemon, Sparta

lacer torn, rent

lacertus, m. shoulder, upper arm

lacrima, f. tear

lacrimō (1) cry

lacrimōsus full of tears, sorrowful, weeping, grievous

laedō, -ere, laesī, laesum harm

laetitia, f. happiness, joy, gladness

laetor (1) be happy

leatus happy

laevus left

lambō, -ere, lambī, lambitum lick

languor, -ōris, m. weakness, faintness

laniō (1) tear at

lapidōsus stony, gritty

lāpsus, -ūs, m. fall, falling

lār, -is, m. household god

largītiō, -ōnis, f. generosity, bribery

largus ample, bountiful

lassus tired

lātē far and wide, broadly

latebrōsus hidden, secret

lateō, -ēre, latuī hide, hide from, lie hidden

Latiāris of Latium, Latin

Latīnus of the Latins

Latīnus, m. Latinus, king of Latium

Latium, n. Latium

lātrātor, -ōris, m. one who barks

latus, -eris, n. side, beam (of ship)

lātus (*adj.*) wide

laudō (1) praise

Laurēns, -entis Laurentian, of Latium

laureus of laurel

laurus, f. laurel tree, bay tree

laus, laudis, f. glory, praise

lavō, -āre, lavī, lautum wash

laxus loose

lectīca, f. litter

lēctitō (1) be in the habit of reading

lectus, m. bed, couch

Lēdaeus of Leda

lēgātus, m. commander, ambassador, deputy, envoy

legiō, -ōnis, f. legion

lēgitimus lawful, legitimate

legō, -ere, lēgī, lēctum choose; gather; read

leniō, -īre, lenīvī, lenītum soften, soothe

lēnis gentle

lentus slow

lētum, n. death

levis light, fickle, unimportant, inconstant

lēvis smooth

levō (1) relieve, lessen

lēx, lēgis, f. law

libellus, m. little book, accusation

libenter willingly

līber free

līberī, m. pl. children

līberō (1) free, set free

lībertās, -ātis, f. freedom

libertus, m. freedman, ex-slave

libet, libuit it pleases

libīdō, -inis, f. passion, lust, desire

lībō (1) skim

Libycus Libyan

licet, licuit it is allowed, possible

licet although

līctor, -ōris, m. lictor

lignum, n. wood, fuel

līgō (1) bind, harness

līmen, liminis, n. threshold

lingua, f. tongue, language

linter, lintris, f. boat, barge

linteum, n. linen cloth, sails

lippus having sore/inflamed eyes

liquēscō, -ere, licui melt

liquidus clear, liquid

liquor, liquī waste away, dissolve

litō (1) obtain favourable omens

littera, f. letter (of alphabet)

    litterae, f. pl. letter (written to someone)

lītus, litoris n. shore, beach

līveō, -ēre be discoloured

līvidus bruised

loca, -ōrum, n. pl. places, region

locō (1) place, locate

locus, m. place

longē a long way off, far away, in the distance

    longē ac lātē far and wide

longus long, far

loquor, loquī, locūtus sum speak

lōrīca, f. cuirass, breastplate

lubet = libet it pleases

lūbricus slippery, sinuous

luctor (1) wrestle

lūctuōsus mournful, grievous

luctus, -ūs, m. grief, mourning

lūdibrium, n. plaything, sport

lūdius, m. stage-player, pantomimist

lūdō, -ere, lūsī, lūsum play

lūdus, m. game

    lūdī, m. pl. gladiatorial games

luēs, -is, f. plague, pestilence

lumbus, m. loin, backside

lūmen, -inis, n. light, eye, lamp

lūna, f. moon

lupātus with jagged teeth

lupus, m. wolf

lūsus, -ūs, m. game

lūx, lūcis, f. light, day

luxuriēs, -iēī, f. excess

Lycius Lycian

lympha, f. water

macer lean, skinny

maciēs, -iēī, f. leanness, thinness, wasting

macte virtūte esse to increase in courage, to continue to be courageous, to be blessed

macula, f. stain, blemish, disgrace

madeō, -ēre, madui be wet

maereō, -ēre be sad, grieve, lament, bewail

maeror, -ōris, m. grief

maestus sad, mournful, sorrowful

magis more

magister, m. master, helmsman

magistrātus, -ūs, m. magistracy, magistrate

magnanimus brave, heroic

magnificentia, f. magnificence, splendour

magnitūdō, -inis, f. large size

magnus big, large, great

maiōrēs, -um, m. pl. ancestors

malignus evil, spiteful

mālō, mālle, māluī prefer

mālum, n. apple

mālus, m. mast

malus *(adj.)* evil, bad

    malum, n. trouble, danger, misfortune, disaster

mandātum, n. order, instruction

mandō (1) entrust

māne early, in the morning

maneō, -ēre, mansī, mansum remain, stay

Mānēs, -ium, m. pl. shades, spirits of the dead, gods of the Underworld

manifestus clear, evident

manipulus, m. maniple, company (of soldiers)

mānō (1) flow, drip, spread abroad, pervade

manus, -ūs, f. hand; band of men

mare, maris n. sea

margarītum, n. pearl

marīnus of the sea

marīta, f. spouse

maritimus maritime, of the sea

marītus, m. husband

marmor, -ōris, n. marble, stone

marmoreus of marble

Martiae Īdūs, f. pl. the Ides of March

māter, mātris, f. mother

māteria, f. stuff, substance

māternus of a mother

mātrimōnium, n. marriage

mātrōnālis befitting a married woman

mātrumōnium = mātrimōnium

mātūrus mature, speedy

Māvors, Māvortis, m. = Mars, Martis, m. Mars

maximē very much, most of all

medicāmen, -inis, n. drug

medicātus, -us, m. charm

medicus, m. doctor

mediocris moderate

medius middle, in the middle

melior better

membrum, n. limb

memor + *gen.* mindful, remembering

memoria, f. memory, recollection

mēns, mentis, f. mind

mēnsa, f. table

mēnsis, -is, m. month

mercēs, -ēdis, f. pay, reward

mereō, -ēre, meruī, meritum deserve, earn

    meritum, n. service, kindness

mēta, f. end, winning line, turning post

metuō, -ere, metuī, metūtum fear

metus, -ūs, m. fear

meus, mea, meum my

micō, -āre, micuī dart, flash

mīles, militis, m. soldier

mīlitāris military, of soldiers/army

mīlitia, f. military service

mīlle, pl. mīlia thousand

    mīlle passūs a mile; **duo mīlia passuum** two miles

minae f. pl. threats

minimē not at all, not in the least

minister, m. servant, accomplice, agent

minitabundus threatening

minor smaller, younger

minu' = minus less

mīrāculum, n. portent, wonder, surprise

mīrificus wonderful, admirable

mīror (1) wonder at, be full of wonder, be amazed

mīrus wonderful, amazing

misceō, -ēre, miscuī, mistum/ mixtum mix

miser miserable, wretched, sad

miserābilis unhappy, miserable, wretched

misereor, miserērī, miseritus sum pity

miseret it causes pity

miseria, f. wretchedness

mittō, -ere, mīsī, missum send

mixtus mixed, sharing

modestus well-behaved, moderate, modest

modicē moderately, slightly

modicus modest, moderate, small, simple

modo ... modo ... now ... now ...

modus, m. measure, way, kind, tune, rhythm

moenia, moenium, n. pl. walls, defences

mōlēs, -is, f. burden, mass. bulk

molestia, f. misery, annoyance

molestus troublesome, tiresome

molliō, -īre, mollīvī (-iī), mollitum soften, make easier

mollis soft, gentle, calm, tender
mollitia, f. pleasantness, softness
moneō, -ēre, monuī, monitum
    warn, advise
mōns, -tis, m. mountain, rock, cliff
monstrō (1) show
mōnstrum, n. monster, portent
mora, f. delay, hindrance
morbus, m. sickness, disease
mordeō, -ēre, momordī, morsum
    bite
moribundus dying
morior, morī, mortuus sum, die
moror (1) delay, hold up, wait
mors, -tis, f. death
mortiferē terminally
mōs, mōris, m. custom
    mōris est it is the custom
mōtus, -ūs, m. motion, movement
moveō, -ēre, mōvī, mōtum move
mox soon, from now on
Mucius of Mucius
mucrō, -ōnis, m. blade, sharp point
mūla, f. mule
mulcātus battered, bruised
Mulciber, m. Vulcan
muliebris womanly
mulier, -eris, f. woman
muliercula, f. prostitute
multitūdō, -inis, f. crowd
multō (*adv.*) much
multus much, many
mūlus, m. mule
mūnicipium, n. town
mūnīmentum, n. defence,
    protection
mūniō, -īre, mūnīvī, mūnītum
    fortify, build, make a road
mūnītiō, -ōnis, f. fortification
mūnus, -eris, n. gift
murmur, -is, n. murmur
mūtātiō, -ōnis, f. change
mūtō (1) change
mūtus dumb, silent
mūtuus mutual
Mycēnae, f. pl. Mycenae, a city in
    Greece

nam, namque for
nancīscor, -ī, nactus sum obtain
nārrō (1) tell, relate
nāta, f. daughter
nātālis of birth, **(dies)** birthday
nātiō, -ōnis, f. tribe, race
natō (1) swim, float
nātūra, f. nature
nātus born, originated
    nātus, m. son
nātu by birth
nauarchus, m. ship's captain

naucula = navicula, f. small boat
nauta, m. sailor, boatman
nāvālis of ships, naval
nāvigātiō, -iōnis, f. sailing
nāvigium, n. ship
nāvigō (1) sail
nāvis, -is, f. ship
-nē (denotes a question)
nē that ... not, so that ... not
nē ... quidem not even, nor
nec, neque and not
nec ... nec ..., *also* **neque ... neque ...**
    neither ... nor ...
necdum and not yet
necessārius necessary
necō (1) kill
nectō, -ere, nexuī/nexī, nectum
    link, intertwine
nēdum still less
nefārius wicked, unspeakable
nefās, n. *(indecl.)* crime, impious/
    wicked action
neglegentia, f. negligence, lack of
    care
negō (1) deny, say no
nēmō no one, nobody
nemorōsus well-wooded
nempe clearly
nemus, -oris, n. grove, wood
nepōs, -ōtis, m. descendant, *pl.*
    children's children
Neptūnius of/belonging
    to Neptune
nēquāquam in no way, not at all
nequeō, -īre, nequīvī, nequītum
    be unable to
nēquīquam in vain
nēquitia, f. vice
nervus, m. bowstring
nesciō, -īre, nescīvī, nescītum not
    know
    nescio quid something
nescius unaware
nēve and not, that not
nex, necis, f. death, murder
niger black, dark
nihil nothing
nīl = nihil
nimbus, m. cloud
nimium too much
nimius excessive
nisi unless, except
nīsus, -ūs, m. effort, exertion
niteō, -ēre, nituī shine, gleam,
    sparkle
nitidus shining
nītor, nītī, nīsus/nīxus sum lean
    on; strive, endeavour
niveus snowy, snow-white
nix, nivis, f. snow

nō (1) swim
nōbilis of noble birth, noble, famous
nōbilitās, -ātis, f. high birth
nōbilitō make famous, render
    superior
nocēns guilty, at fault
noceō, -ēre, nocuī, nocitum + *dat.*
    harm
nocturnus nocturnal, of the night
nōlō, nōlle, nōluī not want
Nomades, Nomadum, m. pl.
    nomadic tribes of Africa,
    Numidians
nōmen, -inis, n. name
nōminō (1) name, call
nōn not
nōn modo ... sed etiam ... not only
    ... but also ...
nōndum not yet
nōnne? surely?
nōnnūllī, -nūllae, -nūlla some,
    several
nōnus ninth
nōs, nostrum we, us
noscō, -ere, nōvī, nōtum know
noster, nostra, nostrum our
notābilis remarkable, out of the
    ordinary
notō (1) mark out, note
nōtus familiar, well known
Notus, m. the south wind
novellus young, tender
novem nine
noverca, f. stepmother
novissimus final, last
novus new, fresh
nox, noctis, f. night
noxa, f. harm, injury
nūbēs, -is, f. cloud
nūbila, n. pl. clouds
nūbilis of marriageable age
nūbō, -ere, nūpsī, nūptum + *dat.*
    marry
nūdō (1) reveal
nūdus bare
nūllus not any, no
num whether
num ...? surely not?
nūmen, -inis, n. deity, divinity,
    divine power
numerō (1) count; recall, remember
numerus, m. number, measure
nummus, m. coin
numquam never
nunc now
nuncupō (1) call, name, express
nūntiō (1) announce
nūntius, m. messenger, message,
    news
nūper recently, not long ago

nūpta, *f.* bride
nūptiae, *f. pl.* marriage
nūptiālis nuptial
nurus, -ūs, *f.* daughter-in-law
nūtus, -ūs, *m.* nod, command, order

ob + *acc.* because of
obdūrō (1) persist, endure
obiciō, -ere, obiēcī, obiectum throw
obiurgō (1) chide, rebuke
oblīquus slanting
  ab oblīquō from the side
oblīviō, -ōnis, *f.* forgetfulness
obloquor, -loquī, oblocūtus sum speak against, accompany (in music)
obruō, -ere, obruī, obrutum cover over, bury, sink
obscurus dark, hidden, unknown, shady, uncertain
obsequor, -sequī, obsecūtus sum + *dat.* comply with
obses, -idis, *m.f.* hostage
obsideō, -ere, obsēdī, obsessum occupy, settle upon
obsidiō, -ōnis, *f.* siege
obstinātus determined, steady, stubborn
obstipēscō, -ere, obstipuī be astounded
obstō, -āre, obstitī, obstatum + *dat.* stand in the way of
obsum, obesse, obfuī/offuī + *dat.* be a disadvantage to
obtegō, -ere, obtēxī, obtectum cover
obtineō, -ēre, obtinuī, obtentum hold, possess, govern (a province)
obtruncō (1) strike, kill
obvius hostile, in the way, on the way
occāsiō, -ōnis, *f.* opportunity
occidō, -ere, occidī, occāsum fall, set, die
occīdō, -ere, occīdī, occīsum kill
occultō (1) conceal
occumbō, -ere, occubuī, occubitum go down, set, die
occupō (1) seize, gain, reach
occurrō, -ere, occurrī, occursum + *dat.* meet, run/come to meet
occursō (1) come together, rush against, attack, collide
ocrea, *f.* greave, leg armour
Octōber, -bris of October
octōgintā eighty
oculus, *m.* eye
ōdī, ōdisse *(perf. with pres. meaning)* hate

odium, *n.* hatred
odor, -ōris, *m.* scent
odōrātus sweet-smelling, fragrant
Odyssēa, *f.* Odyssea, a port in Sicily
offēnsus offensive, odious
offerō, -ferre, obtulī, oblatum offer
offeror appear, show oneself
officium, *n.* duty, business
offirmō (1) secure, strengthen, keep firm/steadfast
ohē! hey!
oleō, -ēre, oluī smell, be fragrant
ōlim once, some time ago
olīvum, *n.* olive-oil
ōmen, -inis, *n.* omen
ōmentum, *n.* fat, bowel, fatty entrails
omnigenus of all kinds
omnīnō completely
omnis all, every
onus, oneris, *n.* burden. load
opācus dark
operiō, -īre, operuī, opertum cover up, hide
opēs, *f. pl.* wealth
opīmus rich, fat
opīnor (1) think
oportet, oportuit one should
opperior, -īrī, opperitus sum wait, wait for
oppeto, -ere, oppetīvī, oppetītum meet
oppidulum, *n.* little town
oppleō, -ēre, opplēvī, opplētum fill
opportūnus convenient, suitable, advantageous
opprimō, -ere, oppressī, oppressum crush, press down, weigh down, burden
oppugnatiō, -ōnis, *f.* attack
ops, opis, *f.* help, need, wealth, power, strength
optimus best
opto (1) desire, wish for, pray
opus est + *abl.* there is a need
opus, operis, *n.* work, achievement
ōra, *f.* shore
ōrārius of the coast, coastal
ōrātor, -ōris, *m.* orator, speaker
orbis, -is, *m.* circle, world
  orbis terrārum, *m.* world
orbitās, -ātis, *f.* bereavement, state of being orphaned
orbus bereft, deprived
ōrdō, -inis, *m.* line, order, rank, row
Oriēns, -tis, *m.* the east
orīgō, -inis, *f.* origin, source
orior, -īrī, ortus sum arise, dawn, be born
ōrnātus, -ūs, *m.* dress, costume
ōrnō (1) adorn, decorate

ōrō (1) pray, plead, beg
ōs, ōris, *n.* face, mouth
os, ossis, *n.* bone
ōsculum, *n.* kiss
osseus bony
ostendō, -ere, ostendī, ostentum show, reveal
ostentō (1) show, point out
ostentum, *n.* prodigy
ōstium, *n.* entrance
ostrum, *n.* purple
ōtium, *n.* leisure, free time, peace
ovīle, -is, *n.* sheepfold

pābulum, *n.* fodder, grass
paeān, paeānis, *m.* hymn
paedagōgium, *n.* paedagogium, sleeping-quarters of young slaves
paedagōgus, *m.* tutor
paelex, -icis *f.* mistress, love-rival
paelicātus, -ūs, *m.* prostitution
paene almost, nearly
palaestra, *f.* wrestling-ground, exercise area
palam openly
palātium, *n.* palace
palātum, *n.* palate
palla, *f.* robe, cloak, mantle
pallēns pale
pallium, *n.* cloak
palma, *f.* palm, hand, palm tree
palūs, -ūdis, *f.* marsh
palūster marshy, swampy
pandō, -ere, pandī, passum extend, open, spread out
pānis, -is, *m.* bread
pār, paris equal, similar
parcus sparing, moderate, thrifty, frugal
parēns, -tis, *m.f.* parent
  parentēs, *m. pl.* ancestors
pariēs, -ētis, *m.* wall
pariō, -ere, peperī, paritum/ partum give birth to, produce, procure
pariter equally, together
parō (1) prepare
parochus, *m.* local officer
pars, -tis, *f.* part
partim ... partim ... partly ... partly ...
parturiō, -īre, parturīvī bring forth
partus, -ūs, *m.* birth, offspring
parvus small
pascō, -ere, pavī, pastum feed, graze, pasture
pascuum, *n.* pasture
passim everywhere
passus. passūs, *m.* pace, step
pāstor, -ōris, *m.* shepherd

pateō, -ēre, patuī be open
pater, patris, m. father
   patrēs, -um, m. pl. senators
paternus of a father
patientia, f. patience, sufferance
patior, patī, passus sum suffer, endure
patria, f. country, homeland
patrius of a father, of the native land
paucī few, a few
paucitās, -ātis, f. shortage, small number
paulisper for a short time
paulō, paulum a little, for a little while
pavor, -ōris, m. fear, alarm
pāx, pācis, f. peace
peccō (1) sin, do wrong
pecten, -inis, m. plectrum
pectus, -oris, n. breast, chest, heart
pecūnia, f. money
pecus, -oris, n. cattle
pedester on foot
peior worse
pelagus, n. sea
pelliciō, -ere, pellexī, pellectum seduce
pellō, -ere, pepulī, pulsum banish, drive out
Penātēs, -ium, m. pl. household gods
pendeō, -ēre, pependī hang, dangle
pendō, -ere, pependī, pēnsum pay
penetrō (1) penetrate, reach, gain entrance
pensum, n. task
per + acc. through, all over, along
peragō, -ere, perēgī, perāctum complete
percellō, -ere, perculī, perculsum strike down
percipiō, -ere, percēpī, perceptum perceive, take possession of
percūnctor (1) investigate, make a full enquiry
percurrō, -ere, per(cu)currī, percursum pass quickly over
percutiō, -ere, percussī, percussum hit
perditus desperate
perdō, -ere, perdidī, perditum destroy, ruin
perdomō, -āre, perdomuī, perdomitum tame thoroughly
perennis endless, eternal
pereō, -īre, periī, peritum die, perish
perfacilis very easy
perferō, -ferre, pertulī, perlātum endure, see something through

perficiō, -ere, perfēcī, perfectum complete, fulfil, accomplish
perfidus treacherous, untrustworthy
perflō (1) blow through, blow over
perfodiō, -ere, perfōdī, perfossum pierce through
perfringō, -ere, perfrēgī, perfrāctum break through, smash
perfugiō, -ere, perfūgī flee
perfundō, -ere, perfūdī, perfūsum pour over, cover/fill with
pergō, -ere, perrēxī, perrēctum press on, go ahead with
perīculum, n. danger
perinde just as
perlegō, -ēre, perlēgī, perlēctum read through
permisceō, -ēre, permiscuī, permistum/mixtum mix up, mingle, confound, disturb thoroughly
permultī very many
perniciēs, -iēī, f. destruction, ruin
pernoctō (1) pass the night
pernōtēscō, -ere, pernōtuī become widely known
perobscūrus very obscure, under cover
perpaucī very few
perpetuus continual, ongoing
perpōtō (1) drink heavily
perquam very much
persaepe very often
persequor, -sequī, persecūtus sum pursue
persuādeō, -ēre, persuāsī, persuāsum + dat. persuade
pertemptō (1) agitate thoroughly
perterritus terrified
pertinācissimē most stubbornly, very obstinately
pertineō, -ēre, pertinui tend, lead towards, concern, be of interest to
perveniō, -īre, pervēnī, perventum reach, arrive at
pervincō, -ere, pervīcī, pervictum overcome completely
pēs, pedis, m. foot, paw
pessimus worst
pestilēns unwholesome, dangerous
pestis, -is, f. plague, death
petō, -ere, petīvī, petītum seek, make for, fancy, ask for, attack
phantasma, -ātis, n. ghost
philosophus, m. philosopher
Phoebus, m. Phoebus, Apollo
Phrygius Phrygian, Trojan
pictus ornate, embellished

pietās, -ātis, f. duty
piger lazy, sluggish
piget regret
pignus, pignoris, n. pledge, bond
pigritia, f. sluggishness, reluctance
pila, f. ball
pīlum, n. spear, javelin
pinna, f. feather
pīnus, f. pine tree
pīrāta, m. pirate
piscātōrius for fishing
piscis, -is, m. fish
piscōsus fishy, full of fish
pius dutiful
placet, -ēre, placuit + dat. it pleases, suits
plācō (1) appease
plaga, f. blow, stroke
plānus flat, level, obvious
plaudō, -ere, plausī, plausum beat out
plausus, -ūs, m. applause
plēbs, plēbis, f. people
plectō, -ere punish
plēnus + abl. full, well supplied, ample
plērīque many, most
plērumque for the most part, usually
plūrēs more, many
poena, f. punishment
   poenās dō pay the penalty, be punished
polus, m. pole, heavens
Pompēiānus of Pompey
pōmum, n. apple
pondus, -eris, n. weight
pōnō, -ere, posuī, positum place, put; remove
pōns, -tis, m. bridge
Ponticus from Pontus
pontus, m. sea, wave
populātiō, -ōnis, f. plundering
populus, m. people
porrigō, -ere, porrēxī, porrēctum stretch out, hold out, offer
porta, f. door, gate
portendō, -ere, portendī, portentum portend
porticus, -ūs, m. colonnade
portō (1) carry
portus, -ūs, m. harbour, port, haven
poscō, -ere, poposcī demand, ask for
possum, posse, potuī can, be able
post + acc. after, behind
postea afterwards
posteāquam after
posterus next
   posterī, m. pl. descendants
postis, -is, m. post, door-post

postpōnō, -ere, postposuī, postpositum esteem less than

postquam after, when

postrēmus final

postrīdiē on the next day

postulō (1) demand, require

potens powerful

potentia, *f.* power

potestās, -ātis, *f.* power

potior, potīrī, potītus sum + *gen.* win, take possession of

potis possible

prae + *abl.* before, in front of

praebeō, -ēre, praebuī, praebitum offer, provide

praeceps headlong, steep, sheer, impetuous, hurried

praeceptor, -ōris, *m.* teacher

praecīnctus girded, (with clothes) tucked up

praecipiō, -ere, praecēpī, praeceptum + *dat.* instruct, teach

praecipitō (1) throw headlong

praecipuus especial

praeclārus brilliant

praecordia, *n. pl.* breast, vitals, heart

praeda, *f.* booty

praedicō (1) declare, proclaim

praedīcō, -ere, praedīxī, praedictum say beforehand, foretell

praedō, -ōnis, *m.* brigand, pirate

praefātus mentioned before, stated before

praefectus, *m.* commander

praegredior, -ī, praegressus sum go ahead of, precede

praemittō send in advance

praemium, *n.* prize, reward, profit

praenūntius foretelling

praepōnō, -ere, praeposuī, praepositum prefer

praeruptus steep

praescrībō, -ere, praescrīpsī, praescrīptum suggest

praesēns present, before their eyes

praesidium, *n.* garrison, defence, protection

praestō, -āre, praestitī, praestitum/praestātum stand out, excel in; provide; show

praesum, -esse, praefuī + *dat.* be in charge of

praetendō, -ere, praetendī, praetentum extend, put in front of

praeter + *acc.* except, apart from

praetereā moreover, and what is more

praetereō, -īre, praeteriī, praeteritum pass, go past, be gone

praeterita, *n. pl.* the past

praetervehor, -vehī, praetervectus sum sail by, pass by

praetor, -ōris, *m.* praetor, governor

praetōrium, *n.* praetor's headquarters

praetūra, *f.* praetorship

prandeō, -ēre, prandī, prānsum have breakfast/lunch

prandium, *n.* breakfast, lunch

prāvitās, -ātis, *f.* crookedness, vice

precor (1) pray (to)

premō, -ere, pressī, pressum prevail, overpower

pretium, *n.* price, reward

prex, precis, *f.* prayer, plea

prīdem in the past

prīdiē the day before

prīmus first

    prīmā lūce at dawn

    prīmō, prīmum at first

prīnceps *adj.* leading

prīnceps, -ipis, *m.* emperor, chieftain, leading figure in the state

prīncipium, *n.* beginning

prior, prius earlier, first, former; before

prīscus ancient, of old

prīstinus former, ancient

prīvātus, *m.* private citizen

prīvignus, *m.* stepson

prō + *abl.* for, in proportion to

proavia, *f.* great-grandmother

probō (1) approve

prōcēdō, -ere, prōcessī, prōcessum advance, proceed, make progress

procella, *f.* gale, storm, whirlwind

prōclīvis downhill

procul at a distance, far away

prōcumbō, -ere, prōcubuī, procubitum prostrate oneself

prōcurrō, -ere, pro(cu)currī, procursum run forward

procus, *m.* suitor

prōdeō, -īre, prōdiī, proditum go forward, come before, appear

prōdigium, *n.* omen, portent

proditiō, -ōnis, *f.* betrayal, treachery

prōdō, -ere, prodidī, proditum bring out, betray, hand down, declare

prōdūcō, -ere, produxī, productum produce, beget

proelium, *n.* battle

prōferō, -ferre, prōtulī, prōlātum bring forward, put off, delay

proficīscor, -ī, profectus sum set out

profiteōr, -eri, professus sum admit voluntarily, confess

prōflīgō (1) decide (battle)

profugus refugee

profundus deep

prōgeniēs, -iēī, *f.* children, descendants, race

prōgredior, -gredī, progressus sum advance, go out

prohibeō, -ēre, prohibuī, prohibitum prevent

proiciō, -ere, prōiēcī, prōiectum throw away/down, give up

proinde and so, therefore

prōlābor, -ī, prōlāpsus sum slip, fall

prōlēs, -is, *f.* offspring

prōlūtus washed, soaked, drunk

prōmissus long, hanging down (of hair/beard)

promittō, -mittere, prōmīsī, prōmissum promise

prōmō, -ere, prōmpsī, prōmptum bring forward, make known

prōmunturium, *n.* mountain ridge, viewpoint

prōnus forward, face down, crouching

prope *(adv.)* almost, nearly

prope + *acc.* near

prōpellō, -ere, propulī, propulsum drive away, drive back

properē quickly, in haste

properō (1) hurry, rush to

properus quick, speedy

propinquitās, -ātis, *f.* closeness, proximity

propinquus close, near

    propinquī, *m. pl.* relatives, kinsfolk, family

propius close, more closely, too/rather close

prōpōnō, -ere, prōposuī, prōpositum propose, intend, display, imagine, conceive

proprius of one's own, native, particular

propter + *acc.* because of, owing to

prōpugnātor, -ōris, *m.* fighting man, defender

prōra, *f.* prow

proripiō, -ere, prōripuī, prōreptum snatch away

prōrsus absolutely

prōrumpō, -ere, prōrūpī, prōruptum break through

prōscrībō, -ere, prōscrīpsī, proscrīptum write up, advertise

prōsequor, -ī, prōsecūtus sum pursue

prōsiliō, -īre, prōsilui jump up, leap forth

prospectus, -ūs, m. view, sight, prospect

prosperus favourable

prōspiciō, -ere, prōspexī, prōspectum look out, look out at

prōsternō, -ere, prōstrāvī, prōstrātum overthrow

prōsum, prōdesse, prōfuī + *dat.* be an advantage to

protegō, -ere, protexī, protectum protect, cover

prōtendō, -ere, prōtendī, prōtēnsum/protentum stretch out

prōtinus straightaway

prout + *subj.* as

prōvectus advanced

prōvehō, -ere, prōvēxī, prōvectum carry forward

prōvideō, -ēre, provīdī, provīsum foresee

prōvincia, f. province

proximus nearest, next to

prūdenter wisely, sensibly

prūdentia, f. prudence, wisdom

pūbēs, pūbis, f. signs of manhood, young men, men

pūblicē at public expense

pūblicus public

pudīcitia, f. chastity

pudīcus chaste

pudor, -ōris, m. shame, decency

puella, f. girl

puellāris girlish

puer, m. boy, slave

pugillārēs, pugillārium m. pl. writing tablets

pugiō, -ōnis, m. dagger

pugna, f. fight

pugnō (1) fight

pulcher beautiful, handsome

pulchritūdō, -inis, f. beauty

pulpitum, n. stage

pulsō (1) beat

pulvis, -eris, m. dust

puniō, -īre, pūnīvī, pūnītum punish

pūnītor, -ōris, m. punisher, avenger

puppis, -is, f. stern, ship

pūrgō (1) cleanse, clear

pūriter purely

purpureus bright, radiant

pūrum, n. clear, bright sky

putō (1) think

putrefaciō, -ere, putrefēcī, putrefactum make to crumble/rot, break up

putrefiō, -fierī, putrefactus sum decompose

quadrīduum four days

quadringentī four hundred

quadrirēmis, -is, f. quadrireme

quaerō, -ere, quaesīvī, quaesītum seek, search for, ask

quaesō, -ere, quaesīvī ask

quaestor, -ōris, m. quaestor

quālibet everywhere

quālis what sort of

1 quam how

2 quam than

quam celerrimē as quickly as possible

quam diu as long as

quamlibet however

quamquam although

quamvīs although

quandō when

quandoquidem since

quantō ... tantō ... as much as ..., so ..., the more ... the more ...

quantus how big, how much

quārē why, for which reason

quārtadecimānī, m. pl. the men of the Fourteenth Legion

quasi as if

quater four times

quatiō, -ere shake

quattuor four

-que and

quemadmodum how

quercus, -ūs, f. oak tree

querimōnia, f. complaint

queror, -ī, questus sum complain

quī, quae, quod who, which

quī ... ! what ... !

quia because

quicquid whatever

quīcumque whoever, whatever

quid why?

quīdam someone, a certain

quidem indeed

quidquid whatever

quiēs, -ētis, f. rest

quiēscō, -ere, quiēvī, quiētum rest, sleep

quiētus quiet, at rest, uneventful

quīn but rather, why ... not ... ?

quīn etiam even more so

quīn immō indeed, on the contrary

quīnam 'as to which'

quīnque five

quīntus fifth

quīntus decimus fifteenth

quippe certainly, surely, indeed; for

quis, quid? who, what?

quisquam anyone, anything

quisque each

quīvīs anyone

1 quō in order that

2 quō? whither? to what place?

quō ... pactō how

quoad until, whilst

quōcumque wherever

quod because

quondam one day, once

quoque also, too

quōquō modō in whatever way

quot? how many?

quot ... tot ... as many as ... so many ...

quotiēns how often, whenever

racēmus, m. bunch of grapes

radiāns shining, gleaming

radius, m. rod, spoke, beam, ray

rādīx, -īcis, f. root

rādō, -ere, rāsī, rāsum shave, scratch, graze

raeda, f. carriage, wagon

rāmulus, m. little branch, sprig

rāmus, m. branch

rāna, f. frog

rapāx grasping

rapidus rapid, quick, devouring, swirling

rapiō, -ere, rapuī, raptum carry off, snatch, seize, grab

rārus scattered

ratiō, -ōnis, f. reasoning, method, plan, rule

ratis, -is, f. ship

recēdō, -ere, recessī, recessum go back/away, depart, leave

recēns recent, fresh

recenseō, -ēre, recēnsuī, recēnsum/recēnsitum count, survey, review

recidō, -ere, recidī, recāsum rebound

recidō, -ere, recīdī, recīsum cut short

recipiō, -ere, recēpī, receptum get back, take, receive

me recipio retreat

reciprocus turning back, tidal

recitō (1) read out, recite

recognoscō, -ere, recognovī, recognitum recognise, recall, review

recoquō, -ere, recoxī, recoctum cook, melt, forge again

recordor (1) call to mind, remember

rēctē rightly

rēctus straight, right

recūsō (1) refuse, say no

reddō, -ere, reddidī, redditum give back, restore

redeō, -īre, rediī, reditum go back, come back, return

redigō, -ere, redēgī, redāctum reduce

redimō, -ere, redemī, redemptum buy

redintegrō (1) restore

reditus, -ūs, m. revenue

redūcō, -ere, redūxī, reductum lead/draw back

reductus remote, lonely, secluded

redux coming back, being brought back

referō, referre, rettulī, relātum bring, carry back, speak, report, tell

refoveō, -ēre, refōvī, refōtum revive, refresh

refulgeō, -ēre refulsī reflect, flash back

rēgaliōlus, m. small bird, wren, king-bird

rēgia, f. palace

rēgīna, f. queen

regiō, -ōnis, f. region

regius of the king, royal

rēgnum, n. kingdom, reign, rule

regō, -ere, rēxī, rēctum rule, control, drive

regredior, -gredī, regressus sum go back, return

reiciō, -ere, reiēcī, reiectum reject, refuse

relanguēscō, -ere, relanguī fall

religiō, -ōnis, f. religion, ritual

religō (1) tie up

relinquō, -ere, reliquī, relictum leave, leave behind

reliquus remaining

reluctor (1) struggle against, obstruct

remaneō, -ēre, remānsī remain, stay behind

rēmex, -igis, m. rower

rēmigium, n. oars, rowing

remissiō, -ōnis, f. break, recreation

remittō, -ere, remīsī, remissum send back, let go, give up

remoror (1) delay again

removeō, -ēre, remōvī, remōtum move back

remūnero (1) pay back

rēmus, m. oar

renūntiō (1) report

reor, rērī, ratus sum think

repente suddenly

repentīnus sudden

reperiō, -īre, repperī, repertum find

repetō, -ere, repetīvī, repetitum recall

repō, -ere, repsī creep, crawl

repōnō, -ere, reposuī, repos(i)tum place, lay to rest

repugnō (1) fight back, oppose

requirō, -ere, requīsīvī, requīsītum ask, seek

rēs, rēī f. thing, matter, affair, event, property

   rēs novae, f. pl. revolution

   rēs publica, f. state, republic

rescīscō, -ere, rescīī, rescītum find out

resīdō, -ere, resēdī sit back down, remain, settle

resistō, -ere, restitī, restitum + *dat.* resist

resonō (1) resound

respectō (1) look around

respiciō, -ere, respexī, respectum consider, look back, round, pay attention to

respondeō, -ēre, respondī, respōnsum reply

restinguō, -ere, restīnxī, restīnctum put out (fire)

restituō, -ere, restituī, restitūtum restore, give back

restō, -āre, restitī remain

rēte, -is, n. net

reticeō, -ēre, reticuī keep silent

retinācula, n. pl. halter, reins

retineō, -ēre, retinuī, retentum keep to, maintain, hold back, hold on to

retrahō, -ere, retrāxī, retractum pull back

retroversum back, for the return

reus, m. a person accused/committed for trial, defendant

revellō, -ere, revellī, revulsum/ revolsum tear out, uproot

revertor, -ī, reversus sum return

revocō (1) recall, call back

rēx, rēgis, m. king

Rhēnus, m. the river Rhine

rhētor, rhetoris m. teacher of rhetoric

rīdeō, -ēre, rīsī, rīsum laugh, smile

rigeō, -ēre be stiff, stand on end

rīma, f. hole, chink, crack

rīpa, f. river bank

rīsus, -ūs, m. laughter

rīte duly, properly

rītus, -ūs, m. custom, usage

rīvus, m. stream

rōbur, -oris, n. oak tree; strength, maturity

rogitō (1) ask repeatedly

rogō (1) ask, ask for

Rōma, f. Rome

Rōmānus Roman

rōstrātus adorned with beaks

rōstrum, n. beak, curved end of ship's prow

ruber red, reddish-orange

rubēscō grow red

rudēns, -entis, m. rope, **pl.** rigging

rudis rough

rūmor, -ōris, m. rumour

rumpō, -ere, rūpī, ruptum break

ruō, -ere, ruī, rutum rush

rūpēs, -is, f. rock

rūrsus again

Sabīna, f. a Sabine woman

sacer sacred

sacerdōs, -ōtis, m. priest

sacrificium, n. sacrifice

sacrō (1) consecrate, devote, make/ perform (a vow),

saeculum, n. age, century

saepe, often

saepiō, -īre, saepsī, saeptum block

saeviō, saevīre, saeviī, saevītum rage

saevus savage, cruel

sagittiferus carrying arrows

sāl, -is, m. salt

salignus made of willow

saltus, -ūs, m. glade

salubris healthy

salūbritās, -ātis, f. health-giving properties

salūs, -ūtis, f. health, safety, hope of safety

salūtō (1) greet

salvēre iubeō greet, welcome, hail

sānctitās, -ātis, f. sanctity, piety

sānctus sacred

sanguineus blood-red

sanguis, -inis, m. blood

sānus healthy, in one's right mind

sapiēns wise, sensible, shrewd

sapientia, f. wisdom, philosophy

sarcina, f. burden, baggage

satelles, -itis, m. attendant, bodyguard

satiō (1) sate, satisfy

satis enough

saucius, wounded, injured

saxum, n. rock, stone

scaena, *f.* stage
scelerātus wicked
scelestus wicked
scelus, -eris, *n.* crime
scēptrum, *n.* sceptre
scientia, *f.* knowledge, expertise, skill
sciō, -īre, scīvī, scitum know
scīscitor (1) enquire
scissus torn
scītor (1) enquire, consult
scortum, *n.* prostitute
scrība, *m.* secretary
scribō, -ere, scrīpsī, scriptum write
scrīnium, *n.* book-box, file
scrīptor, -ōris, *m.* writer
scūtum, *n.* shield
sē, sēsē himself, herself, itself, themselves
secō, -āre, secuī, sectum cut, cut through
sēcrētus withdrawn, apart, cut off
   sēcrētum, *n.* secret, mystery
sector (1) follow, pursue
secundus second, favourable, on one's side
   secunda, *n. pl.* successes, good fortune
secūris, -is, *f.* axe
secus otherwise
sed but
sedeō, -ēre, sēdī, sessum sit, settle
sēdēs, -is, *f.* home, seat, dwelling
sēdō (1) calm, allay
sēdulus busy, attentive
seges, -etis, *f.* corn, grain
Segestānus of Segesta
sēgnis sluggish, inactive, slow
sēgniter slowly
sēmel once
sēmet himself
semper always
senātus, -ūs, *m.* senate
senecta, *f.* old age
senex, senis, *m.* old man
sēnsus, -ūs, *m.* sense, emotion
sententia, *f.* opinion
sentiō, -īre, sēnsī, sēnsum feel, notice
sepeliō, -īre, sepelīvī, sepultum bury
septem seven
septimus seventh
sequor, sequī, secūtus sum follow
serēnus clear, bright
sermō, -ōnis, *m.* tale
serpēns, -tis, *m.f.* serpent
serviō, -īre, serviī, servitum + *dat.* be a slave
servō (1) keep, preserve, save

servolus, *m.* young slave
servus, *m.* slave
seu ... seu ... whether ... or
seu if, or
severitās, -ātis, *f.* severity
sex six
sī if
   sī minus if not
   sī quis ... if any man ... , if anyone
sīc thus, in this way
siccus dry
Siculus Sicilian
sīcut, sicuti as, just as, as if
sīdō, -ere, sidi sit, settle, stick
sīdus, -eris, *n.* star, constellation, season
siet = sit
significō (1) make a sign, indicate
signō (1) seal
signum, *n.* sign, signal, military standard, constellation
silentium, *n.* silence
sileō, -ēre, siluī be silent
silva, *f.* wood
similis + *dat.* like, similar to
similiter in similar fashion
simpliciter simply
simul at the same time
simulācrum, *n.* statue, vision, apparition
simulō (1) pretend
simultās, -ātis, *f.* quarrel
sincērus pure
sine + *abl.* without
singularis singular, outstanding
singultus, -ūs, *m.* sobbing
singulus each, every individual, single, every single
sinister left
sinō, -ere, sīvī, situm allow
sinus, -ūs, *m.* lap, embrace, curve, hollow, fold (of clothing)
sī qua if any
siquis if anyone, anyone who
sistrum, *n.* sistrum, rattle
Sisyphius of Sisyphus
sīve ... sīve ... whether ... or ...
socer, *m.* father-in-law
socius, *m.* ally
sōcordia, *f.* sluggishness, lethargy
socrus, -ūs, *f.* mother-in-law
sōl, -is, *m.* sun
sōlācium, *n.* solace, consolation
soleātus wearing sandals or slippers
soleō, -ēre, solitus sum be used to, make a habit of
solidus firm
sōlitudō, -inis, *f.* loneliness, isolation
sollemne, *n.* solemn rite, ritual

sollicitus anxious, disturbed, causing anxiety
solum, *n.* ground
sōlus alone, lonely, only, on one's own
solvō, -ere, solvī, solūtum loosen, untie, break down, remove
somnus, *m.* sleep
sonitus, -ūs, *m.* sound
sonō, -āre, sonuī, sonitum resound, be heard
sonor, -ōris, *m.* sound, noise, din
sonus, *m.* sound
sōpiō, -īre, sōpīvī, sōpītum put to sleep
soror, -ōris, *f.* sister
sors, -tis, *f.* fate, lot
sospes, -itis safe
sospitō, -āre preserve, protect
spadō, -ōnis, *m.* eunuch
spargō, -ere, sparsī, sparsum throw about, scatter, shower
spatior, -ārī, spatiātus sum walk
spatiōsus large, ample, spacious
spatium, *n.* distance, duration
speciēs, -iēī, *f.* appearance
spectābilis spectacular, worth looking at
spectāculum, *n.* sight, spectacle, show
spectātor, -ris, *m.* spectator
spectō (1) look at, watch
spernō, -ere, sprēvī, sprētum disdain, scorn, reject, make light of
spērō (1) hope, expect
spēs, -eī, *f.* hope
spīritus, -ūs, *m.* breath, spirit
spoliō (1) plunder, rob
sponte of its own accord
spūmō (1) foam
squālor, -ōris, *m.* dirt, filth
statim at once, immediately
statīva, *n. pl.* halt, stationary camp
statua, *f.* statue
statuō, -ere, statuī, statūtum resolve, determine
stella, *f.* star
   stella crīnīta, *f.* comet
sternō, -ere, strāvī, strātum bedeck, spread, cover, overthrow
stertō, -ere, stertuī snore
stilus, *m.* implement for writing on wax tablets
stīpendium, *n.* pay
stirps, -is, *f.* root, stem, offspring, descent. lineage
stō, stāre, stetī, statum stand
strāgēs, -is, *f.* destruction
strātum, *n.* bed, blanket

strēnuus energetic, active

strepitus, -ūs, m. loud noise, rattle, jangle

strīdēns screaming, screeching, creaking

stridor, ōris, m. creak, scream (any harsh, shrill sound)

stringō, -ere, strīnxī, strictum draw (a sword)

struēs, struis, f. pile

struō, -ere, strūxī, structum pile up

studiōsus enthusiastic, keen

studium, n. enthusiasm, zeal, application

stultus stupid

stupeō, -ēre, stupuī be dumbstruck, be stunned

stuppeus made of tow (flax)

Stygius Stygian, of the River Styx

suadeō, -ēre, suāsī, suāsum + dat. urge, recommend

suavitās, -ātis, f. sweetness

sub + acc./abl. under, beneath

subdō, -ere, subdidī, subditum place, insert

subdūcō, -dūcere, subdūxī, subductum withraw

subeō, subīre, subiī, subitum come up to, come to mind

subiectus bordering on

subitō suddenly

subitus sudden

sublābor, -lābī, sublāpsus sum sink into

sublīmis high, lofty, exalted, on high

submergō, -ere, submersī, submersum sink, drown

subolēs, subolis, f. offspring

subrēpō, -ere, subrēpsī, subrēptum creep

subsequor, -sequī, subsecūtus sum follow, follow closely

subsidium, n. help

subsistō, -ere, substitī stop, pause, stay for a while

subtrahō, -ere, subtrāxī, subtractum take away from under, remove

subveniō, -īre, subvēnī, subventum + dat. help

succendō, -ere, succendī, succēnsum set fire to

successor, -ōris, m. successor

succurrō, -ere, succurrī, succursum + dat. help

sūcus, m. juice, sap

suffrāgatiō, -ōnis, f. electoral support

suffrāgātor, -ōris, m. election campaign helper, supporter

suffrāgium, n. vote

suggredior, -gredī, suggressus sum approach

sum, esse, fuī be

summittō, -ere, summīsī, summissum produce, send off, lower, allow to grow

summus highest, greatest, top (of)

sumō, -ere, sumpsī, sumptum eat, consume, take up

sūmptus, -ūs, m. cost, payment

suntō let (them) be

super remaining

super + abl. about

super + acc. above, over, on top of, besides

superbus proud, splendid

superī, m. pl. the gods

superior higher, previous, former

supernē above

superō (1) overcome, defeat

supersum, -esse, superfuī + dat. survive

supīnus backwards, lying on the back

supplex suppliant

supplicium, n. punishment, penalty

suprā (adv.) / (prep. + acc.) above, over

suprēmus final, last

surgō, -ere, surrēxī, surrēctum get up, stand up, rise

sūs, suis, m.f. pig

suscipiō, -ere, suscēpī, susceptum undertake, take on

suscitō (1) rouse to flame

suspectō (1) suspect, distrust

suspēnsus in suspense, in doubt

suspectus suspect

suspiciō, -ere, suspexī, suspectum look up

suspicor (1) suspect

suspīrō (1) sigh

sustineō, -ēre, sustinuī, sustentum hold, support, maintain, keep in check

suus, sua, suum his, her, its, their (own)

tabella, f. message, writing-tablet

tabernāculum, n. tent

tabidus lingering

tabula, f. board, plank, writing-tablet

taciturnitās, -ātis f. maintaining silence

tacitus silent, in secret

taedet, taeduit it is tiring

taedium, n. weariness, burden

taenia, f. ribbon

taeter grim, foul, vile

tālāris reaching down to the ankles

tālis such

tam so

tamen however

tametsī even though

tamquam as if, like

tandem at last, finally; 'I ask you!'

tangō, -ere, tetigī, tāctum touch

tantum only

tantus so great, such a great

tardus slow, late

taurus, m. bull

tēctum, n. roof, house

tegō, -ere, tēxī, tēctum hide, cover

tellūs, -ūris, f. ground, earth

tēlum, n. shaft, arrow, spear, weapon

temerārius rash

temere blindly

temerō (1) violate, dishonour

temperantia, f. restraint, self-control

temperō (1) control, moderate

tempestās, -ātis, f. storm, weather

templum, n. temple

tempora, n. pl. temples of the head

temptō (1) try, attempt, make an attempt on, attack

temptābundus trying, testing

tempus, -oris, n. time

tēmulentus drunken

tendō, -ere, tetendī, tentum/ tensum stretch/hold out, make for

teneō, -ēre, tenuī, tentum hold

tener tender, soft

tentōrium, n. tent

tenuis slender, slim, slight

tenus + abl. as far as, up to

tepidus warm

ter three times

tergum, n. back

terō, -ere, trīvī, trītum tread; rub

terra, f. earth, land, ground

terreō, -ēre, terruī, territum frighten

terrestris land-based, of/on the land

terribilis terrible, dreadful, frightening

terror, -ōris, m. terror, fear

tertius third

testāmentum, n. will

testis, -is, m.f. witness

testor (1) declare

tētē = te

Teucrī, m. pl. Trojans (descendants of Teucer)

textum, n. fabric

thalamus, m. marital bedchamber, marriage

theātrum, n. theatre

Thrāx, Thrācis, m. Thracian

Thrēicius Thracian
thymum, *n.* thyme
Tiberis, -is, *m.* the River Tiber
tībīcen, -inis, *m.* piper
timeō, -ēre, timuī fear, be afraid
timidus fearful, timid
timor, -ōris, *m.* fear
tintinō (1) make a ringing sound
titubō (1) stagger, stumble
titulus, *m.* notice, honour, glory, distinction
tolerō (1) bear, endure
tollō, tollere, sustulī, sublātum raise, lift up, hold up, remove
tonans thundering
  Tonāns, Tonantis, *m.* the Thunderer (the god Jupiter)
tonitrus, -ūs, *m.* thunder
tōnsus shorn, shaved
torpeō, -ēre, torpuī be numb, be paralysed
torpēscō, -ere, torpuī grow numb
torpor, -ōris, *m.* paralysis, numbness, torpor
torqueō, -ēre, torsī, tortum whirl around, fling
torreō, -ēre, torruī, tostum dry, scorch, burn
torridus hot, heated
tortilis twisted, coiled
torus, *m.* couch, funeral bier; marriage, marriage bed
tot so many
totidem the same number
totiē(n)s so often
tōtus whole
  tōtum fully, completely
tractātus, -ūs, *m.* procedure
trādō, -ere, tradidī, traditum pass on, hand down, say, tell
trāgula, *f.* spear fitted with a throwing strap
trahō, -ere, trāxī, tractum pull, drag
trāiciō, -ere, traiēcī, traiectum shoot across, cross, thrust through, pierce
trānō (1) swim across
tranquillus calm, settled
trans + *acc.* across
trānscendō, -ere, trānscendī, trānscēnsum cross, climb over
transeō, -īre, transiī, trānsitum go past, cross over, transfer
trānsfīgō, -ere, trānsfīxī, trānsfīxum pierce through
trānsigō, -ere, trānsēgī, transāctum pierce through
trecentī three hundred

tremō, -ere, tremuī tremble, quake, quiver
trepidāns anxious, in distress
trepidō (1) tremble in alarm
trepidus alarmed, anxious
trēs, tria three
tribunal, -ālis, *n.* platform
tribunus, *m.* tribune
  tribunus mīlitum, *m.* military tribune, commander
tridēns with three teeth, three-pronged, triple
trīduum, *n.* the space of three days
triplex threefold, triple
trīstis sad, mournful, grim, harsh
triumphō (1) triumph
triumphus, *m.* triumph
Trōia, *f.* Troy
Trōiānus Trojan
tū you (sing.)
tuba, *f.* trumpet
tueor, -ērī, tuitus sum keep watch over, protect
tum then, at that time
tumēscō, -ere, tumuī swell
tumidus swelling, swollen
tunc then
tunica, *f.* tunic
turba, *f.* crowd
turbidus disturbed, violent
turbo (1) confuse, disturb
turbō, -inis, *m.* whirlwind, tornado
turdus, *m.* thrush
turpis shameful, foul
turriger turreted, crowned with turrets
turris, -is, *f.* tower
turrītus towered, turreted
tūs, tūris, *n.* incense
Tuscus Tuscan, Etruscan
tūtus safe
tūus your (sing.), yours
Tȳdīdēs, *m.* son of Tydides, Diomedes
Tyndaritānus of Tyndaris
tyrannus, *m.* ruler
Tyrius Tyrian

ūbertim copiously, in floods
ubi where? where, when
ubīque everywhere
ūdus damp, wet
ulcīscor, -ī, ultus sum avenge
ūllus any
ultimus last; worst, most remote, most distant
ultor, -ōris, *m.* avenger
ultrā + *acc.* beyond
ultrā (*adv.*) on the other side, further, beyond
ultrō suddenly, of one's own accord

umbō, -ōnis, *m.* shield
umbra, *f.* ghost, shade, shadow
umerus, *m.* upper arm, shoulder
umquam ever
ūnā together (with)
unda, *f.* wave, stream, surge
unde from where
undecimus eleventh
unguentum, *n.* perfume, ointment
unguis, -is, *m.* talon, nail (of a person)
ūniversī, *m. pl.* the whole body, everyone together
ūniversus whole
ūnus one
urbs, -is, *f.* city
ūrēns burning
urgeō, -ēre press, drive, force
urna, *f.* water-pot, jar
ūrō, -ere, ussī, ustum burn
ūsitor (1) use frequently
ūsque as far as, continuously, all the way up to
ūsus, -ūs, *m.* use; experience; service, advantage
ut, utī + *subj.* so that, in order that; when; as, like; how
ut + *indic.* as
utēnsilia, -ium, *n. pl.* equipment
uter? which of two?
uterque both, each (of two)
uterus, *m.* womb
ūtilis useful
utinam would that
ūtor, utī, ūsus sum + *abl.* use, have dealings with
utpote because of
utrimque on both sides
uxor, -ōris, *f.* wife

vacuus empty
vādō, -ere go, proceed, rush in
vadōsus shallow
vadum, *n.* shallow water
vae ah! woe! alas!
vāgīna, *f.* scabbard
vagor (1) wander
vagus wandering
valē, valēte goodbye, farewell
valedīcō, -ere say farewell to
valeō, -ēre, valuī, valitum be strong, prevail, be well
valētūdō, -inis, *f.* health, state of health; ill health
validus strong, sturdy
vallis, -is, *f.* valley
vāllum, *n.* rampart
vānus of no substance
vappa, *f.* flat, bad wine
varius different, various
vastus desolate, huge, immense